Ferrari

... a dream born in the snow

The story of the Prancing Horse from 1898 until today

SEP
Editrice

"I am devoted to my land, dare I say it, fiercely.
Especially today, for reasons connected to my family's tragic history.
This devotion did not exist before, when I worked in Turin, Milan or Switzerland.
They were places which meant more to me than my flat, monotonous,
foggy land with its exaggerated summer heat, without a lake,
without a beach and with a few plain hills on the horizon.
However I don't know if I could have obtained the same results
if I had stayed there"

Enzo Ferrari
from his autobiography "Ferrari 80"

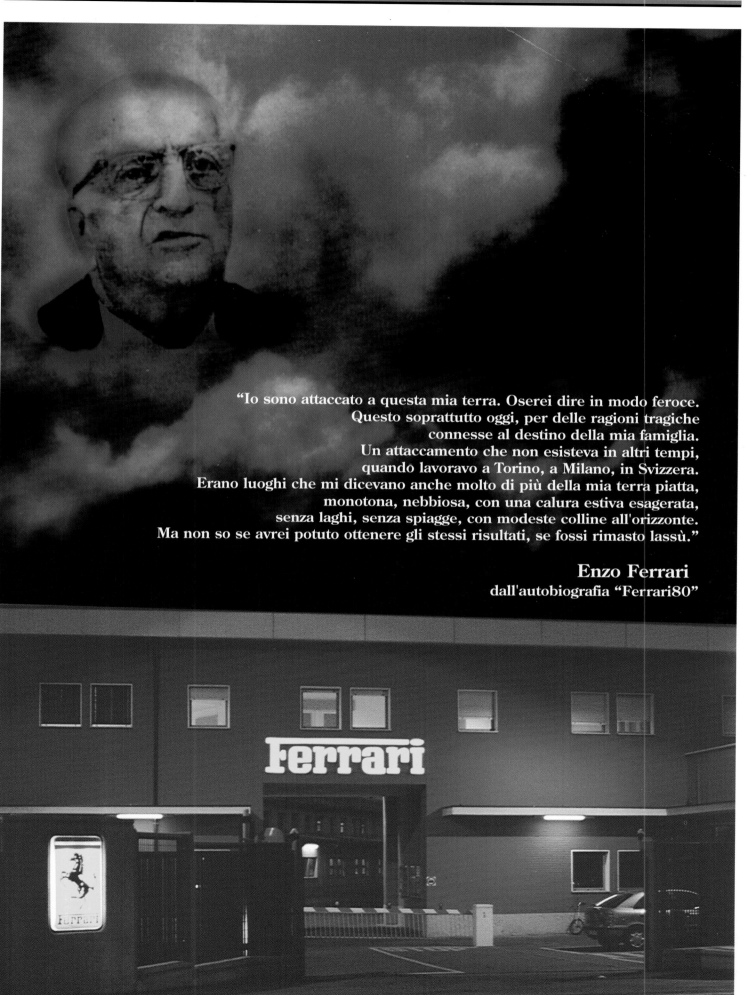

"Io sono attaccato a questa mia terra. Oserei dire in modo feroce.
Questo soprattutto oggi, per delle ragioni tragiche
connesse al destino della mia famiglia.
Un attaccamento che non esisteva in altri tempi,
quando lavoravo a Torino, a Milano, in Svizzera.
Erano luoghi che mi dicevano anche molto di più della mia terra piatta,
monotona, nebbiosa, con una calura estiva esagerata,
senza laghi, senza spiagge, con modeste colline all'orizzonte.
Ma non so se avrei potuto ottenere gli stessi risultati, se fossi rimasto lassù."

Enzo Ferrari
dall'autobiografia "Ferrari80"

I would like to thank Roberto Boccafogli, the author of this book, for having understood the spirit of the project, which was not simply a "rewrite" of the history of Ferrari. It is instead an analysis of the legend through minor and major details, long-forgotten curiosities as well as a recollection of well-known and not so well-known fact ... always working closely with everyone who assisted us in the project. In producing the book, we met dozens of people and it was fantastic to appreciate the warmth with which they welcomed us, opened their homes to us and patiently put up with our interest and that of our photographers.

The Editor

Thanks to everyone and in particular to:

Renzo and Alvaro Cernesi, Gisberto Leopardi and Sergio Vezzali, Luigi Montanini "Pasticcino", all the men who have given their everything to Ferrari in the company and at the race-tracks, to Don Erio Belloi, parish priest of Maranello, to Riccardo Andreoni of Ferrari for checking the statistics and finally to Pietro De Franchi, Ferrari Club Italy secretary.

Umberto Masetti, 1950 and 1952 World Motorcycle Racing Champion

Antonio Magro and Elvira Ruocco of Alfa Romeo

Paolo Montagna and Paolo Moroni of the Milan Automobile Club

Paolo D'Alessio, whose colour plates of Ferraris from 1948 to 1988 illustrate the book

Finally, for the photographs:

Gabriella Coltrin, the wife of the late Peter Coltrin as well as our photographers Serafino Celso and Giulio Guerrieri who often worked in technically harsh situations,

Carlo Rezzonico, who shot the cover photos which were then computer-edited

and the firms and photographic archives which contributed to the extraordinary images in this book..

The stylized car designs in the headings were produced of Diego Galbiati..

FERRARI - A Dream born in the Snow
© 1997 Worldwide - SEP Editrice - Milano (Italy)

Author:: Roberto Boccafogli
English version: Julian Thomas

Photographic archives:

Gabriella Coltrin	C.O.N.I.Press Office
Expressen	Shell Italiana Press Office
Alfa Romeo archives	MilanAutomobile Club - archives
Bryn Williams - Colin McMaster	Ferrari Press Office- Maranello
Tazio Nuvolari Museum - Mantua	La Libertà di Piacenza
Mario Arquati	Auto Italiana
Sport Mecanique - France	Autosprint
Opel Italia Press Office	Williams Grand Prix - UK
Automobile Club de Monaco	UMI - USA
Corriere della Sera	Gazzetta dello Sport
Car Magazine - Japane	Autosport - Japan

Photographs: Serafino Celso, Giulio Guerrieri, Carlo Rezzonico

Colour Plates and Technical Drawings: Paolo D'Alessio

Graphic Design: Diego Galbiati

Technical Coordination: Ermenegildo Chiozzotto

Editing and Information: Tina Caiazza,Chiara Mendella,Francesca Vallardi

Photolithograph: FCM - Marcallo C. (MI) **Printing:** Alfa Print - Busto A. (VA)

ISBN 88-87110-00-X   Printed in Italy - July 1997

CONTENTS

FERRARI - A dream born in the Snow

BIBLIOGRAPHY
Many quotes in the text come from the following books:

- Ferrari l'unico
  Nada Editore 1988

- F1 33 anni di Gran Premi
  iridati - Conti Editore 1982

- Ferrari 80 - Edizione
  Fuori Commercio 1980

- Ferrari
  La Storia di un mito -
  RCS Supplemento della
  Gazzetta dello Sport 1996

- Marlboro Grand Prix Guide
  Edizione 1997

- Museo Alfa Romeo -
  Catalogo - Automobilia 1985

- Museo Storico Alfa Romeo -
  Alfa Romeo 1983

- Bandiera a Scacchi -
  Vallardi 1993

- The Legendary Italian
  Grand Prix - ACM 1989

INTRODUCTION

MARANELLO

The soul of Ferrari and its all-enveloping substance can be sensed as one arrives from Modena in the direction of Maranello. Here, near the Appenines and Mount Abetone, one is in the middle of tidy fields, the quintessence of perfect productivity in every season. Faithful to this rule, Enzo Ferrari and Ferrari were born in this area. In the beginning, Ferrari was just a small idea, the result of a childhood dream.

"When I grow up, I'm going to be a racing-driver", said a young Ferrari to his close friend Peppino one hot August evening. Together, the two boys were leafing through a newspaper which reported the exploits of Raffaele De Parma, a driver of the time and one of the stars of the Indianapolis race. *"A good idea"*, was the reply. *"That must be a great job"*. These were far-off memories from a time when Italy almost had no experience of the motor car, let alone speed and racing. Those words however contained something special: a foreshadowing of a legend not born from chance but from real human ambition. It eventually turned

into a reality which formed part of the story of a man, a marque and most of the sport of motor racing. From the early years of the twentieth-century until today, the wide-eyed dream of Enzo Ferrari has become a reality which today guarentees worldwide fame and fortune for Maranello. Every motor racing fan, especially F1 enthusiasts, knows about Ferrari, the flaming red Ferrari and the Ferrari legend with its drivers, its engineers, its victories and defeats which are all inextricably linked with a unique historical roll of honours. Everyone who reads detailed newspaper accounts and who follow the television commentary of the races can learn a lot about the technology, the aerodynamics and the latest carbon-fibre applications. But they can never get the real feeling of Maranello that makes Ferrari something more than just a mere motor racing team. All one has to do however is visit Maranello once. A short, unhurried visit is all that is required to understand the hidden but visible meaning of this small town in the Modena industrial hinterland. 1800 of the slightly more than 15,000 inhabitants work for Ferrari and for the legend and history of the Prancing Horse. A legend that will never die; a legend born in the nineteenth-century and ready to race into the year 2000 in top gear; a legend rejuvenated by the alternating fortunes of Ferrari since the death of its founder almost ten years ago. At Maranello there is an overriding sensation: Ferrari is the phenomenon which helped to industrialize this predominantly agricultural area until the start of the Second World War, a pillar of industrial society on a world scale. At Maranello and the surrounding areas, Ferrari means cars, races and victories.

Maranello, just a few minutes from Modena by car, at the foot of the Appenines. The legend of the Prancing Horse was born here and developed over the years. The Ferrari company was first a small-time firm, but then became a worldwide industrial and sporting phenomenon. Young Enzo Ferrari's dream ("I'm going to be a racing driver when I grow up") far exceeded his own expectations ...

But it also means work: work and economic security, where until half-a-century ago fields were the only thing which made the difference between making ends meet and widespread hunger.

The factory, the racing headquarters, the Fiorano test-track, just a few metres away from the monument dedicated to Gilles Villeneuve in the street named after him as well as the street dedicated to Ascari, the Ferrari Museum, the Ferrari shop which is visited by customers from all over the world in search of Ferrari-related products; the Cavallino restaurant, in front of the main company entrance, where even today it is not unusual to

The "Cavallino" in front of the main Ferrari entrance is not just an excellent restaurant. Inside, life revolves around the scarlet red cars and their race wins. Trophies, helmets signed by drivers, racing-car parts: the restaurant is a gallery of Ferrari

7

INTRODUCTION

The Ferrari Gallery appears on the road leading to Fiorano. It is the only real official souvenir outlet for the Prancing Horse marque in the world. At Maranello, the shops sell motor sport articles, gadgets and items ... but Ferrari-related products sell the most.

Other page: Enzo Ferrari has been depicted in stamps, bas-relief and statues, made from piston-heads. The bust which has special importance for the "tifosi" is the one dedicated to Gilles Villeneuve, put up in 1982 a few metres from the entrance to Fiorano

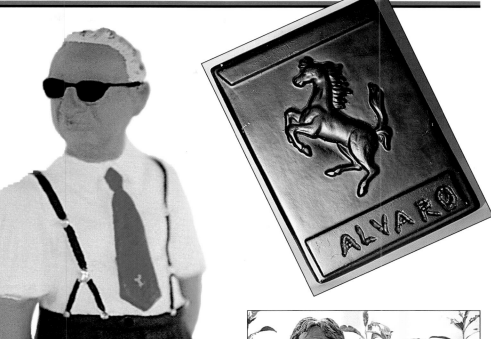

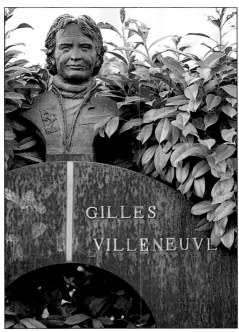

INTRODUCTION

bump into Ferrari figures of the past and the present, such as the unforgettable Umberto Masetti, world motorcycling champion in 1950 and 1952. Everything and everyone at Maranello "breathes" Ferrari.

Such as Alvaro Cernesi, employee in the engine paint-shop department and son of a worker who accompanied Enzo Ferrari in the good old days. His father started work in the factory in the first half of the century with registration number 22. His son remembers this with pride and adds: *"See these overalls? On the left there is the Prancing Horse and I feel its heart beating next to mine".*
These overalls, which for an outsider are totally normal, for Cernesi are something quite unique and special and are never removed except ... during working hours.
So as not to get them dirty ...
The same could be said about Gisberto Leopardi.
"Everything I have I owe to Ferrari",

he tells frankly while showing us his pretty house on the outskirts of Maranello, immersed in the green countryside where the Abetone state road begins to climb. He continues: *"I used to work in the rice-fields. The pay was meagre: twenty kilos of rice to help the family get by".*
Then suddenly, came Ferrari. In a way which could best be described as romantic. After successfully completing a mechanical engineering course, young Leopardi realized that his only hope lay in the newly-created car industry. How could he get in? Simple: the most direct way possible. One day he waited for Enzo Ferrari on the steps of the town hall. He went up to him and said point-blank: *"Ferrari, I've finished my course, but my stomach is empty ...".*
And that is how on 10 April 1947, 17 year-old Leopardi started work in the Cavallino factory. Almost fifty years of work and races, trips home and abroad full of adventure and hard work and yet a marvellous experience. A story which only came to an end when he reached retirement age, but which has carried on today with a series of souvenirs, photographs, result-sheets and circuit and pit passes. Items of memorabilia which in all parts of the world are exchanged at high prices by collectors and which for these men mean simply a succession of events in a life filled by a passionate love for their work. There are many

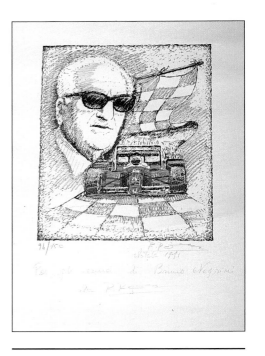

*Two "dynasties" of Ferrari mechanics. Left: Alvaro Cernesi with his father, who, in the 1940s, was registered worker number 22 at Maranello.
Bottom left: Gisberto Leopardi proudly stands before his "personalized" tools, and with his Ferrari employer's identity card*

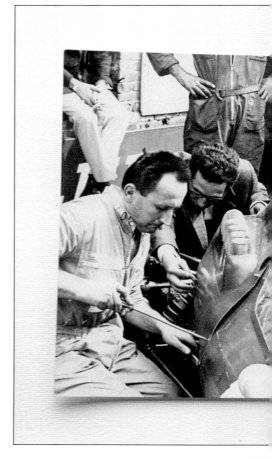

others like Leopardi; men often linked by having their roots in Maranello and the surrounding area.

But above all linked by a history, the pace of which is dictated by the same metronome. Sergio Vezzali was Gilles Villeneuve's chief mechanic. Before he was with the Canadian, he worked with Niki Lauda, whom today he remembers as *"... the best, the most generous with us mechanics: after each win, he never failed to give us a present, sometimes a big one"*.

Sergio Vezzali, Ferrari F1 mechanic at the time of Niki Lauda and Gilles Villeneuve. The framed photographs portray him in the pits in the 1960s, in a briefing with Enzo Ferrari. Alongside: Vezzali with the crown and sceptre of "King of the Box", as he was called affectionately by his colleagues when he retired

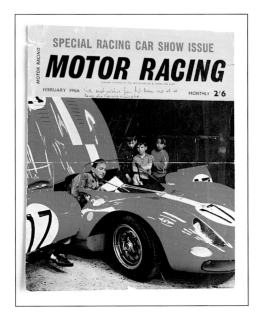

(8) and Villoresi (2) in the first two rows. Below, Enzo Ferrari discusses 312 F1 with mechanic Sergio Vezzali in 1968.

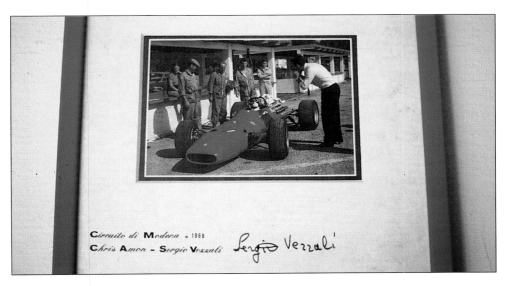

Circuito di Modena - 1969
Chris Amon - Sergio Vezzali   Sergio Vezzali

INTRODUCTION

Vezzali's house, like Leopardi's and who knows how many other ex-colleagues, is packed with memories: souvenirs, photos and artefacts, trophies and copies of menus from the traditional and regular company meals offered by Ferrari to celebrate Christmas or other happy occasions, such as when they successfully completed a job within an impossible time-scale.

And what memories! Memories of days spent working on the racing-cars, suddenly interrupted by a half-whispered word or one that everyone could hear.

"Maraja, maraja!"

(Watch out! Watch out!)

"Daddy's coming".

That's what they called him: Daddy: a mixture of respect, fear and affection. Ferrari came into the factory and the chatter faded away, cigarettes smoked during work (absolutely forbidden!) were put out in a hurry.

He came every day at about 10.30 in the morning. And he always, at least once a day, visited every sector.

A sudden and important presence, which brought everything to a complete standstill.

On catching a worker hiding a cigarette in his pocket, he would say half-smilingly:

"You'd better put that out otherwise you'll burn your overalls". Few words, often abrupt and without raising his voice. With a few exceptions ... *"We all knew when there was a meeting going on - recalls Vezzali - And if things were not going well, you could hear the shouting, sometimes even the cursing. There was no answering back. Shortly after, they all came out of his office, their eyes lowered. No-one answered back to him: not even Forghieri or the young Montezemolo".*

Ferrari instilled fear, but also totally backed his workers. *"In all my years of working for Ferrari - recalled the ex-racing mechanic Leopardi - I never received my wages late, not even in hard times for the company. For Ferrari, there was always money for those who worked, it was always the most important thing".*

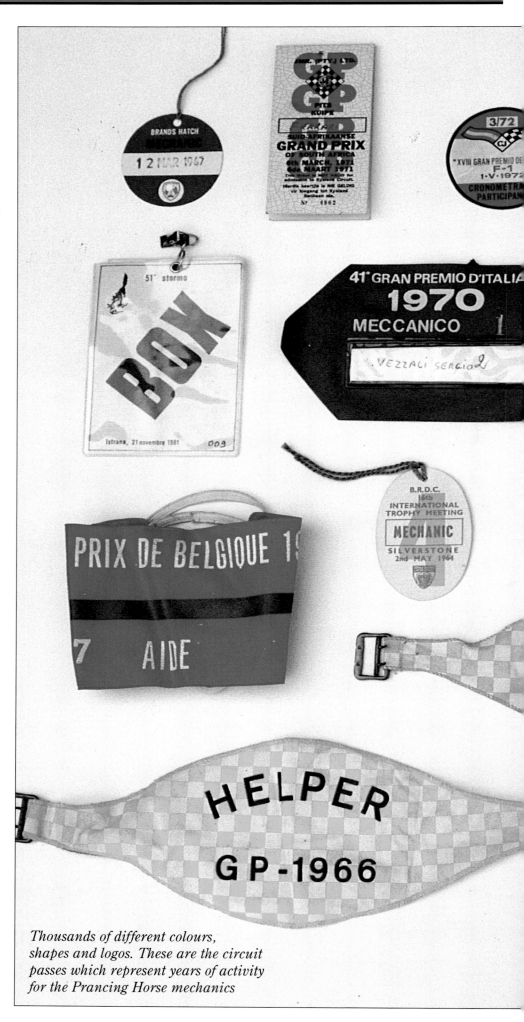

Thousands of different colours, shapes and logos. These are the circuit passes which represent years of activity for the Prancing Horse mechanics

1970 PERFORMANCE UNION 76 TRIALS

3° GRAN PREMIO S. MARINO
FOCA
Agip   Alitalia

TEMPORADA INTERNACIONAL
SP YPF
CONTROL N° 3392
MECANICO
PUERTA N°. 11
ENERO 1970
11   18

FOCA
VEZZALI-GANDARELLI
THE HOLDER OF THIS CREDENTIAL
NUMBER · MUST BE GIVEN
FREE ACCESS
FORMULA ONE CONSTRUCTORS ASSOCIATION

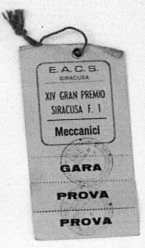

E.A.C.S.
SIRACUSA
XIV GRAN PREMIO
SIRACUSA F. 1
Meccanici
GARA
PROVA
PROVA

Player's
GRAND PRIX CANADA
GP   N° 466
GP TEAM
Sept. 20/1970   LE CIRCUIT

FOCA
VEZZALI GANDARELLI
FOCA ARE THE OWNERS OF THIS
CREDENTIAL NUMBER
AND CAN WITHDRAW IT AT ANY
TIME WITHOUT NOTICE
FORMULA ONE CONSTRUCTORS ASSOCIATION

Automobilclub von Deutschland
Wiesbadener Automobilclub
JIM CLARK
Gedächtnis-
Rennen
13. April 1969
Zulassung
N°. 1391
SICHTBAR TRAGEN!
Helfer
5
Name
(Nicht ausgefüllte Zulassungs-
karten sind ungültig und wer-
den eingezogen)

HELPER 1964

Monaco 79
37ème
Grand Prix
Automobile
F.1.C.A.
PISTE
STANDS

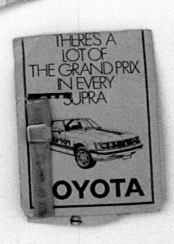

THERE'S A LOT OF THE GRAND PRIX IN EVERY SUPRA
TOYOTA

AUTOMOBILE
FORMEL 1 GP
WM-LAUF
16. 8. 1970
ÖSTERREICHRING
ICHRING

INTRODUCTION

These small memories also help to build the legend.
For Enzo Ferrari, an expert businessman, solidarity had absolute value. On his death, the parish priest of Maranello, don Erio Belloi, was approached by Ferrari's son, Piero:
"Father has arranged for this cheque to be left to the parish".
Ferrari had shown this sort of generosity on many other occasions: the land, where the parish sports fields are now situated, was a gift from him.

A view from the bridge on the dividing-line between Maranello and Fiorano. From this vantage point, one can see part of the circuit of Fiorano: thousands of Ferrari fans gather here when the scarlet cars are testing

"Ferrari was very close to us", recalls the parish priest today. *"On numerous occasions, he used to phone and say to me: Father, things have gone well for me today, if you come and visit me I've got something for you"*.
This solidarity was not only addressed to the Church.

In Modena, you might meet up with one of the taxi drivers, Vincenzo Ferrari. No relation, just the same surname. Vincenzo tells his story:

"In 1982 Enzo Ferrari made a donation of ten million lire to our new cooperative. He said he thought Modena should have a radio taxi cooperative, even though he would almost certainly never use it".

This relationship with Modena's public taxi system is one that has continued over the years. In front of the taxi rank can be found the barber's shop where Ferrari stopped every morning: a shave and a trim before going to work at Maranello.

Above: the barber's shop in Modena where Ferrari stopped every morning and the adverts for the taxi company he financed

The parish church of Maranello in a print from the first half of the century. On the avenue which can be seen on the left, is the main entrance of Ferrari. On the death of Enzo in 1988, parish priest Don Erio Belloi had this beautiful stained-glass window fitted in the church in his memory

MARANELLO - Chiesa Parrocchiale e Strada Abetone-Brennero

This is also Ferrari, and this is also his story. A story born in Modena, nourished by skill and inventivity, but also by the food and Lambrusco wine typical of the area, which Enzo Ferrari liked so much.

On his arrival at Ferrari in 1987, technical director John Barnard ordered a ban on the consumption of wine at the midday canteen. A small revolution ensued: the Maranello workers could not understand this restriction and maintained that it was an insult to their professionalism. Barnard had no way of knowing that the history which had beckoned him to that position had also been written at a table with a dream.

A DREAM BORN IN THE SNOW

Did Enzo Ferrari believe in destiny? A clear-cut answer on the subject has never been available, neither from him nor his closest collaborators. Many clues however, first small and then increasingly larger, imply that in any case destiny believed in Ferrari. This seemed to be the case in a freezing cold month of February 1898, the starting-point for a journey towards a legend, towards an industrial, sporting and social phenomenon, an adventure which can only be called unique in the world.

The snow was too high - recalled Ferrari himself quoting his mother - and they had to wait a couple of days before heading for the registry office to report the happy event. It was strange then that the weather bulletins of the time, which can still be consulted in the town hall of the Emilian city, only speak of cold weather and rain, not snow. Was it the 18th or the 20th? The halo of mystery which surrounds this event is the best way to begin an exceptional story.

The news and the details of those days and those places are exact. They speak the language of Modena of the end of the nineteenth century: a city which was not particularly large, but already flourishing and open to the wonders of industrialization. Alfredo Ferrari was a man who today would be called a small busines-

Reginald Walker, born in Durban, South Africa on 16th March 1889, won the 100 metres event at the London Olympics in 1908 with a time of 10.45 secs, ahead of the American James Rector and Canada's Robert Kerr. At the time 19 years of age, Walker still remains today the youngest-ever Olympic 100 metres champion.

Half-hidden in the outskirts of Modena, Enzo Ferrari's birthplace is still perfectly preserved today. The only indication of its origins lies above the roof of the side of the building, where part of the writing "Officina meccanica Ferrari" is still visible

Enzo Ferrari was born two years before the start of the twentieth century in a building on the outskirts of Modena, in via Paolo Ferrari 5. Here was the steel workshop founded by his father, Alfredo. The name of the street is purely a coincidence and does not justify any further research. The question of his date of birth however is another matter.

According to his own personal version of the facts, and confirmed every year by the telegram of birthday wishes received from his mother, Adalgisa, Ferrari was born on Thursday 18th February. But files in the registry office record the date of 20th February. The reason for this discrepancy appears to be a purely technical hitch.

sman. His steel workshop occupied the ground floor of a building similar to many others in the outskirts of Modena. Above the road-level entrance, the sign read "Officina meccanica Alfredo Ferrari", still visible today as the building has been saved from the industrialization of the area of the past few decades. Above, the windows of the first floor where the Ferrari family lived a quiet middle-class life thanks to the father's business: construction work for the State Railways company.

The early years of young Enzo had no connection whatsoever with the motor car, at the time virtually unknown and which would only become important for the family after the first decade of the twentieth century.

The idea of competition came soon however.

Enzo Ferrari, together with his brother Alfredo, two years his senior, had a very early passion: athletics. There was a canal behind the family house: on its gravel bank, a row of poplar trees formed the backdrop to running races between the two brothers and their friends. Almost every evening, they would run the 100 metres with the impossible aim of equalling or even beating the Olympic record of the day: 10.45 secs held by Reg Walker.

Young Enzo was fast but his brother was faster. In the long-distance races however, it was difficult to compete with their friend Carlo, the barber's son.

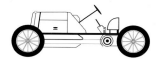

*A young Enzo Ferrari together
with his elder brother Alfredo in
the early years of the 20th century*

One day his father took him and his brother to a motor race: the track wound its way around what was called Circuito di Bologna, deep in the countryside in the form of a triangle, two sides of which were the long straights of the via Emilia and the via Persicetana. Ferrari's official autobiography describes the emotion the youngster felt as having been "violent". Victory went to Felice Nazzaro after a perfect race, even though the fastest lap was set by Vincenzo Lancia. Ferrari watched, observed and made a note in his mind as if etching it in stone.

He was impressed by a measure studied by the organizers to keep the massive numbers of spectators under control: a 15 metre strip of field running alongside the track had been flooded with water. A poor but genial idea: spectators were always enthusiastic about being sprayed or soaked by water, but this solution made it safe for them as the pool of water acted as a run-off area for the cars.

Life in those days was a provincial microcosmos: calm and well-to-do, therefore serene. One of father Alfredo's friends was Anselmo Chiarli, the owner of the wine-making firm of the same name and the godfather of Enzo, whose second name was in fact Anselmo. On top of his interest in athletics and a school performance which left a lot to be desired, Enzo spent long afternoons with his brother in the gym, roller-skating or fighting with sticks. He soon demonstrated ability with a pistol, which enabled the young Ferrari to be good at something and beat his brothers and friends.
But his passion for cars and speed was just around the corner.

TENOR?
RACING DRIVER!

In 1908 Ferrari was ten years old: everything was ripe for a revolution which was destined to overturn the boundaries of the world he knew. The virtually unknown motor car started to take up young Enzo's thoughts.

*Journalism was one of Ferrari's earliest
passions. This famous article was published in the
Gazzetta dello Sport on Monday 16th November 1914* **17**

THE IDEA

One year later, another race: the Record del Miglio. The setting for the race was a long straight of provincial road linking Modena with Ferrara. To get there, the Ferrari father and brothers had to walk across more than three kilometres of fields. Once they arrived at the scene of the action, the eyes of young Enzo began to record the details and etch them once again in his memory. There was no tarmac at the time, and neither was there the liquid called "Fix", a special mixture that would be spread on the surface to stop the dust from forming. The race was held on a gravel road, which dozens of voluntary workers from the Modena Automobile Association dampened with buckets of water and farm barrels to make it more compact and less dusty. Victory went to De Zara: his average speed of more than 140 kph, remarkable for the time, gave Enzo Ferrari a real thrill, but a number of other steps had yet to be taken before he entered the world of motor cars.

Basically there were two obstacles standing in his way. The first was the many temptations which every adolescent embraces, selects and discards.

14th April 1923: Ugo Sivocci and Antonio Ascari finished 1st and 2nd in the Targa Florio.
Alfa Romeo celebrated with a team photograph: Enzo Ferrari is first left; alongside him is the engineer
Rimini and the Baroness Avanzo

One of Enzo's interests in the first decade of the century was music. At home, Saturday evenings were always dedicated to music, a family love which ended up involving the two sons. Many friends also made a name for themselves in this field, such as the tenor Bussetti, a former farrier who performed at the New York Metropolitan. The other temptation was journalism. The years to come would demonstrate the connection between the future constructor and writing. In 1914 Enzo freelanced with the daily newspaper La Provincia di Modena.

This was followed by football correspondent for La Gazzetta dello Sport: a memorable article "Inter defeat Modena 7-1", published on Monday 16th November 1914, is a historical testimony of this.

But the second, more serious obstacle was represented by the First World War. Ferrari went to war in a rather particular way: he was taken on as instructor in the turner's workshop of the Modena fire-brigade, a position which at first enabled him to avoid military service. Another sign of the destiny was that the turning workshop was to be converted into a factory to eventually become the largest manufacturing plant for Fiat agricultural vehicles.

Back to the war, which tore through Ferrari's life like a tornado. The conflict left Italy far worse off and 1917 brought about mass conscription for many young men who had managed to avoid being called to arms. Ferrari was forced to join the Artillery on the Bergamo Alps.

He was only able to return home following a serious (and never exactly specified) illness which led him to convalesce in Brescia Hospital and then, thanks to his mother's intervention, in nearby Bologna Hospital. In 1918, the final year of the war, Ferrari's life had totally changed. Two years previously, he had lost his father and his much-loved brother Alfredo almost at the same time.

Alone with his mother, young Ferrari had to start to get a grip on his life. He was not in any immediate difficulty, thanks to a small inheritance from his father's business. But he needed to find work quickly.

Twenty years old, without any real job experience but with a tireless resolve to do something important, Ferrari accepted with gratitude the help of his mother, who managed to obtain an interview for him at Fiat in Turin. It was the 1918-1919 winter but not even his position as an ex-serviceman saved him from the courteous refusal of the Turin manufacturer, which was also in the reconstruction phase. In the biting cold, which swept throughout the main city of Piedmont, Ferrari felt disheartened, alone and without any hopes for the future.

Many years later, after a happier episode which occurred in the same place, he told of how he had felt discouraged at Parco del Valentino, seated with his head in his hands on a snow-covered bench.
He didn't know at the time, but the motor car and racing bug, long dormant, was about to break out. Enzo Ferrari remained in Turin and found work in the workshop of an engine tuner from Bologna, Giovannoni.

Enzo Ferrari's career as a driver began in 1919 with a C.M.N. car. Ferrari made his debut in the Parma-Berceto mountain time-trial event, finishing fourth overall

It wasn't much, just demolishing lorry chassis and turning them into motor cars. But Enzo soon began to make contacts in the world of racing by frequenting the Bar del Nord in Porta Nuova, where dozens of people from motor racing organized meetings. Drivers mostly, including the Nazzaro brothers, Bergese and Salamano; as well as Bonacini, who had been Bordino's mechanic before the war and was soon to become Ferrari's adviser.

Another bar, the Vittorio Emanuele in Milan, a city which attracted everyone looking for work, opened the door towards the Lombardy metropolis. Thanks to the insistence of Ugo Sivocci, a former cyclist even though less famous than Ferrari's brother Alfredo who had been in the same team as the champion Costante Girardengo, Enzo went to C.M.N. in Milan. There, since the end of the war, the construction of tractors for wartime activity had given way to a factory which fitted engines on chassis derived from the Isotta Fraschini. For C.M.N., Ferrari first began work as a test-driver, and then - despite his mother's objections - as a driver.

It was thanks to Sivocci, a driver who was destined to lose his life at Monza four years later, that Ferrari's passion became uncontrollable ... so much so that he invested his first earnings in the purchase of a racing C.M.N. and entered the first running of the "Parma-Berceto mountain time-trial". It was 1919 and a fourth place overall convinced him to follow a path which he already felt was a vocation.

That same year, again on Sivocci's insistence, he took part in the "Targa Florio". This was a magnificent story and deserves to be told. His participation in the classic Sicilian event began with him driving across almost all of Italy; then from Naples to Palermo by ship. He finished the race, in which he took part in a C.M.N., over the time limit, when the grandstands had already been dismantled. The fault was mechanical, which lost him almost one hour, but also due to a roadblock at Campofelice, where Carabinieri were monitoring a political rally. It was with this excuse that Ferrari, the day after the race, managed to obtain from Vincenzo Fiorio in person an overall ninth place, as well as the reimbursement of his expenses and prize money.

While his career as a driver had begun with tireless resolve, it had now become a burning ambition.

A PASSION FOR ALFA ROMEO

Enzo Ferrari's career as a driver lasted from 1919 to 1931. Twelve years of passion, joys and even victories, some against drivers of the calibre of Tazio Nuvolari. Twelve years which also consolidated the relationship between Ferrari and Alfa Romeo, whose cars Ferrari raced throughout almost all of his career.

The first win with a car from the Alfa Romeo factory - the fifth race of his career - was the 1920 Targa Florio, after three races with an Isotta Franchini 4500 Grand Prix. Ferrari almost won the Sicilian race, but in the end was second with a twin-block four cylinder Alfa 4500. The prize money was 12,000 lire (US$ 7.5): a substantial sum for the time, the equivalent of Lit. 18.000.000 today (US$ 11,250).

Sivocci's Alfa Romeo.
He persuaded Ferrari to become
a driver and shared the wheel
with him in several races.
Sivocci was killed
in 1923 at Monza

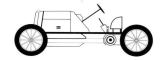

ALFA ROMEO

The Alfa Romeo logo

This is a stylized design of a snake, the symbol of the Visconti, the old noble family of Milan, together with a red cross against a white background, the ensign of the Municipality of Milan. The latter, created in 1045, in turn derives from the union of the ensign of the people (white) with that of the nobility (red).

The evolution of the Alfa Romeo logo
1) *Alfa from 1910 to 1915.*

2) *Romeo was added from 1918 to 1925.*

3) *The World Championship laurels were added from 1925 to 1946.*

4) *From 1946 to 1971 the figure-of-eight knots of the ruling House of Savoy disappeared and were replaced by two insignia.*

5) *The current logo.*

But what was more important was that this result opened the doors to the official team of the Milan manufacturer, whose emblem at the time was the snake of the Viscount, an amaranth-coloured cross and the name Alfa - which stood for Anonima Lombarda Fabrica Automobili. There was still no trace of the word which would complete the marque: Romeo, from the name of the Neapolitan industrialist and politician Nicola Romeo, who only later was to enter the Alfa factory with full support for a sporting programme which would become famous in the history of motor sport. The glorious four-year period from 1921 to 1924 included most of Ferrari's career with Alfa. Wins at the Circuito del Savio (Ravenna), the Circuito del Polesine (Padua) and above all in the 1924 Coppa Acerbo (Pescara) make up a prestigious roll of honours. Ferrari could almost certainly have added another prestigious win, were he not to suddenly withdraw on the eve of the 1924 French Grand Prix in Lyon, where four P2 Grand Prixs had been entered for the race. The drivers were Ascari, Campari, Wagner and Ferrari.

For the world of motor sport, this decision was a bombshell. The withdrawal was announced with a simple telegram. Ferrari was by now a top-level international driver: exhaustion, the official reason for not racing at Lyon, did not fool anyone. It was rumoured that the decision resulted from the insistence of Laura Garello, Ferrari's young and fascinating wife of the past three years, who had no love for the sport. The truth lies elsewhere. Even if one accepts exhaustion as the reason, at the time Ferrari was not just content with being a driver and only a driver.

A MOTIVATOR OF MEN

The race in which he failed to take part in France in 1924 was, if not a pretext, at least a curious coincidence. For some time Ferrari had had a growing desire, which given his character, was becoming an overwhelming ambition: to be more involved in Alfa Romeo's racing programme; Not only as a driver, not only as the final performer in a project which was born by chance. In 1923 he suggested to Alfa that they "poach" a young engineer, his great friend Luigi Bazzi from Fiat. The move was a success and Bazzi became the man behind the legendary 2000 cc six-cylinder P1. It was also this engineer who suggested to Ferrari another young and brilliant engineer, who was also soon to defect from Fiat: Vittorio Jano.

The Four-Leaved Clover

This symbol, a prominent feature on every Alfa Romeo sportscar and racing car, appeared for the first time in 1923 on the front of the RL Targa Florio model, which dominated the race of the same name, finishing first, second and fourth. The Alfa RL won the Circuito del Savio race the same year with Enzo Ferrari. The 3154 cc engine had six cylinders and 95 bhp of power. Top speed was 157 kph.

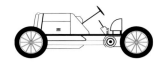

Ferrari came to Turin in September of the same year. Like he did five years previously, although this time not to look for work: instead to offer it. With that typical look of his, despite being just 25, Ferrari knocked on the door of the Jano house on the third floor of a building in via San Massimo. To Jano's wife, who opened the door, he said candidly that he intended to convince her husband to leave Fiat for Alfa Romeo. Signora Jano began to laugh: the totally Piedmontese mind of her husband would never let itself be persuaded to upset the family in this way; Ferrari must have seemed like a madman. Then the engineer arrived and listened to Ferrari: they hit it off straight away and got on famously. The next day he signed a contract at Alfa headquarters.

This episode, a spontaneous one which had no profit-making or heirarchical aims, was just the first step towards making Ferrari totally independent in motor racing. Many years later, he rejected the label of "constructor" which many people called him. He always liked to call himself a "motivator of men", a continuous source of ideas, questions, ambitions and projects which sometimes were totally out of line. The Ferrari of the 1924-1926 three year period kept far away from the steering-wheel. Instead he began to explore every detailed aspect of a racing programme.

He also had to deal with the death of a number of close friends, events which were a severe test for his totally positive nature and his tireless energy.

In 1923 his close friend and great inspiration Sivocci lost his life in a

Lyons, 1924: Antonio Ascari's Alfa P2 in the French GP. Enzo Ferrari did not take part in the race: the first of two he decided to miss

1924 Parma-Berceto mountain time-trial: Antonio Ascari and Ramponi immediately after the victory with the Alfa RLTF

crash at Monza on what many years later would be called the A-scari Curve.

This was followed by the deaths of Giuseppe Campari and Antonio A-scari: the former was a colleague at Alfa, the latter an acknowled-ged champion.

These events however only managed to slow down for a few days Ferrari's own pro-fessional drive towards his one ambition: design and construct increasingly fa-ster cars and assemble complete, perfect and winning teams around them. With this goal in mind, he even invented a number of totally new roles. He did not miss one important race and there were with whom he did not maintain almost daily contacts, always on an equal basis.

He even started up the idea of sponsorship in motor racing, get-ting some of the leading technical suppliers to give financial backing to his first great invention in 1929: Scuderia Ferrari.

Vittorio Jano

The golden age of Alfa Romeo in racing started with Jano, who immediately be-came the undisputed leader of the tech-nical department in Milan. He would continue with Ferrari, where superb te-chnical preparation would allow the thin and severe Turin manager - the method of work imposed by him at Alfa was de-fined by Ferrari as 'military discipline' - to anticipate and perfect dozens of diffe-rent theories and technical applications, including the 6, 8 and 12 cylinder world championship-winning engines.

The Turin engineer was one of those many cases in which a man, an engi-neer, a driver, forged a bond with Ferra-ri that would go down in the history of motor racing. More often than not, they were ties which went far beyond mere professional respect. Relations which were not always (in fact, almost never) serene, and were often prolonged six or seven days of the week, from early in the morning to late in the evening: always discussing, planning, comparing projects during working hours which were regularly extended to include lun-ch and often dinner.

Vittorio Jano was born in Turin but grew up and was professionally trained in Milan. The chief engineer of the Alfa factory was the man behind Alfa Romeo's golden age in motor racing. A French advertising poster (above) for Alfa's international successes in 1924

in the world

1913 - Woodrow Wilson became President of the United States of America. Henry Ford created the world's first car manufacture production line in his Detroit factory.

1914 - On 28th June the heir to the Austrian throne, Archduke Franz Ferdinand, and his wife Sofia, were assassinated in Sarajevo, sparking off the First World War.

1914 - The Panama Canal, joining the Atlantic and Pacific Oceans, was opened in Central America.

1915 - On 7th May, a German submarine sank the steamship Lusitania. 128 Americans on board lost their lives.

1918 - Germany surrendered on 11th November, bringing an end to the First World War.

in motor sport

1916 - In a motor race at Indianapolis, drivers wore a steel protection helmet for the first time ever.

Antonio Ascari

For Ferrari, and for every member of the Milan racing team in the 1920s, Antonio Ascari was known simply as "the Master".

Born in Casteldario, province of Mantua, where Tazio Nuvolari also came from, Ascari began his career in his own workshop where he prepared cars in the very early 1900s. He soon became part of the Alfa Romeo scene and was Alfa's representative for Lombardy. But he was also involved in other different fields, as demonstrated by a spell in Brazil where, together with his two brothers, he helped to build a narrow-gauge railway.

At the wheel of a racing car, Antonio Ascari showed all his talent: an exuberant, attacking driver, constantly going for top performance and maximum speed, rather than for tactics. One episode demonstrates this more than any other.

The 1924 Italian Grand Prix was held at Monza. Ascari was entered in an Alfa Romeo and a message was received in his pits from Arturo

A child in the cockpit of the 1925 Alfa P2. From left to right, Antonio Ascari, Ferrari and Ramponi

Spa-Francorchamps, 1925. Ascari's Alfa P2 refuelling in the pits and celebrations after winning the race

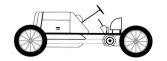

Mercanti, the race director as well as practically the founder of the Autodromo di Monza. "If Ascari continues to take the 'curvetta' in such a dangerous way - read the message - I will be forced to disqualify him". The Mantua driver's control around the bend was slipping as he tried to drive each lap faster than the last. Ascari was to lose his life on the circuit of Monthlery in France in 1925. He left a young son, Alberto, who would do more than just keep the family flag flying.

Monthlery, 1925: the same bend and two dramatically different moments for Antonio Ascari, who was killed at the age of 37, when his car overturned

Giuseppe Campari

Giuseppe Campari became well-known in 1920. The Milan driver started off his career in the automobile sector at Alfa Romeo, which he joined young as test-driver. In his memoirs, Ferrari remembers him as an extraordinary driver, almost an acrobat in a way. Tall, rather chubby, with black hair, very shy and incapable of speaking in public, he was always hot and sweating.

Campari however started off a friendship with Ferrari which went further than a mere commitment to the sport. Campari soon confessed to his young Alfa team-mate from Modena his other two great passions: singing and cookery. His love for singing extended to his marriage, in the 1920s, to the famous opera-singer Lina Cavalleri. His love for cookery would be remembered by Ferrari in a curious

*April 1931:
Giuseppe Campari and
Tazio Nuvolari during
a break in the Mille Miglia*

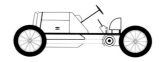
anecdote: one evening, Ferrari was invited together with some friends to Campari's house in the San Siro area of Milan to try out his speciality: riccioline (a short, twisty pasta) in sauce.

A curious Enzo went into the kitchen, where the "cook" was bent over preparing the sauce, unaware that his sweat was dripping into the pan. Without saying a word, Ferrari was the only person present who managed to avoid eating the dish,

saying he was allergic to it. Campari lost his life at Monza in 1933, when he crashed on some oil, the same fate which befell Borzacchini and the Pole Czaykowski.

Campari just before the start of the 1933 Italian GP at Monza. He was destined not to reach the chequered flag. Campari lost his life in a tragic incident when his car went off the road on oil and overturned

in the world

1922 - In Italy after the Fascist March on Rome (24th-28th October), Mussolini was given the task of forming a government (29th October).

1922 - A British expedition led by Lord Carnarvon and Howard Carter discovered the tomb of the Pharaoh Tutankhamen in Egypt.

in motor sport

1922 - The circuit of Monza was inaugurated in the Villa Reale Park. In fact Monza was two tracks which could be linked together a high-speed 4.5 km banked oval and a 5.5 km road course.

1925 - Antonio Ascari died during the French GP. He was born in 1888 near Mantua and started racing with a Fiat in 1919.

1926 - The Avus circuit in Germany held the first German GP. Rudolf Caracciola won in a Mercedes.

1907 PEKING - PARIS RAID

The idea of this raid had been suggested by the Paris daily newspaper "Le Matin".

It was an utterly crazy idea because of its length (15,000 kms) and scarce knowledge of the route. The idea was taken up by only five teams (3 French, one Dutch and one Italian, with the Itala). The route began in Peking (to be reached at drivers' own expense) and then passed through the Gobi Desert, crossing Asia, the Caucasus and Siberia before arriving in Moscow and then Warsaw, Berlin and Paris.

The Italian crew was made up of the 36-year-old Prince Scipione Borghese, a reporter from the Milan newspaper "Corriere della Sera", 33-year-old Luigi Barzini and a mechanic, Ettore Guizzardi. The 7.5 litre, 100 hp Itala weighed 2000 kgs fully-loaded (with 400 litres of fuel and 100 litres of lubricating oil). After leaving Peking on 10th June 1907, the Italian crew was the first to arrive at the headquarters of "Le Matin" in Paris on 10th August.

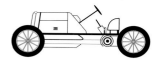

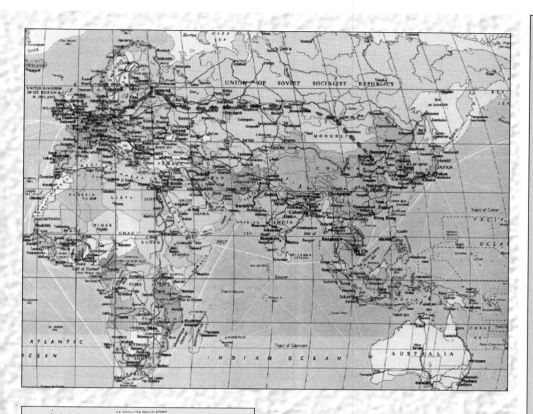

in the world

1927 - Charles Lindbergh completed the first non-stop solo transatlantic flight from New York to Paris (20th-21st May) in the single-engine monoplane, Spirit of St. Louis.

1928 - Alexander Fleming discovered penicillin. He was awarded the Nobel priz for Medicine in 1945.

1929 - On 24th October, the Wall Street Stock Market in New York crashed. It was the start of "The Great Depression", which led to the collapse of thonsands of firms and a massive increase in unemployment.

in motor sport

1927 - The International Association (AIACR) declared it was no longer obligatory to have two seats in motor sport competition. The figure of riding mechanic disappeared.

1929 - The circuit of Monaco-Monte Carlo was created. The street circuit would remain virtually unchanged until the present day.

Raid PEKINO-PARIGI

Arrivato a Parigi il PRINCIPE SCIPIONE BORGHESE
telegrafa alla **DITTA PIRELLI**:

«Parigi 10 Agosto 1907

«**PIRELLI - MILANO**

«Giunto con pneumatici anteriori montati Omsk soddisfattissimo avendo consumate

«soltanto sedici coperture e

«camere aria da Pekino

Borghese»

Peking, 1907: the start of modern-day motor racing. The Itala, driven by Prince Scipione Borghese, accompanied by a mechanic (Guizzardi) and a journalist (Barzini), starts the Peking-Paris Raid from one of the entrances to the Chinese imperial city. They were the first to reach Paris, after encountering numerous difficulties along the route, including the crossing of this stone bridge in Manchuria

THE INVENTOR

In 1929, Alfredo and Augusto Caniato would have found it difficult to believe that they were involved in something destined to become part of the history of motor sport. Hempmerchants from Ferrara, the two brothers were caught up in the wave of enthusiasm and ambitions which Enzo Ferrari managed to generate. It was the Caniato brothers who put in more than 60% (at the time 130,000 lire - US$ 81.25 - out of a total of 200,000 - US$ 125) of the share capital which set up the Scuderia Ferrari joint-stock company. Other shareholders, as well as Ferrari himself, were a driver, Mario Tadini and a photographer, Ferruccio Testi. Alfa Romeo and Pirelli were also minor, but important shareholders.

Scuderia Ferrari was thus created on 29th November 1929, registered by the court of Modena. The initial idea dated back to a few months earlier during a dinner in Bologna. The idea was to help the shareholders race by preparing and running the cars; to organize the necessary technical and sporting back-up and race not only as an activity reserved for a rich élite, but as an outlet for anyone interested in racing who from now onwards would only have to concentrate on just that.

Not even Enzo Ferrari could have imagined it, but his was a unique idea. Having taken Alfa Romeo to the top after removing it from the hands of Fiat, the 31 year-old from Modena became totally involved in motor sport throughout the second half of the 1920s by playing a variety of different roles. He took up racing once again and had a steady job in the Alfa factory working as commercial representative for Emilia-Romagna and the Marche. Above all however, he was thinking, elaborating and making plans. He was constantly inventing and instilling his enthusiasm in others to build up an organization that would top Alfa Romeo itself as far as both prestige and results were concerned. Moreover, his earlier passion for driving racing cars was becoming increasingly replaced by the desire to make his name in the sport with total authority and commitment. The debate no longer revolved around whether Ferrari was a great driver or not: results show that although he might not have been an Ascari or a Nuvolari, he owed nothing to fortune on the track. By now the manager had replaced the driver and the truth was emerging: showing ability behind the wheel of a racing car was only the last - and decisive - phase of the road towards winning. The whole process began much earlier, with the choice of cars, their preparation and the knowledge of races, circuits and regulations; finally with the swift decision-making processes which understand and put into action everything required to arrive first at the chequered flag.

Ferrari at the end of the 1920s was basically an inventor. From his boundless imagination and his total ambition, a project was born out of nothing and grew to become a real company business. Just ten years back, alone and lonely from the family misfortunes of the years of the First World War, he could never have imagined this turn of events. Help obviously came from his new family. Married to the young Laura Garello from Turin, Ferrari was to become a father at the start of the 1930s. The birth of his son Alfredino would be the decisive factor in ending his driving career and at that point, in 1931, the Modena "Manager" was to all effects a point of reference for Alfa Romeo and its motor racing.

Right from the start Scuderia Ferrari exclusively raced Alfa Romeo cars. After the pensioning off of the 6C with 1500 and 1750cc engines, which Ferrari experimented with from 1927 when he resumed racing, the start of the 1930s saw the Scuderia involved with the Alfa Romeo P2 and P3. These cars were to become famous for the first epic battles between champions such as Tazio Nuvolari and Achille Varzi. "Nivola" in fact won the Trieste-Opicina mountain time-trial on 15th June 1930, the first victory for the Scuderia, defeating an array of other Alfa Romeos and numerous Lancias and Bugattis. Two weeks later came the next win, with an Alfa P2, in the mountain race from Cuneo to Colle della Maddalena.

Ferrari was a young entrepreneur: 32 years old and full of hundreds of innovative ideas. The success of the Scuderia was quite exceptional, but one year's activity was sufficient to give cold feet to Ferrari's shareholders who decided not to continue the business due to the efforts required. Their pulling-out however failed to discourage the Modena entrepreneur, who saw that it was necessary to capitalize on success.

In 1931 the Scuderia entered a total of ten cars for the Mille Miglia. The following year Ferrari managed to acquire all the P3s produced by the Milan constructor, becoming the technical-sporting arm of Alfa, which was more than happy to entrust its Modena partner with all of its sporting activity. 1932 was the turning-point, on a company and organizational level, for Scuderia Ferrari. As well as his fellow shareholders, Ferrari began to employ professional drivers. Antonio Varzi and Luigi Fagioli, Campari and Arcangeli, Borzacchini and Chiron, as well as the brilliant Guy Moll began to appear at the wheel of Scuderia Ferrari cars. But one name stood out amongst all the others: Tazio Nuvolari, who was always to remain "the alter ego" of Enzo Ferrari.

August 1930: Scuderia Ferrari has just been formed and most road races were held on gravel surfaces, like these hairpin bends near St Moritz

in the world

1931 - On 11th December, the Statute of Westminster (UK) sanctioned the birth of the Commonwealth and the independence of Australia, New Zealand, Canada and South Africa.

1933 - In Germany on 30th January, Adolf Hitler became Chancellor with a government backed by high finance and large industry.

1933 - The Reichstag Fire on 27th February, caused by the Nazis but blamed for propaganda purposes on the Communists, created a pretext for a decree to be approved by Hindenburg which suspended the fundamental rights of the Constitution: it was the start of the Third Reich.

in motor sport

1932 - Ferdinand Porsche founded the company of the same name for the design and construction of racing cars.

1935 - On 28th July, more than 200,000 people watched the German GP at the Nurburgring. The outcome was supposed to have been a foregone conclusion between 5 works Mercedes and 4 factory Auto Unions. But Germany hadn't reckoned with Italy: Tazio Nuvolari won in an Alfa Romeo, run by Enzo Ferrari.

NUVOLARI

Everything and more about Tazio Nuvolari has been handed down to the present day by historical news items. This means that the figure of "Nivola" has emerged from the legend itself. Six years older than Ferrari (he was born on 16th November 1892 at Castel d'Ario, a few kilometres from Mantua), Nuvolari was already a top driver when he joined the Scuderia. Small, with smiling eyes worn on a thin and nervous body, the champion from Mantua seemed to be born to be a part of motor racing history. He used to race and win on bikes. When he switched to cars, maybe because he was used to the superior balance required on two wheels, he did extraordinary things. He had no fear of speed: on the contrary, it spurred him on. But his class behind the wheel would be directly proportional to the number of curves waiting to be tackled. Curves: he called them resources of the track, each one of them was for him a challenge, whatever the risk.

In October 1930, when he signed an exclusive contract for 1931, except for three motor bike races which he was particularly fond of, it was clear that Nuvolari was soon to become the flag-bearer of Scuderia Ferrari. This immediately lead to the start of a string of events, sometimes sensational, which made Nivola's legend and motor racing history. At the 1930 Mille Miglia, he was driving an Alfa Romeo, identical to that of Varzi who started one minute before him. Nuvolari was to catch him by surprise at the end of the final night of the race, overtaking him with his headlights turned off so as not to be noticed. It was not important that the dark of the night had been replaced by the early light of dawn: the legend had been made.

Tazio Nuvolari won many races for Scuderia Ferrari. The historic victories were the 1932 Targa Florio, with a final time which was only to be bettered twenty years later. A sensational victory also came at the 1935 German GP, where Nuvolari's tiny Alfa managed to win on the impossible curves of the old Nurburgring circuit against the powerful and dominant Auto Union and Mercedes squads, the hosts, who were widely expected to walk away with an easy win.

At Brno in Czechoslovakia, again in 1935, Nuvolari finished second with his left rear tyre down to the rim.

A special mention is reserved for his victory in the 1936 Vanderbilt Cup, organized in the United States which aimed to start up motor racing competition between Europe and America.

The Italian driver was the driving force behind the growing technical side of the Scuderia, which was mo-

The Alfa Romeo P3 (1932)

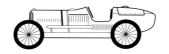
re and more involved in research and testing, even though always for Alfa Romeo. In 1935 Ferrari's organization constructed a "monster" of a car, fitted with two eight-cylinder Alfa engines (one at the front and one at the rear), capable of taking Nivola to a new maximum speed record of 364 kph and an average of more than 323 kph over the mile,

Tazio Nuvolari: the legend began on two wheels but he soon switched to cars. This was the start of a unique relationship of friendship and rivalry, admiration and brotherly love between 'Nivola' and Enzo Ferrari

in the world

1936 - The Spanish Civil War broke out after the revolt of Generals Francisco Franco, Mola, Sanjurjo and Goded (backed by Germany, Italy and Portugal) against the Republican government of Manuel Azana.

1937 - The German Air Force devastated the Basque town of Guernica during the Spanish Civil War on 26th April. The massacre provided the inspiration for a monumental oil painting by Pablo Picasso.

in motor sport

1936 - Tazio Nuvolari, driving an Alfa Romeo, won the Vanderbilt Cup in the State of New York, 10 minutes ahead of Wimille (Bugatti 4900). Fiorello La Guardia, mayor of New York, thanked him publicly on behalf of millions of immigrants in the United States.

1937 - An Auto Union driven by Bernd Rosemeyer made history by breaking the 400 kph limit for the first time on an autobahn near Frankfurt, Germany.

speeds which were reached on a stretch of the motorway from Florence to the coast.

The idyllic relations between Nuvolari and Ferrari were interrupted in 1936. The driver, aware that he was the reason for the fortunes of the Modena entrepreneur, wanted to become an equal partner in the company. But that wasn't all: he also wanted the new company to be called Scuderia Nuvolari Ferrari. This situation has its roots in a conflict of personalities, both strong and determined, between the driver and the businessman. A conflict only in part, full of mutual admiration and friendship, but one which had the capacity to surprise: Ferrari showed shrewdness and organizational and administrative ability; Nuvolari gave a constant display of extraordinary courage. On his departure for the 1932 Targa Florio from Modena, the driver discovered he had a return ticket, and he realized this was an opportunity to make a gibe at Ferrari:
"They say you're a good administrator - said Nivola to an astonished Ferrari

- but I realize it's not true. You should have booked me a one-way ticket: when you leave for a race, there is always the possibility that you'll come back in a wooden coffin".
What an extraordinary personality! In any case, there are many such anecdotes aptly describing the relationship linking the driver and the constructor until 1953, the year of Nuvolari's death. A relationship between two giants of motor racing, who began to understand that they were just that, but managed to respect each other all the same.
After Nuvolari wanting to become partner of Ferrari, the relationship between the two was punctuated by divorces and reconciliation. At the 1936 Circuito di Modena on the street circuit prepared on the narrow roads of the town in Emilia, the Monument Chicane was probably the most difficult curve, forcing the drivers to use their arms on the

1930: the Alfas of Scuderia Ferrari began to become more numerous: the 1750 SS of Lord Howe-Birkin (below) at the Le Mans 12 Hours. The same car driven by Nuvolari at the Targa Florio (alongside) and the driver after victory in the Mille Miglia the same year

1939 - On 1st September, Germany invaded Poland without declaring war. The Second World War began.

1940 - (August-October) In the Battle of Britain, Goering's Luftwaffe was unable to overcome the British fighters and anti-aircraft attack, which had help from the discovery of radar.

1941 - On 22nd June, Hitler gave the go-ahead for Operation Barbarossa, attacking the USSR without declaring war.

1941 - On 7th December, the Japanese carried out a surprise attack on the US naval base at Pearl Harbour (Hawaii). The USA entered the war the next day.

The New York Times.

JAPAN WARS ON U. S. AND BRITAIN; MAKES SUDDEN ATTACK ON HAWAII; HEAVY FIGHTING AT SEA REPORTED

1943 - On 25th July, Mussolini was ousted after being outvoted by the Grand Council: control of the Italian government was taken over by Marshall Badoglio, who with the consent of the King, opened peace negotiations with the Allies.

1943 - At the Tehran Conference on 28th November, Roosevelt, Churchill and Stalin discussed the invasion of Europe, scheduled for May 1944, and post-war political issues regarding Germany and Poland.

steering-wheel. The curve was also Ferrari's favourite observation point, but that year he was without Nuvolari, who had moved to Maserati. It was at the Variante del Monumento that the driver, oblivious to the difficult nature of the curve, on every lap passed his hand over his nose in a gesture mocking the astonished Ferrari. Memories of days gone by ...

The two, in any case, took different paths. Nuvolari raced with other cars: Cisitalia and Auto Union, as a replacement driver after the tragic death of Bernd Rosemeyer. With the German car, Tazio amazingly won the race on 22nd October 1938 at Donington Park in Britain, making up time on Lang's Mercedes after a pit-stop of almost a minute. He took the lead four laps from the end to the cheers of the spectators, thus earning the title of "master" from all the other drivers.

Nuvolari and Ferrari found themselves back together again in 1947, the year of the birth of the first real Ferrari racing car. One year later Nuvolari dominated the Mille Miglia with a Ferrari 166 powered by a two-litre 12-cylinder engine, but a few hours from the finish in Brescia a broken leaf-spring pin interrupted the legendary cavalcade.

"Bad luck, you'll win next year", said Ferrari in an attempt to cheer up the 56 year-old driver.

"Ferrari", came the reply (he had always called him Ferrari). *"At our age, there aren't many days left like this. Remember that, and try and enjoy them to the utmost, if you can"*. Nuvolari died five years later on 11th August 1953. In a way he would surely have preferred not to: in a bed, after trying to avoid for many years the terrible destiny which had taken away both his sons at an early age, a destiny which made him lucidly but desperately in charge of his own fate.

With this letter, signed by Minister Falcone Lucifero, the Royal House expressed its condolences for the death of Tazio Nuvolari in 1953. Eighteen years before, in 1935, the contract between 'Nivola' and Scuderia Ferrari was three pages long

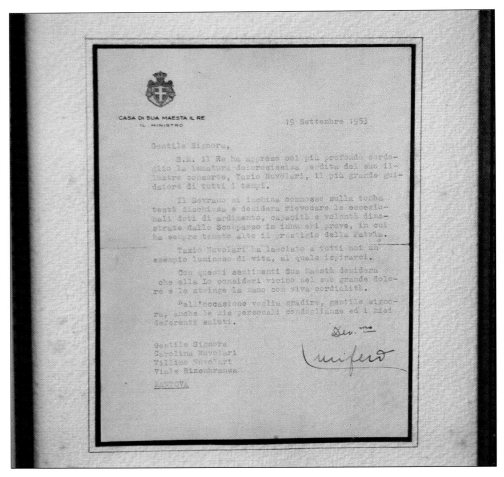

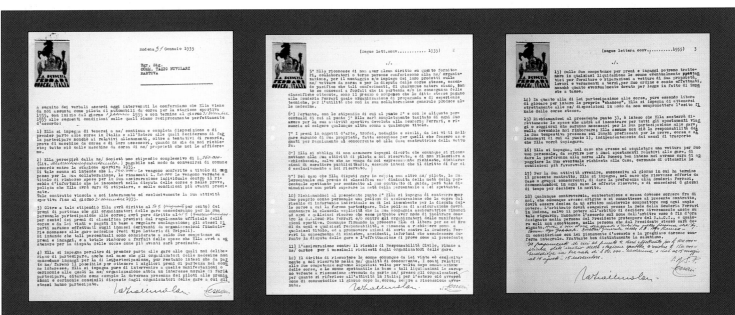

AWAY FROM ALFA

Destiny often plays strange tricks, unpredictably yet inevitably taking its course. This was the case of Alfa Romeo from 1937 onwards. A complex string of events, with an initial serious consequence, that arrived at a turning-point, deciding the fate of a man, a marque and the future of motor racing.

Half-way through the 1930s, Alfa was in the middle of a serious crisis, results-wise. The sporting regulations introduced in 1934 stipulated a maximum weight of 750 kilograms for cars. Everything else was free: including the type and power of the engine. The technical regulations ended up by penalizing the cars from the Milan manufacturer. Above all against the German competitors - Mercedes and Auto Union - which

made good use of an avant-guard iron and steel industry and a budget far greater than anything the Italian manufacturer could pour into motor racing. The greater agility guaranteed by a smaller structure allowed Scuderia Ferrari to intervene more easily and above all more rapidly in this difficult technical scene. Already in 1935 the Scuderia had constructed the twin-engined "Bimotore", powered by two 8-cylinder units, whose main feature was its exceptional performance, despite it also having major mechanical problems. In a lightened version weighing less than a ton, the "Bimotore" set the above-mentioned land speed record on the Florence-Livorno motorway. But in the heavier, more reliable version for racing, the car literally tore up its tyres, thus requiring numerous pit-stops which wiped out the

advantage from its greater performance. One year later, Alfa Romeo commissioned Scuderia Ferrari to construct a new car: the 158, powered by a supercharged 8-cylinder engine. This was a car with a great potential, so much so that Alfa sent to Modena one of its top engineers, Gioachino Colombo, to design it together with Ferrari's engineering staff.

The situation began to become dramatic. The Milan manufacturer continued to support the Scuderia, but in a particular way and with particular agreements. It proposed the purchase of 80% of Ferrari's organization, leaving him with the task of representing Alfa in competition. Ferrari was waiting for this moment and replied with a counter-proposal: close down the Scuderia and hand over to Alfa the technical material of the team, cars included.

In exchange, he was to ask for and obtain the creation of a new structure in Milan, Alfa Corse, of which he would become sole director with full powers.

In a certain sense, it was blackmail.

"I will give you greater, more dedicated support", was Ferrari's reply, *"on condition that from now on the company guarentees its total commitment to competition and that I am the one who runs it"*. The idea must have come as a shock to Alfa Romeo and its Director-General, Ugo Gobbato, but in any case it was swallowed and accepted. This transformed the moment of crisis of the Milan constructor into a clear take-over by Ferrari. In any case Ferrari was the one who had the big ideas. The Scuderia itself, a splendid and revolutionary invention in the ever-changing world of motor sport, was limited by its size. Clearly Alfa Romeo guarenteed a different future, other means and other possibilities.

That was the start of Alfa Corse, but soon the expectations of the Modena constructor came face to face with cold reality. Even colder in a way because Ferrari soon discovered he was not the only real boss. He was put in charge of the sporting division, but as head of the special **39** projects division, there was a certain Ricart, a man almost the same age as Ferrari with whom he came into direct competition. Of Spanish origin and an extrovert and authoritarian engineer, Wilfred Ricart had managed to obtain the total confidence of the Alfa Romeo Director-General. Sparks immediately flew between him and Ferrari on a personal level. It was a clash which magnified the lack of synergy between the working methods of the man from Modena and those of the Alfa of the day. Ferrari maintained that the entire competitions programme must be in the hands of a small and agile structure, capable of resolving problems in a short time. Gobbato thought differently, and in this he was backed by Ricart. The Alfa Romeo management maintained that races, although independent, must in any case be run with cars which incorporated the technical capacities of the entire company.

Ferrari tried to prevail in every way possible. He attempted to convince the Director-General that Ricart was clearly a genius, and for this reason his efforts must be directed to higher activities than mere racing. He tried to make friends with the Spaniard, but to no avail. Ferrari was to remember this in one of his best books "Ferrari 80" with a few sharp words:

"Ricart had smooth greasy hair. He dressed elegantly but looked rather oriental, with long-sleeved jackets which hid his hands. When he held out his hand, you could feel inert flesh, rather like that of a corpse".

He continued with a funny anecdote:

"He used to wear shoes with enormous rubber soles. They were so big that one day I asked him why he wore them. He replied calmly that an engineer had to take certain precautions: a well-sprung step prevented disturbances and vibrations from going to the brain".

Ferrari was astounded: he felt he was reaching boiling-point. That was when the 158 began to cause problems. Ferrari wanted to exploit its potential which he maintained was still vast; instead Ricart thought it was outdated and pressed for the

construction of a new car, with a 12-cylinder rear-located engine. This was never going to work and when Enzo Ferrari pointed it out to the Director-General, the reply was exactly one from someone expecting such a protest. Divorce came immediately: in September 1939 Alfa Romeo recognized the severance pay for almost twenty years of close collaboration, demanded a commitment from Ferrari not to become involved in motor racing for four years, and wound up the rapport with immediate effect.

Thus ended a chapter of motor sport history. Ferrari lost: the clash between his personal desire for innovation and inventive energy and the working methods of a large company saw him end up in a minority. The order to not become directly involved in motor sport for four years reveals just how much re-

spect Alfa Romeo had for the 41 year-old "motivator of men" from Modena. On the other hand, Ferrari was a man of extraordinary sensibility and could see that four years were soon to pass by in haste: the Second World War was just around the corner and all signs pointed to it being a long one ...

1935: a group photo for the first appearance of the Alfa Romeo Bimotore with Nuvolari at the wheel. A picture from Monza the same year (the other page, below) of the Trossi Monoposto, powered by a curious 16-cylinder engine with volumetric compressor which was capable of producing more than 250 hp. 1936 saw the first appearance at Monza of the Alfa Romeo driven by Dreyfuss, closely watched by Vittorio Jano. The Alfa 12 cylinder of Nuvolari at Monza (the other page, above). Chicanes had already been invented

Nivola's secret

In 1931 Enzo Ferrari was still active as a driver as well as being the owner of Scuderia Ferrari. He was to hang up his gloves at the end of this season, helped a little in taking his decision by the birth of his son Alfredino. One day, during practice for the Circuito delle Tre Province race, he asked Nuvolari if he could sit beside him in an Alfa 1750 leased to him by the Scuderia for that race. Nivola was suspicious: he had seen Ferrari at the wheel of a much more powerful 8-cylinder Alfa Romeo 2300. Nevertheless, he agreed to the request. From the tale of that experience as co-driver, written by Ferrari in his book "Piloti, che gente ..." (Drivers, what people ...), comes possibly the clearest and most colourful explanation of the mystery which made Nivola such a great and legendary driver.

"At the first curve - wrote Ferrari - I had the clear sensation that Tazio had made a mistake and we were to end up in the ditch. I braced myself for the impact. Instead we ended up at the start of the next straight with the car perfectly in line. I looked at him: his rugged face was calm and normal, not the face of one who has just luckily escaped from a spin. At the second and third curve, I had the same impression. At the fourth and fifth it all became clear to me: out of the corner of my eye, I noticed that throughout the Parabolica curve Tazio never once took his foot off the accelerator; on the contrary he pushed it flat to the floor. As the curves flashed by, I discovered his secret. Nuvolari went into the bend earlier than driver instinct would have told me. But he approached it in an unusual way, suddenly pointing the nose of the car at the inside edge, right at the point where the curve began. With his foot down - clearly in the right gear for the curve before pointing the car - he let the car go in a controlled skid on all four wheels, taking advantage of the centrifugal force and holding it with the traction force of the driving wheels. Throughout the entire radius of the curve, the nose of the car shaved the inside stone edge, and when the curve finished and the straight began, the car would be in the normal position to continue the race, without any corrective manoevres". Just for the record, the Circuito delle Tre Province was won by Nuvolari. Ferrari was second.

Circuit of Biella, 1935. The acrobatic driving style of Nuvolari was something which his rivals had no chance of emulating

The Vanderbilt Cup

This was the first important motor race competition between Europe and America. The Vanderbilt Cup was a well-established race over the on side of the Atlantic, more important than the Indianapolis 500, but in 1936 it was even more prestigious than ever. The Roosevelt Field circuit was set up for the event on Long Island. A 34-strong American team lined up against the expedition from Europe, made up of Alfa Romeos, Bugattis and Maseratis. At the last moment an entry was received from Scuderia Ferrari for three Alfa Romeo 12Cs for Nuvolari, Brivio and Farina. The result was sensational. Nivola totally annihilated the opposition: pole position, fastest lap and victory in a race led from start to finish, almost half-an-hour ahead of the local favourite Mauri Rose, the first of the Americans, but only sixth overall.

To drive home the sensational result, Nuvolari collected prize-money of $85,000 (an exorbitant amount for the time), but broke into a cold sweat on the steamship on the trip home, when he thought he had left the winning cheque in his hotel. Luckily though, he found it.

Nuvolari won the 1936 Vanderbilt Cup and the Italian press celebrated the victory. In the group photo on arriving in New York, the driver can be seen together with the captain of the transatlantic liner Rex, Brivio; on the right, Farina, Bazzi and the journalist Canestrini

The Prancing Horse emblem

A black horse on a yellow background, with its front legs in the air, viewed from the left. Today this is the universally recognized symbol of Ferrari and many other companies over the years have come to realize this - at their own expense - after having, maybe involuntarily, copied it to publicize their own products. The prancing horse appeared on Scuderia Ferrari cars in 1932 at the Spa 24 Hours race.

Ferrari remembered that the idea hadbeen offered to him nine years before. On his first victory as a driver, at the 1923 Circuito del Savio, he was given the prize by Countess Paolina Baracca, the mother of Air Force pilot and First World War ace, Francesco. The Countess offered Ferrari the horse logo which was on the fuselage of her son's fighter airplane so that he could use it for his racing cars. Ferrari accepted with gratitude. Since 1932 the black horse on a yellow background - the historic colour of Modena - has identified all the cars, competition and production, from Enzo Ferrari's activity.

The sponsors

History has already credited Enzo Ferrari's intuition in coming up with the idea of sponsorship. It was in 1929, the first year of the Scuderia; the involvement of Alfa Romeo and Pirelli in the initial share capital was aimed above all at ensuring maximum technical collaboration from the two companies. But as well as tyres and cars, the two Milan companies also made a financial contribution: 5,000 lire (US$ 3.125) from Pirelli and 10,000 (US$ 6.25) from Alfa, thus paving the way for the numerous marques which were involved from then onwards: Shell (fuels and lubricants), Bosch (electrical equipment), Rudge Whitworth (wheels), Champion (spark plugs), Siata (shock absorbers) and Memini (carburettors). In addition to supplying their material free of charge, these companies guaranteed financial support in exchange for which Ferrari gave them advertising space in the end of season company magazine and their names on the lorries which transported the cars to the circuits. With this sensational new idea, Enzo Ferrari succeeded right from the start in financing his racing activity, improving the overall situation with the many "paying" drivers. The figures were quite substantial, with Shell in 1932 paying the Scuderia the tidy sum of 100,000 lire. (US$ 62.5). Today that would be around 150,000,000 lire (US$ 93,750) ...

"La storia del cavallino rampante è semplice e affascinante. Il cavallino era dipinto sulla carlinga del caccia di Francesco Baracca, l'eroico aviatore caduto sul Montello, l'asso degli assi della prima guerra mondiale.
Quando vinsi nel '23 il primo circuito del Savio, che si correva a Ravenna, conobbi il conte Enrico Baracca, padre dell'eroe; da quell'incontro nacque il successivo, con la madre, contessa Paolina.
Fu essa a dirmi, un giorno: « Ferrari, metta sulle sue macchine il cavallino rampante del mio figliolo. Le porterà fortuna ». Conservo ancora la fotografia di Baracca, con la dedica dei genitori, in cui mi affidano l'emblema. Il cavallino era ed è rimasto nero; io aggiunsi il fondo giallo canarino che è il colore di Modena".

A meteoric Guy Moll

It is no secret to reveal that out of all his drivers, Ferrari has always loved the most instinctive and exciting ones, drivers who manage to put on a show thanks to their inborn sense of speed and their ability to overcome the risk threshold. Guy Moll, in this sense, would be paralleled by Ferrari to the recent phenomenon called Gilles Villeneuve. Born of an Algerian father and Spanish mother, Guy Moll began to make his name in motor racing and Ferrari immediately gave him an

Alfa from the Scuderia. It was the 1934 Monaco Grand Prix: Moll won by overtaking Chiron on the final curve, repeating Nuvolari's victory of two years before. It was love at first sight between Ferrari and Moll. Unfortunately however it was not destined to last: Moll lost his life at the Coppa Acerbo that same year. The memory remains of Moll as a splendid, exciting meteor.

Victories of Ferrari at the wheel

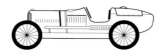

Ferrari competed in 40 races from 1919 to 1931, with a break from 1925 to 1926. He won a total of 9 races:

1923 Circuito del Savio

1924 Circuito del Savio
Circuito del Polesine
Coppa Acerbo

1927 Circuito di Alessandria
Circuito di Modena

1928 Circuito di Alessandria
Circuito di Modena

1931 Bobbio-Passo del Penice
mountain time-trial

Scuderia Ferrari raced from 1930 to 1937, competing - always with Alfa Romeos - in a total of 225 races, with 144 victories. The best year was 1935 with 30 victories out of 35 races.

Photo album of racing in the 1920s and 1930s.

1) 1936 Monaco GP: Brivio ahead of Farina and Nuvolari, all in 8-cylinder Alfa 3800s
2) Enzo Ferrari and Nuvolari at the 1924 Circuit of Savio. The car is a Chiribiri and Ferrari went on to win
3) The prancing horse of Scuderia Ferrari can be seen on the Alfa Tipo B of Nuvolari, winner of the Circuit of Biella race
4) 1935: Enzo Ferrari behind Nuvolari who is preparing for his first test with the Alfa Romeo Bimotore
5) Montecarlo 1935: the pile-up at the chicane in front of the port
6) The triumph of 'Nivola' in an 8-cylinder Alfa 2300 at the 1931 Targa Florio
7) 1938 Le Mans 24 Hours: the 8-cylinder Alfa 2900 of Biondetti-Sommer
8) 1936 Hungarian GP: the number 24 Alfa 8C of the winner Nuvolari, whose teammate Tadini finished fourth
9) 1933 Coppa Principessa di Piemonte: the Alfa 1500 SS of women drivers Peduzzi-Restelli
10) The start of the 1932 Monaco GP: Nuvolari and Caracciola on the front row in 8-cylinder Alfa Romeo 2300Ms.
11) Rome, 1931, the Autodromo del Littorio: Nuvolari drove the 8-cylinder Alfa 2300 Monza to victory in the duel with a Caproni 100 aeroplane
12) 1934 French GP: victory went to Luis Chiron, in the middle between Varzi and Trossi, all driving Tipo B Alfa Romeos

THE NEW 12 CYLINDER ENGINE

Let us go back to the precise moment when Ferrari left Alfa Romeo. The amount of severance pay given to Enzo Ferrari by the Milan manufacturer was never officially made known, even though sources put the figure at about 1,000,000 lire (US$ 625) at the time; a considerable sum enabling Ferrari to purchase the beautiful Palazzo dei Cento Caproni, one of the finest buildings in Modena. It also allowed him to buy land at Maranello, and maybe just then the Modena constructor was unaware that he he was laying the first stones of his legendary future.

As mentioned, Ferrari left Alfa with one clear aim: to demonstrate to the management of the Milan manufacturer who Ferrari was and what he could achieve in motor racing. He was of course forced to abandon racing for four years, but this was easily got round by plans to build a car for private drivers: the 815. As he could not use the logo of the Scuderia, the Auto Avio Costruzioni Ferrari was born. With the first of the two 815s constructed, Alberto Ascari, the son of Antonio who had flanked the Modena constructor in his first steps in the sport,

made his racing debut at the 1940 Mille Miglia. The race was much shorter, a triangle connecting the towns of Brescia, Cremona and Mantua. The 815 made a brilliant start before retiring with mechanical problems. The project was a good one, but the car was built too hastily. It was also spring 1940: Italy was about to become involved in the Second World War and thoughts were lying elsewhere.

At the start of the conflict, the work of the small group of engineers in the headquarters at Viale Trento e Trieste in Modena became first difficult and then impossible. The main cities of northern Italy were hit by bombs and everything had to be moved to Maranello, especially after the new laws on industrial decentralization. Despite being caught up in a war, the workforce under Ferrari grew from 40 to more than 150. Work was not hard to find. Ferrari was asked to construct mechanical parts for the National Aeronautics Company in Rome; later he also obtained the tender for the construction of industrial machinery for the production of ball bearings.

These weeks were packed with drama: bombing raids and war incidents quickly followed and not even the Maranello factory was spared when it was hit in a couple of air raids at the end of 1944 and the start of 1945, the final year of the war.

The building in the centre of Modena, purchased at the end of the 1930s, where Enzo Ferrari lived until the final days of his life

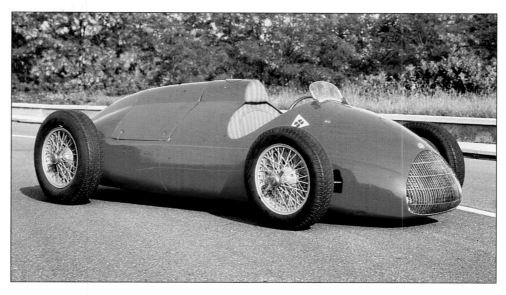

When the engineer Colombo, the designer of the Alfa 158, came to Maranello in the spring, he found Ferrari impatient to get going again.

By now he was thinking of racing-cars day and night. He also had a new revolutionary aim in mind: a car constructed around a 12 cylinder engine. Raymond Sommer, a French driver who was very famous at the time, never failed to impress upon Ferrari his personal view of this particular engine configuration, which he considered to be the choice of the future. Convincing Ferrari was not difficult: in the 1920s he had already been impressed by an American car, purchased by Antonio Ascari, which had a V12 engine. This was followed by the US Army Packards which arrived with the liberation of Italy

at the end of the war. Finally at Alfa Romeo, there was the idea of Ricart, who was convinced he could construct a rear-engined 12 cylinder 1500cc car. It was at this stage that Enzo Ferrari, not in the least perturbed by the events of the war which had just ended after a period of terror in northern Italy, began to nurture splendid projects for the relaunch of motor sport.

THE FIRST REAL FERRARI

May 11th 1947 marked the debut of the first real Ferrari racing team at the Circuito di Piacenza. The race was a minor one and the spectators were unaware of the fact that the first chapter of a motor sport legend was being written. The Ferrari 125 at this debut had been designed two years beforehand. Since then, much importance had been given to the design, construction and testing of the 12 cylinder engine, which ran for the first time on the test-bench in autumn 1946. At Piacenza there were two cars in the newly-created colours of the Prancing Horse: they were driven by the future World Champion Nino Farina and Franco Cortese. The former decided to abandon the venture on the eve of the race, unhappy with the performance of the car in practice. Cortese however carried on: he was leading the race until two laps from the end and retired with fuel-pump problems. All things considered, it wasn't such a bad debut.

Two weeks later, on Sunday 25th May, there was a race in Rome. At the Caracalla circuit, it was Cortese who again set the pace. This time there were no mechanical problems and he won easily. The enthusiasm amongst the team was evident, but nobody - not even Ferrari - could have guessed that this victory was the start of a legend. The run of vic-

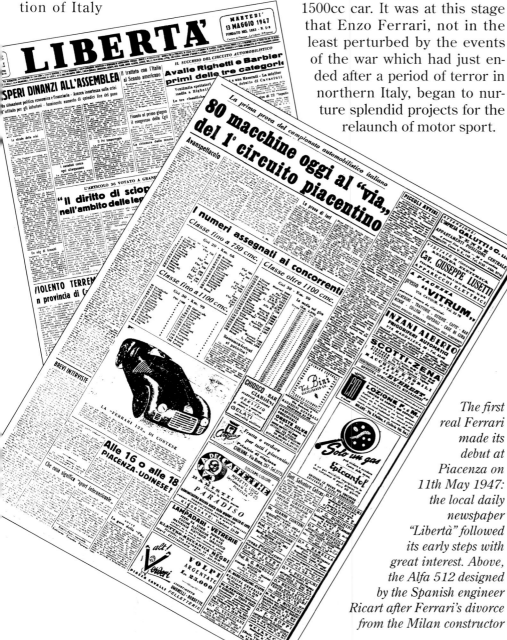

The first real Ferrari made its debut at Piacenza on 11th May 1947: the local daily newspaper "Libertà" followed its early steps with great interest. Above, the Alfa 512 designed by the Spanish engineer Ricart after Ferrari's divorce from the Milan constructor

tories continued. Cortese won again, as did Nuvolari soon afterwards. After enthusiastically agreeing to drive the new car, he triumphed in two races. At the end of the season in autumn, the Grand Prix version of the Ferrari 125 made its debut. It was driven by Sommer, who won the Turin GP. Success for the 125, a car which could be raced in different categories thanks to simple modifications to the bodywork and the fairings, was complete and immediate.

This was in spite of the fact that the first real Ferrari had sprung from the constructor's own technical conviction that the engine was always more important than the chassis.

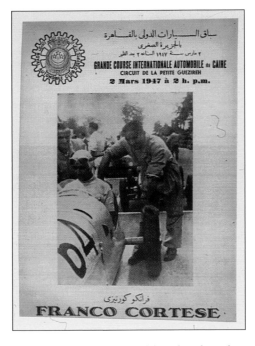

FRANCO CORTESE

A conviction he would only abandon later, on the path towards technical perfection, paving the way to other wins and increasingly sophisticated cars, which would come to dominate in the technical sector.

For Enzo Ferrari, the Grand Prix won by Sommer stretched far beyond its technical importance. The finishing line for the 125 Grand Prix at the Circuito del Valentino was in fact just a few feet away from that famous bench where Ferrari

Racing at the Circuito del Valentino in Turin. On the other page, the 1948 Ferrari 125 Grand Prix

had cried silent tears at the end of the First World War. Then he was alone, after the death of his father and without his much-loved brother Alfredo. He was unemployed without any immediate hope of finding work. That was 1919, now it was 1947. How life had changed over the years ....

Almost thirty years which transformed the face of the world, society, the motor car and motor racing. Thirty years in which Ferrari was "invented". Two years after the end of the Second World War, Ferrari was one of the new men on the Italian industrial scene. In racing, the stage for his real, indestructible ambition, the Modena constructor was the point of reference. He loved racing, but had abandoned the career due to a combination of professional and family reason.

A new profession, a motivator of men and ideas, had taken over. His driving ambition was to give life to a completely new role in racing: constructor, sporting director, technical adviser; the role of husband and father was not an easy one for a racing-driver, who has to win, win and win again. All of these conditioning factors undoubtedly influenced the decision to bring an end to his career as a racing-driver. But all things considered, Ferrari himself felt he never had what it took to become a great champion.

"Even if I had worked hard at it - he admitted one day - I wasn't sure I could have been a great racing-driver. I had my doubts at the time ...".

The doubts, in a way, also involved a technical aspect. The racing-driver in Ferrari respected the motor car and did everything he could to go easy on it. A racing-driver who wants only to win, who must win, thinks in a completely different way. The constructor in Ferrari could give his best to this role, dividing his massive desire to reach the top with this particular aspect. Furthermore, he was entirely at home in this role, and could totally respect the engineering techniques which were his guiding light. From this point onwards, the scarlet red cars had become a cornerstone of road racing competition and were now ready to make a triumphant entry into the circuits.

FROM THE ROAD ... TO FORMULA 1

At the end of the 1940s Enzo Ferrari had reached a key point in his life. At fifty years of age, he was above all a lonely man. Only this time, not in the negative sense of the word. In the much more positive and reassuring sense of man and manager who did not have to ask for anyone's agreement before taking a decision. Ferrari was very much his own man. The racing team was based on various strong personalities, but only Ferrari was at the helm. The days at Alfa Romeo were long gone. And so were the days with the Spaniard, Ricart, with his crazy pretences, with his absurd way of dressing, of speaking, of walking on rubber so as not to disturb his brain waves.

"I am in charge of Alfa Romeo - said Gobbato at the moment of the disagreements which led to the divorce of 1939 - *and I cannot accept your suggestions without reserve. Or in any case without discussion*".

"*I'm leaving Alfa* - was Ferrari's reply - *and it's Alfa's decision. But for this reason I will not change my way of being and thinking*".

History. Or maybe prehistory. The Milan manufacturer, which remained under Ricart's control, never again produced a winning racing-car. The Spanish engineer, who stayed with Alfa until 1945 as Director of Special Projects, was by then a man of the past. Ferrari, on the other hand, was looking with great interest towards everything that moved, changed, and promised innovation and developments in the competitions sector. On the horizon there was a new category of cars and races called Grand Prixs, destined to become the first Formula 1 in 1950. The path towards Grand Prixs on a continuous and worldwide basis was however still a long one. Ferrari approached it by dominating the road races of the day. In 1948 Clemente Biondetti and Giuseppe Navone won the Mille Miglia with a Ferrari 166S. For the Prancing Horse manufacturer, it was the first victory of international importance, but it was dulled by the disappointment which befell Nuvolari. Called upon to take part in the Mille Miglia just one day before the start, Nuvolari was given the Scuderia Inter 166S with number 1049 on its bodywork. His co-driver was the mechanic Sergio Scapinelli: together they took the lead on the stretch of road to Pescara. When they got to Rome, they had a twelve-minute lead. At Livorno, the lead was twenty minutes. At Bologna, thirty-five. Before Rome, the number 1049 Ferrari had lost its

breakage of the rear leaf-spring pin which was to prove fatal.

Ferrari, watching the race, was following the situation which was about to bring an end to Nuvolari. The racing-driver from Mantua was 56 years old, Ferrari six years younger. They were linked by a special bond of affection. Eleven years before, in 1937, Tazio was in the United States to defend the Vanderbilt Cup he won the year before. During those days, his oldest son Giorgio had died. Ferrari had had to inform Nuvolari in a touching telegram:

"We have accompanied your Giorgio. Your mother and his mother have born the loss with great strength. Stay calm. Brotherly yours, Enzo Ferrari".

In 1948, after recovering from the disappointment of his retirement at Villa Ospizio near Reggio Emilia close to the finish of the Mille Miglia, Nuvolari asked the parish priest of the town if he could go and have a nap in the bed of his rectory.

Nivola's season was over, but another

reopened with renewed energy: the victory by Biondetti was the first of six successive Ferrari wins at the Mille Miglia.

The red cars began to win regularly. In 1949 Biondetti repeated his victory in the Mille Miglia, this time co-piloted by Salami in a 166MM Barchetta Touring. Four more victories followed in the next four years. Meanwhile the Ferrari name was also beginning to be known at circuits on the other side of the Alps. Still in 1949, Luigi Chinetti and Lord Seldson alternated behind the wheel and triumphed at the Le Mans 24 Hours. A few weeks later Chinetti repeated the feat, this time with the Frenchman Jean Lucas, at the Spa-Francorchamps 24 Hours in Belgium. The Maranello cars were becoming enormously popular. Circuit races attracted massive numbers of spectators and received considerable coverage from newspapers and radio stations all over Europe. At the end of the 1940s and the start of the new decade, cars from Maranello also tackled the legendary Central American race: the Carrera, more than 3000 kilome-

bonnet, which they had never been able to close and which the driver pulled off while they were on the road at high speed. It was also possible that the fact that the car was without a rear mudguard caused the

With the Ferrari 125, Alberto Ascari obtained a superb victory in the European GP at Monza

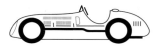

tres from the United States to Mexico and then on to Guatemala, almost always in the middle of a festive and multi-coloured tunnel of spectators. But Formula 1 was just around the corner and Enzo Ferrari could not - and did not want to - remain indifferent. Great Britain, Montecarlo, Indianapolis, Switzerland and Belgium, France and finally Italy, with its Grand Prix at the Autodromo di Monza which had seen Ferrari and Alberto Ascari take victory in 1949. The first season of the newly-created Formula 1 in 1950 was a lengthy and complex one, imposing major production and technical efforts. The main competitors were Alfa Romeo, together with other important manufacturers such as Maserati, Talbot and Gordini. There was a real danger that the whole series would fizzle out. The Maranello manufacturer could only rely on the 125 Gran Premio, an updated but three-year-old car. The whole idea started off as a great adventure. If things went well, it would have been the right springboard for a young and ambitious factory such as Ferrari. If things went badly however, the whole project could have had dramatic repercussions ....

One soul, three faces

The Ferrari 125 was a twin-seater with the steering wheel on the right, long and bulky like all the competition cars of the early post-war period. A simple change of bodywork enabled the "Sport" to be turned into the "Competizione" version: the former was more massive and had covered wheels; the latter was thinner and with motorcycle-type mudguards. Under the bonnet of both versions could be found a 1500cc 12 cylinder 60° Vee engine. Power output was a respectable 90 hp for the Sport and around 120 hp for the Competizione version with a top speed of close to 220 kph. The Gran Premio version of the 125 had even greater performance.

in the world

1944 - On 22nd January, the Allies landed in Italy at Anzio near Rome. On 6th June, it was the turn of northern Europe. Under the command of General Eisenhower, the Allies landed in Normandy in Operation Overlord.

1945 - In Italy on 27th April, Benito Mussolini was captured at Dongo on Lake Como while trying to flee to Switzerland. He was tried and shot by partisans. Three days later, Hitler and Goebbels committed suicide in a Berlin bunker with the city surrounded by Soviet troops.

1945 - On 7th-8th May in Reims, the Wehrmacht unconditionally surrendered to the Anglo-American forces and in Berlin to the Soviets; the new US President Harry S. Truman, Churchill and Stalin announced to the world the end of the war in Europe.

1945 - The US Air Force dropped two atomic bombs on Hiroshima and Nagasaki on 6th and 9th August respectively.

1945 - The Second World War ended on 2nd September with the surrender of Japan.

1947 - In August, the independence of India and the secession of Muslim Pakistan was proclaimed.

1947 - BENELUX, a customs union between Belgium, the Netherlands and Luxembourg, was formed.

1948 - On 30th January in India, Gandhi was assassinated by a Hindu fanatic.

1948 - On 14th May, the State of Israel was created following the withdrawal of British forces from Palestine. Ben Gurion was the new President.

1949 - On 1st October, the People's Republic of China was proclaimed with Mao Tse-Tung as Chairman and Chou En-Lai as Prime Minister.

in motor sport

1946 - On 9th June, the first post-war Grand Prix was held at St. Cloud outside Paris. The race was won by Sommer in a Maserati.

1949 - Juan Manuel Fangio arrived in Europe from Argentina to race with "sponsorship" from the Automobile Club and the Argentine government; at 38, he immediately won the Pau GP in a Maserati.

1950 - The World F1 Drivers' Championship was created. The first winner was Italy's Giuseppe Farina in an Alfa Romeo, who won three races (Britain, Switzerland and Italy).

1951 - Disc brakes were fitted for the first time ever to a racing car at the 500 Miles of Indianapolis.

75 years of Monza

On 26th February 1922 Vincenzo Lancia and Felice Nazzaro laid the first stone of the Monza Racing Circuit, which was President of the Milan Automobile Club, Senator Silvio Crespi's dream come true. Since that first stone, the circuit has always been under pressure from the supporters of the artistic heritage of the Royal Park of Monza ... as it still is today. In fact, just two days after construction started, the Secretary of State for Education asked for the work to be stopped. The real construction work began in May and the track was completed in a record time of three months. 3500 people were employed and a 5 km long internal "railway" was used for the work.

On 28th July, Nazzaro and Bordino tried out the track in a Fiat 350 and on 20th August the first race was held there. Since then, the F1 Italian Grand Prix has always been held at Monza, with only a few exceptions: the Livorno circuit for the 1937 race and the Dino Ferrari circuit at Imola in 1980. In 1981 the Italian Grand Prix returned to Monza, while Imola has always hosted the San Marino Grand Prix.

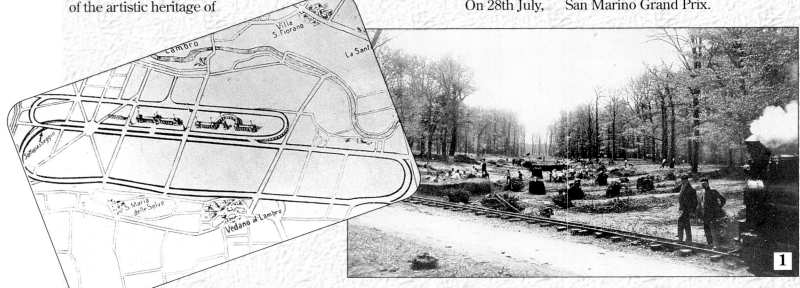

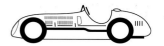

THE ITALIAN GP FROM 1921 TO 1996

Date	Circuit	Distance	Winner	Car	Average
1921	Brescia (*)	km. 519	Goux	Ballo	144.737
1922	Monza	km. 800	Bordino	Fiat	139.853
1923	Monza	km. 800	Salamano	Fiat	146.502
1924	Monza	km. 800	Ascari Antonio	Alfa Romeo	158.896
1925	Monza	km. 800	Brilli Peri	Alfa Romeo	152.596
1926	Monza	km. 600	Charavel	Bugatti	138.204
1927	Monza	km. 500	Benoist	Delage	144.928
1928	Monza	km. 600	Chiron	Bugatti	159.898
1930	Monza (**)	km. 240	Varzi	Maserati	150.444
1931	Monza	10 ore	Campari-Nuvolari	Alfa Romeo	155.775
1932	Monza	5 ore	Nuvolari	Alfa Romeo	167.521
1933	Monza	km. 500	Fagioli	Alfa Romeo	174.740
1934	Monza	km. 500	Fagioli-Caracciola	Mercedes	105.175
1935	Monza	km. 503	Stuck	Auto Union	137.080
1936	Monza	km. 502	Rosemayer	Auto Union	135.352
1937	Livorno (*)	km. 350	Caracciola	Mercedes	131.310
1938	Monza	km. 419,5	Nuvolari	Auto Union	155.726
1947	Milano (*)	km. 345	Trossi	Alfa Romeo	113.194
1948	Torino (*)	km. 360	Wimille	Alfa Romeo	113.263
1949	Monza	km. 504	Ascari Alberto	Ferrari	169.039
1950	Monza	km. 504	Farina	Alfa Romeo	176.542
1951	Monza	km. 504	Ascari Alberto	Ferrari	185.910
1952	Monza	km. 504	Ascari Alberto	Ferrari	177.099
1953	Monza	km. 504	Fangio	Maserati	178.130
1954	Monza	km. 504	Fangio	Mercedes	180.210
1955	Monza	km. 500	Fangio	Mercedes	206.791
1956	Monza	km. 500	Moss	Maserati	208.787
1957	Monza	km. 500,250	Moss	Vanwall	193.563
1958	Monza	km. 402,500	Brooks	Vanwall	195.077
1959	Monza	km. 414	Moss	Cooper	200.177
1960	Monza	km. 500	P. Hill	Ferrari	212.534
1961	Monza	km. 430	P. Hill	Ferrari	209.387
1962	Monza	km. 494,500	Graham Hill	B.R.M.	198.940
1963	Monza	km. 494,500	Clark	Lotus Climax	205.575
1964	Monza	km. 448,500	Surtees	Ferrari	205.634
1965	Monza	km. 437	Stewart	B.R.M.	209.961
1966	Monza	km. 391	Scarfiotti	Ferrari	218.748
1967	Monza	km. 391	Surtees	Honda	226.119
1968	Monza	km. 391	Hulme	McLaren	234.022
1969	Monza	km. 391	Stewart	Matra Ford	236.523
1970	Monza	km. 391	Regazzoni	Ferrari	236.698
1971	Monza	km. 316	Gethin	B.R.M.	242.615
1972	Monza	km. 317	Fittipaldi	J. Player Sp.	211.812
1973	Monza	km. 317,625	Peterson	J. Player Sp.	213.449
1974	Monza	km. 300,560	Peterson	J. Player Sp.	217.420
1975	Monza	km. 300,560	Regazzoni	Ferrari	218.034
1976	Monza	km. 301,600	Peterson	March	199.749
1977	Monza	km. 301,600	Andretti	Lotus JPS	206.014
1978	Monza	km. 232	Lauda	Brabham	207.526
1979	Monza	km. 290	Scheckter	Ferrari	212.185
1980	Imola (*)	km. 300	Piquet	Brabham	183.440
1981	Monza	km. 301,600	Prost	Renault	209.045
1982	Monza	km. 301,600	Arnoux	Renault	219.500
1983	Monza	km. 301,600	Piquet	Brabham	217.548
1984	Monza	km. 295,800	Lauda	McLaren	220.514
1985	Monza	km. 295,800	Prost	McLaren	227.565
1986	Monza	km. 295,800	Piquet	Williams	228.373
1987	Monza	km. 290	Piquet	Williams	232.636
1988	Monza	km. 295,800	Berger	Ferrari	228.528
1989	Monza	km. 307,400	Prost	McLaren	232.119
1990	Monza	km. 307,400	Senna	McLaren	236.569
1991	Monza	km. 307,400	Mansell	Williams	236.749
1992	Monza	km. 307,400	Senna	McLaren	235.689
1993	Monza	km. 307,400	D. Hill	Williams	239.144
1994	Monza	km. 307,400	D. Hill	Williams	236.322
1995	Monza	km. 305,810	J. Herbert	Benetton	233.814
1996	Monza	km. 305,810	Schumacher	Ferrari	236.034

The first designs for the circuit of Monza were drawn up in 1921. It was a figure-of-8 track made up of two perfect ovals, featuring long straights. These are some of the historic moments of the Autodromo and its races:

1) The internal railway used for construction work

2) The underpass at the point where the two sections of the circuit crossed

3) The construction of the banked curve

4) 1923 Italian GP: the Mercedes Benz of Minoia follows the Miller of Murphy

5) The first Italian GP dates back to 1921, but was held at Brescia, not Monza

6) The Automobile Club of Milan was founded on 3rd June 1903 and nineteen years later it gave the go-ahead for the construction of the Autodromo. In the photograph, the first president of the AC Milan, Augusto Massoni, behind the driver of a Serpollet with which in 1904 he made an adventure-filled journey from Paris to Milan

NOTES

(*)   The Italian GP has not been held at Monza five times: the first edition in 1921 (circuit of Brescia), in 1937 on a decision by Benito Mussolini, "Il Duce" (Livorno), in 1947 on the streets around the trade fair in Milan, in 1948 in the Valentino Park in Turin, and finally in 1980 at Imola.

(**) In 1930 the Monza GP was held instead of the Italian GP.

ROAD-RACING DOMINATION

In 1950 Enzo Ferrari began to be just "Ferrari". In the sense that slowly, day after day, victory after victory, he began to unbridle his ambitions, his desire to tackle everything and everyone. To aim for victory without fear of showing what he was capable of doing. When Formula 1 started officially with the British GP on 13th July, it was clear that Ferrari was aiming for a clear role: to be the thorn in the side of Alfa; the richer and more powerful Alfa. It was not going to be easy. The Milan manufacturer entered the famous 158 with Giuseppe Farina and Juan Manuel Fangio. The 158 was the car that had been constructed in the 1930s by Scuderia Ferrari for the Milan manufacturer, which then absorbed the entire sporting and technological side of the Modena group. Since then, 15 years had passed ... and Alfa was still on the track with that single-seater. For Enzo Ferrari, this was already a major victory.

As far as performance was concerned, the Ferrari 125 could not seriously compete with the Alfa. Behind the wheel of the red Ferraris were drivers of the calibre of Alberto Ascari, Gigi Villoresi, Raymond Sommer and at Monza, Dorino Serafini. The English privateer Peter Whitehead also drove in two races. The 1950 Formula 1 World Championship was run over seven races. Six really: the Indianapolis 500 counted on an official level, because it was only disputed by American drivers. Alfa domination was total: six victories out of six "real" races, three for Fangio and three for Farina who became the first World Champion in the history of Formula 1; the very same Farina who, three years before, refused to drive the Ferrari 125 on its debut at Piacenza, judging it to be poorly prepared and uncompetitive. Now, after having abandoned Ferrari for Alfa where he was their favourite, he was World Champion.

At the time, there was not much news about Ferrari in that first world championship year. It was however easy to imagine. With his inborn tendency to think ahead, almost always foreseeing events, the Modena constructor had perfectly understood that in Formula 1 the battle would be played out for the sporting power of tomorrow. For the moment, the field of play was almost exclusively Italian, with Alfa, Maserati and Ferrari. France made a contribution with Talbot and Gordini, but these manufacturers were echoes of the past. It was clear however that the new category, born from the ashes of International Grand Prixs, would end up by attracting new constructors, British, above all: not major manufacturers, but small factories which were already showing some interest in motor racing. Before the British however would come the Germans. For large manufacturers such as Mercedes, the wounds of the Second World War were still wide open but they were seriously thinking about taking to the race tracks. Undoubtedly the memories of the pre-war victories of Auto Union and the knife-edge battles with Italian industry around the 23 crazy kilometres of the Nurburgring had left their mark.

It was the expectation of this sensational rivalry which enabled Ferrari to forget about 1950 - no victories in the World F1 Championship, Alfa dominating with Farina, Fangio and Fagioli filling the top three places. Luckily there were still road races, in which the red Sport Ferraris dominated. The Mille Miglia of that year saw a third successive victory: this time the 185S Touring driven by Giannino Marzotto crossed the finishing-line in Brescia first. A lawyer from the Veneto, a passionate racing-driver and very fast in road races, Marzotto always took the wheel in an impeccable suit, jacket and tie. He won two Mille Miglias with Ferraris. 1950 also saw success in the Paris 12 Hours, thanks to Chinetti who shared the wheel of a Barchetta 166 Touring with Lucas.

More glory and more victories: but Ferrari wasn't satisfied. The young man who had a dream without confessing it entirely, even to himself, had disappeared. In its place was a 52-year-old entrepreneur who had come from nothing and had chosen to remain true to his own ideas, realizing that he could count on a personal genius which in the racing world was second to none. As the second half of the century began, Enzo Ferrari was a man who had done a lot but who still wanted to do a lot more. Even in his family, the situation was far from normal. Dino, the son born in 1931 from his marriage with Laura and the official reason for the end of Ferrari's career as a racing-driver, was now a young man with a passion for engineering. He was soon to gain a degree in mechanical engineering presenting a thesis on engines, much to the pride of his father. Ferrari also had a second son from Lina Lardi, Piero, who was born in May 1945.

With his own personal life having stabilized, victories in Formula now gradually became the number one goal, to which every effort had to be directed and every hour of freedom sacrificed.

Mille Miglia: six out of six

From 1948 to 1953, Ferrari won six successive editions of the Mille Miglia. The series began with the unforgettable domination of Tazio Nuvolari, who retired not far from the finish at Brescia. A wide variety of Ferrari cars and drivers triumphed over those six years:

Year	Drivers	Car
1948	Biondetti-Navone	166S
1949	Biondetti-Salami	166MM Barchetta Touring
1950	Marzotto-Crosara	195S Touring
1951	Villoresi-Cassani	340 America
1952	Bracco-Rolfo	250S
1953	Marzotto-Crosara	340MM

OVERTAKING ALFA ROMEO

For Ferrari, the factory was everything, whether it was morning, midday, afternoon or evening, often after dinner. Work meant everything: it began with a detailed analysis of a technical design; it continued with lengthy sessions at the engine test-bed or at one of the production or assembly divisions; it finished with testing on the track. Often, almost always, it was non-stop. Even lunch and dinner were the subject of endless meetings. In this way the engineering staff worked together as a team. Probably however, in this way they also wore themselves out. In this atmosphere of full immersion, Ferrari began to change his technical staff and chief engineers over and over again, something which during the years became one of the hallmarks of the Ferrari factory in competition. Gioachino Colombo, responsible for the first 12 cylinder Ferrari engine, went back to Alfa. He was replaced by Giuseppe Busso, who was soon flanked by Aurelio Lampredi. The arrival of these two engineers marked the start of Ferrari's assault on the Formula 1 championship. Between one argument and another, Lampredi and Busso constructed the 375 which was entered for the 1951 Formula 1 World Championship.

The single-seater was created in 1950 with a 3300cc 12 cylinder engine and its capacity was increased to 4500cc for the 1951 championship.
The second season of Formula 1 began, as expected, with Alfa dominating. Fangio won on the circuit of Bremgarten in Switzerland, with Taruffi's Ferrari over one minute behind. The second race was at Indianapolis and was deserted by European teams and drivers. The third round was at Spa-Francorchamps: Alfa won again, this time with Farina; Ferrari finished second with Ascari and third with Villoresi, both on the same lap as the winner although some distance behind. Two Sundays later, it was the French GP: Fangio won again with Fagioli in an Alfa; Ferrari was second with the pairing of Ascari-Gonzalez, third with Villoresi and fourth with the British driver Reginald "Reg" Parnell. The positions at the flag were the same, but this time the gap was much smaller. The big event was on 14th July at Silverstone in England. The first surprise came from Gonzalez, who set pole position for Ferrari, interrrupting the domination of Fangio who had been fastest with the Alfa in the three previous races.

Montecarlo, 1950:
the second GP of the first-ever
World F1 Championship

1954 - Stirling Moss won his first F1 race on 29th May at Aintree.

A FERRARI IN EVERY CATEGORY

It was a tough race: 90 laps and more than 400 kilometres long. The fastest lap went to the Alfa of Farina, but at the chequered flag it was Gonzalez's Ferrari 375 which crossed the line first, 51 seconds ahead of Fangio.

It was a historic day for Enzo Ferrari and motor racing in general. The stocky Argentinian, nicknamed "Cabezon" because of his enormous head on top of a not particularly athletic body, took a victory which was to change the face of the sport. It was a victory which came about not through luck or the problems of the other drivers: the victories of Alberto Ascari in the next two Grand Prixs, at Nurburgring and Monza (in Germany ahead of the ever-present Fangio; in Italy in front of the other 375 driven by Gonzalez), demonstrated without a shadow of doubt that the Ferrari phenomenon in Formula 1 was not destined to be a sporadic one. At the end of the championship, the title went to Juan Manuel Fangio, another victory for the Milan cars, but Ascari was second just six points behind. Ferrari had started to make everyone sit up and take notice.

FERRARI STARTS LIFE IN F1

At this point in time, another chapter has to be devoted to the famous, intense and difficult rapport between Enzo Ferrari and Alfa Romeo. It would not be out-of-place to say that since 1939, the year of his divorce from the Milan constructor, Enzo Ferrari had never for one minute ceased to think of Alfa Romeo cars. Especially how to beat them. It is easy to imagine Ferrari the evening of Gonzalez's great victory at Silverstone. In 1951 there was still no television in Formula 1: the news would have filtered through on the radio. Maranello would probably have been informed by phone. The first victory of a single-seater with Ferrari's name in a world championship race, Alfa's domination finally interrupted ...

There was enough material here to touch a man who had devoted two-thirds of his life to the motor car in its various forms and to competition.

A man who immediately grasped what Alfa Romeo had meant to him: the starting point for a career as a splendid soloist. He defined Alfa as his mother: a mother to whom he dealt a death blow at Silverstone.

When Ferrari received a telegram of congratulations the next day from the President of Alfa Romeo, Quaroni, these sentiments uncontrollably burst to the fore.

"My dear friends at Alfa - he began cautiously - *your telegram has prompted me to review the entire history of our memories. I lived twenty years with you, amongst events, facts and men ... and I still remember everything clearly today. For our Alfa (yes, this is what was actually written: "our" Alfa!) the adolescent tenderness of a first love, the pure affection for a mother".*

Years later, Ferrari mentioned that he thought the wheel had turned full circle. From Modena, where he was born, to Turin for his first job. Then to Milan, where he took some of the engineers who made Alfa great in the 1930s. Back to Modena, with only himself as the boss, without having to account to anyone. With him, the legacy of an engineering and sporting know-how picked up elsewhere and which he had brought to Maranello, to begin a new, exciting adventure. In a way, this adventure was only in its early stages. 1952 was the year of the Prancing Horse's total commitment in competition: Formula 1, as well as all the other most important international road and circuit racing events. Four Ferrari 4100s in the colours of Scuderia Guastella (a town in the province of Modena) went to Mexico for the Carrera Panamericana, to be driven by Ascari, Farina, Villoresi and Taruffi. At the Mille Miglia of that year, called "The Race of the Century" for the quality and quantity of cars and drivers entered, Ferrari notched up a fifth success with the pairing of Bracco-Rolfo. The team also went to the United States, where Ascari took part in an unlucky - and not particularly well-organized - expedition to the Indianapolis 500.

Enzo Ferrari with the engineer, Lampedri. Below, the front row of the grid in a heat of the third Autodromo di Monza GP. Note Bracco (8), Ascari (4), Fangio (16) and von Stuck (28). On the other page, the 1951 Alfa Romeo 159

The most important result came from Formula 1. After the official retirement of Alfa Romeo, satisfied after the two successive titles won by Farina and Fangio, the Prancing Horse took on Nino Farina. With the Ferrari 500, a Formula 2 car as per the international regulations of that year, Ascari dominated the season, winning all the Grand Prixs except two: the first on the Swiss circuit of Bremgarten, where Ferrari won, this time with Taruffi, and then the 500 Miles of Indianapolis which finished with the above-mentioned defeat. On 8th September, the day after the Italian GP, the Italian press dedicated full-page headlines to the extraordinary victory of Ascari and the Ferrari 500 at the Autodromo di Monza. It was a triumph of the public ... and of public opinion, for whom Enzo Ferrari was now a hero. The crown had however been mathematically clinched three weeks before with the Milan driver winning in Holland. Success in Formula 1 was accompanied by the title of World Champion in the Sport category (reported in the certificate from the International Federation, as the championship still did not have an official denomination).

At the end of 1952, Enzo Ferrari and Ferrari were one of the great names of motor racing, but they were not resting on their laurels. In 1953 Ascari won the World Championship in an even more impressive way. He won five Grand Prixs in Argentina, Holland, Belgium, Switzerland and Britain, leaving one apiece to his teammates Farina (Germany) and Hawthorn (France). The final round was held at Monza and was won by Fangio in a Maserati. The second successive world championship title for Ferrari was even more prestigious because it was accompanied by the title in the Sport category, which was finally made official and was conquered thanks to wins in the Mille Miglia, the Spa 24 Hours and the Nurburgring 1000 Kms.

This was definitive consacration for the Prancing Horse manufacturer. On the horizon for the 1954 season however, the threat of Mercedes was looming ...

The first victorious Ferrari in F.1

The first Ferrari to win a Formula 1 Grand Prix was the 375, in the hands of José Froilan Gonzalez on 14th July 1951 at Silverstone.
The 375 was designed by Chief Engineer Lampredi to replace the 125 which disputed the entire 1950 season. At first with a 3300cc engine, the 375 was powered by a 60° V12 (obviously front-located at the time) which was then increased to 4100cc and then 4500cc, the version which notched up the first victory in F1.

The two valves per cylinder carburettor-feed engine produced up to 350 bhp at approximately 7000 rpm. It also had a 4-speed gearbox. Suspension was transversal strut at the front and De Dion bridge at the rear. The Ferrari 375 only raced in the 1951 championship: from the following year, it was used for Indianapolis.

ASCARI

Alberto Ascari was unable to defend Ferrari honour against Mercedes. His story with the team, which made him great and which, thanks to his triumphs, reached the top of the world championship, was a strange one. Like all strange stories, it was bound to end in an unusual, traumatic way. Alberto Ascari was the son of Antonio, who left him fatherless way back in 1925, when Alberto was just seven years old. Too old not to forget, too young to derstand.

In any case, confirming the laws of genetic heredity, Alberto Ascari became a great racing-driver. He was unable to demonstrate his talent immediately, because the Alfas were unbeatable and Ferrari was getting angrier race by race, month after month. When the technical picture changed half-way through the 1951 season and the red cars took over, Ascari sat on the throne and never gave it up even for one moment.

A FERRARI IN EVERY CATEGORY

The 1950s: Ferrari racing production. Below, the Ferrari 500 F2 with which Alberto Ascari was crowned World F1 Champion in 1952 and 1953

His tactics in the race were clear: if he took the lead at the start, no-one could catch him. A total contrast to Varzi many years earlier, relentless in wheel-to-wheel battles and brilliant in catching up the leader. A total contrast to the Jim Clark of the 1960s, a racing-driver who will never be forgotten for his incredible fight-backs. Ascari did not exactly have the physique of a racing-driver. Photographs from his two golden years in Ferrari, 1952 and 1953, show him as overweight, with a chubby face and body. Some people even called him "Ciccio Ascari" (Fatty Ascari). This nickname seemed more suitable for a shopkeeper than a racing-driver who succeeded in winning two Formula 1 World Championships. Ascari himself didn't mind. He will be remembered as an almost comical figure under a blue helmet and with a woollen vest, also blue because he was superstitious. Another memory of Ascari however sticks in the mind: his impassiveness, his apparent indifference to tension, fear, and to what today is called stress. Monza, Silverstone, Nurburgring, sun, rain; nothing appeared to move him: as long as his Ferrari did not let him down, Ascari powered away and disappeared. Until the chequered flag. This happened repeatedly,

with disarming ease. The red cars from Maranello won four world championship titles (even though there was still no official title for the constructor) in the 1952-53 two-year period. In Italy, it was the era of Fausto Coppi, the champion cyclist. Apart from the two-wheeled sport of cycling, only football could command mass public attention. Motor racing, even Formula 1, came way down on the popularity scale. But the phenomenon of Ascari-Ferrari began to overturn this heirarchy of values. Television still did not exist, but the newspapers exalted the victories of "Ciccio" with the red Ferrari. Ascari became a personality; the connection with his unforgotten father Antonio

not forgotten, his popularity went beyond the Alps and spread like wildfire throughout Europe.

Maybe it was to this popularity that Enzo Ferrari referred to when in three words he defined the situation of Ferrari-firm and Ferrari-team at the end of 1953. Four years before, after Biondetti's great win at the Mille Miglia, a journalist wrote:

"The Ferrari era has begun".

"No - was the immediate reply of the constructor - *The Ferrari era begins now, and so do the problems of remaining at the top".*

1953 was coming to a close and Ferrari again launched a message:

"It is easy to wake up in the morning as world champion - he declared - *but more difficult to demonstrate that you deserve it".*

That wasn't enough: evidently the person to whom that message was addressed did not hear. Or pretended not to hear. And the messages continued in an even more determined tone:

"One can die of hunger...or indigestion". Historians tend not to agree on one point: Did Ferrari understand Ascari's intentions? If we consider the attention Ferrari devoted to the man instead of the racing-driver, it is easier to answer yes. Ascari in fact was tempted by a stratospheric offer from Lancia, which for 1954 wanted to build a super-team capable of defeating Ferrari.

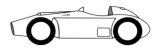

In other situations, with other people involved, this problem could have been easily resolved. The Ferrari-Ascari pairing was unbeatable: why break it up? But certain arguments with the man from Maranello did not work.

On Christmas Eve, Ascari went to Morocco: together with Villoresi, he drove a Ferrari to victory at the 12 Hours of Casablanca. On returning to Italy, he did not go directly home to Milan: he stopped off at Modena for head-to-head talks. After the second, late in the evening, Ascari was seen coming out of Modena headquarters. He was alone and apparently confused: he said goodbye, wished everyone a Happy Christmas and burst into tears. This was, in the motor racing world, the divorce of the century.

This time there were no doubts: the real reason for the split was money. Only money. By joining Lancia, Ascari could earn a lot more than by staying with Ferrari.

"Talking about money - concluded the constructor - *ruins friendships. I didn't want to lose Ascari's friendship".*

Now it was 1954. The Lancia only existed on paper and not on the track. That meant that Ascari was a spectator. Fangio won the first two "real" Grand Prixs for Maserati: Argentina (followed by the Indianapolis 500 for the Americans) and Belgium. On both occasions "El Chueco" (knock-kneed in Spanish) headed home a procession of Ferraris.

Ferrari together with Gigi Villoresi. In 1952-53 however, the attention of the Italian and international press was focussed on the Ferrari-Ascari pairing

At Reims, the scene for the French GP on 4th July, the Mercedes made its appearance. Fangio, who had joined the German manufacturer, dominated qualifying and the race with the W196, winning ahead of his team-mate, the German Karl Kling, in a similar car. Ferrari was in difficulty, one lap behind with Frenchman Roberto Manzon. Two weeks later, Ferrari bounced back. At Silverstone, the aerodynamic Mercedes W196 for Gonzalez (him again, as at Silverstone 1951 against the Alfas) proved to be unsuitable for the circuit and the red cars were back on top. But it was only an illusion. At the German and Swiss Grand Prixs, Fangio and Mercedes steam-rollered to victory ... and Monza was just around the corner. Something happened at the Italian race which was quite exceptional in the history of the Prancing Horse. Despite being contracted to Lancia, Ascari was given a Ferrari for his home race. It was a gesture of friendship by the Modena constructor, even though deep down Ferrari knew that Ascari was just the right man to defeat Mercedes. Ascari knew what he had to do. Starting from the front row of the grid, alongside Fangio's Mercedes, he was right behind him for most of the Grand Prix. The number 16 Mercedes led the race, but the constant counter-steer he had to use in the Parabolica was evidence that the Argentinian driver was having trouble holding off the number 34 Ferrari's attacks. It didn't last long however: Ascari had to stop at the pits with a broken engine. His brief Ferrari in-

in the world

1955 - On 14th May, the Eastern European countries signed the Warsaw Pact, a military alliance in clear opposition to NATO.

in motor sport

1955 - On 26th May, Alberto Ascari was killed at Monza. The two-time World F1 Champion with the Ferrari 500-F2 in 1952 and 1953 was the son of Antonio Ascari.

1955 - The most tragic motor sport incident ever occurred on 12th June at Le Mans. Two drivers, Levegh (Mercedes) and Macklin (Austrin Healey) collided and flew off the track into the crowd. Levegh and 81 spectators were killed.

A FERRARI IN EVERY CATEGORY

terlude came to an end: seven weeks later, at the Spanish circuit of Pedralbes, he made his debut behind the wheel of the Lancia with pole position. For the record, Mike Hawthorn won for Ferrari. For Mercedes, it was a second defeat in a season dominated by Fangio, who won his second world title.

And Ascari? Although he remained great friends with Ferrari, the future was called Lancia. It was however to be a short future. On 22nd May 1955, Ascari ended up in the sea at the GP of Montecarlo. A lot of fear, but few consequences, just a fractured nose. On Thursday 26th May, he was at Monza, where Eugenio Castellotti was testing the Ferrari 3000 Sport. The two drivers stopped for lunch together with Villoresi, who let them go back to the pits

Ascari ahead of Marimon, Fangio and Farina at the 1953 Italian GP. Ascari was killed two years later: alongside, his funeral in Milan. Below, Fangio with his road-going Mercedes at the time of his wins with the Stuttgart manufacturer in F1

without following them.

"After an accident - said Ascari - it's better to get back behind the wheel as soon as possible. Let me have a few laps in your Ferrari".

Was this the reason which led Ascari to try out the Ferrari Sport? Was it that Castellotti had asked Ascari to try out the car? Or was it that Castellotti and Ascari, both official Lancia drivers, had obtained permission from their team to race with that very Ferrari at the Supercortemaggiore GP at Monza the following Sunday? The mystery will never be solved.

Ascari decided to drive during the midday break. He was not wearing overalls but he did have a helmet and a pair of gloves, lent to him by Castellotti, in total contempt of his superstition of always wearing the same colours and items of clothing. He got in the cockpit of the still unpainted Ferrari. Three laps later and the Sport went off

the road at the braking-point for the Parabolica, a few hundred metres after the long curve, which would be later called "Ascari". The only things that remained of that fatal moment for the two-times world champion were a mangled Ferrari and two long rubber tyre-marks on the tarmac.

For the rest, there were only doubts. Some people maintain that his fracturered nose could have caused a blood clot. Another possibility is that a circuit-worker did not expect any cars on the track during the lunch-break and walked over, causing Ascari to brake suddenly to avoid him. A third version, denied by Ferrari himself at the end of the year, maintained that the 3000 Sport was a nervous, difficult and unpredictable car. Even to the point of betraying a two-times world champion.

It is of no importance: Alberto Ascari was killed at Monza on 26th May 1955.

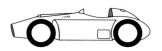

The only Indy 500

Apart from the purely political operation in 1986, when Enzo Ferrari announced to the whole world that he had constructed a Formula Indy single-seater for the US race in response to the hotly-contested regulations in force in Formula 1 at the time, Ferrari has only raced once in the legendary 500 Miles of Indianapolis. It was in 1952, with a 375 for Alberto Ascari, and run at the Brickyard with almost pioneering methods. Only one positive memory remains of that Indy expedition: the classic image of Ascari at the wheel of the single-seater before the race, because the result itself was certainly best forgotten.

In fact, Ferrari was not really interested in racing at Indianapolis, but Ascari and Luigi Chinetti, Ferrari's man in America, insisted and persuaded the constructor to give the green light to the expedition. Only one car was sent to Indianapolis, with virtually no spare parts and with a technical preparation not up to the specific demands of the ultra-fast 500 Mile oval race.

It was necessary to organize a sort of on-the-spot back-up, and it was clear that any attempt to find potential sponsors who were interested in putting their logos on the red car was not going to be successful.

The race was a disaster for Ferrari. Ascari barely managed to qualify and started way down on the grid. A broken joint soon put paid to the expedition. For the record, the race, which also counted for the F1 World Championship, was won in an Agajanian by local ace Troy Ruttman, who with this victory was classified seventh in the world championship at the end of the season.

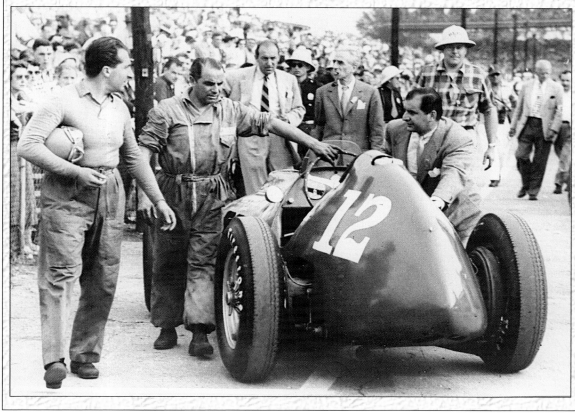

Indianapolis, 1952. Alberto Ascari drove the Ferrari 375 at the 500 Miles, but the improvised nature of the Prancing Horse manufacturer's expedition to America prevented good results from being achieved

Sporting director in a double-breasted suit

It is impossible not to remember the sporting director of Ferrari in the years of the first world titles, Nello Ugolini, as a trim figure, always dressed in a jacket and tie, an exception to the rule even at that time. He had already been sporting director with Scuderia Ferrari from 1934 to 1937, then became involved in football with the Modena and Fiorentina teams until 1952. He returned to Ferrari and stayed there until 1956, when he moved to Maserati. He always wore "civvies" and was never seen without a jacket and tie even when he had a stopwatch around his neck. Ugolini was the symbol of sportsmanship in races of the time.

LANCIA THEN DRAMA

The 1955 world championship season was shaken by the death of Ascari. But things remained the same on the track: the Mercedes were too powerful to fear any other cars.

Apart from a victory for Ferrari, with Trintingnant at Montecarlo, and the Indy 500, the Silver Arrows scored a string of victories in the other Grand Prixs: in Britain at Aintree with Stirling Moss; in the others with Fangio, who took his third world title. The Ferrari of that year was David against Goliath. In the previous year, it had managed to contain the German "general offensive" - rather like in total warfare - better than expected. In Ferrari headquarters at Modena, the constructor however began to think that the Silver Arrows could be beaten ... were it not for Fangio.

The Argentinian driver had by now become a legendary figure and this had led a generation of drivers to emerge from the South American country. It produced champions such as José Froilan Gonzalez, the man behind Ferrari's two "historic"

victories: Great Britain 1951 against the dominant Alfas; the same race in 1954 against the Mercedes powerhorse. But Fangio had something extra, especially in his character. When another Argentinian driver Marimon, was killed during qualifying for the 1954 German GP, Gonzalez broke down in uncontrollable tears; Fangio also suffered, but barricaded himself behind a mask of stone.

Ferrari understood that Fangio was the key to the situation: if he had him in his team, his cars could beat the Mercedes. But the Argentine champion was, for many reasons, not available. The first reason was cost:

"In 1955 Ferrari will be present in races where its means allow it to be present - he announced at the end of 1954 - *means which are very modest".*

This was true, but not entirely. In that period, Ferrari was an industrial phenomenon which employed around 250 people. Racing was possible thanks to a long list of technical suppliers - today they would be called sponsors - which he thanked punctually and publically after each victory, receiving in return generous financing. Another form of help came from private drivers: those who bou-

ght a Ferrari to race, especially on the road but also in circuits. Giovanni Bracco, the famous winner of the 1952 Mille Miglia, one day declared that he had spent - from the 1940s to the 1950s - around 600 million lire (US$ 375,000) to race. A considerable amount, close to one billion lire in today's money (US $ 625,000).

But from a technical point of view, the Mercedes of 1955 were on another planet. They dominated the World Formula 1 Championship, and as if that was not enough, won the World Constructors Championship, thanks also to victory in the Mille Miglia, which was won by Stirling Moss and Denis Jenkinson in an SLR300. This situation underwent a sensational revolution in July when Lancia retired from motor racing. The Turin company was beginning to have financial problems and the death of Alberto Ascari was the "coup de grace". On 5th June, there was the Belgian GP, where Castellotti set the fastest time in qualifying with the Lancia D50. But the decision was in the air. The team run by Gianni Lancia, son of Vincenzo who was one of the first idols of Enzo Ferrari, found itself without any points of re-

ference. No-one was capable of guaranteeing the right technical development. Lancia therefore decided to retire, immediately. The outcome of this decision, which many people said was an unjustifiable surrender, was that Lancia handed over all its cars and material totally free of charge ... to Ferrari, who accepted. In the last few days of July, six of the eight existing Lancia D50s were transported to Maranello. One month later, the Turin cars were tested at the Modena circuit, in preparation for the Italian GP scheduled for 11th September at Monza.

The Ferrari F1 of 1954-55: the 625 (other page); the Shark (above) and the Supershark (below), in detailed pictures from the weekly magazine Auto Italiana in 1955

FANGIO: A LOVE-HATE RELATIONSHIP

1955 drew to a close bringing Ferrari a second unexpected gift. As well as inheriting all of Lancia's technical material, the Maranello team found itself virtually alone in battling for the 1956 World Championship. Its rivals for the new season were called Maserati and Vanwall, the first of the small but innovative British teams (the famous "tuners") which were soon to rewrite the history of motor racing.

THE DRIVER DRAMA

The sudden absence of Mercedes in 1956 helped Ferrari to win the world championship. Officially the reason was " ... *the lack of valid competition*", according to a meagre and pompous farewell statement from the German manufacturer and its Sporting Director Alfred Neubauer. The superiority of the Stuttgart cars was unquestionable, but other events had a destructive role. Amongst these was the tragedy at Le Mans. That race will be remembered as the 24 Hours of the "Apocalypse", the most tragic in the history of motor sport. A Mercedes was involved in an incident and crashed into the stands. The death toll was appal-

July 1955: six of the eight Lancia D50s produced were presented free of charge to Ferrari. They were transported to Maranello, underwent various modifications and became known as Ferraris, one of which (alongside) Fangio took to the world title in 1956

This series of events however led to Mercedes formally withdrawing at the end of the season. After inheriting cars and equipment from Lancia, Ferrari also inherited from the German team the three-times world champion Juan Manuel Fangio. At the traditional end-of-year gathering with the pre-

ling: 81 people lost their lives, wiped out by the fireball which the Mercedes was turned into. Public opinion turned against the sport ... and began to make itself heard. From all sides, criticism was levelled at the races, the risks, the speed and the audacity. Races were cancelled all over Europe after feelings ran wild. Enzo Ferrari chose to speak and publicly defended the Stuttgart manufacturer: figures at hand, figures which no-one chose to consult after the wave of accusations, demonstrated that Mercedes was not to blame. It was not a gesture of courtesy: Ferrari knew more than ever that at that moment motor racing risked extinction. And without races, his work over the years would have been in vain and he too would have died.

D50: from Turin to the Prancing Horse

The Lancia D50 was born on paper in August 1953. The car began to interest Alberto Ascari and Gigi Villoresi almost immediately, and the Ferrari drivers were soon contacted by Gianni Lancia to form part of his future motor sport plans. When it took to the track for first shakedown tests at Turin's Caselle Airport in February 1954, it was characterized by having large side fuel tanks, enveloped by the bodywork but clearly visible. It was also powered by a load-bearing 2488cc V8 engine. It was these two features, lateral fuel tanks and load-bearing engine, which were changed by Ferrari as soon as he took them over.

The front-located engine was balanced by a single fuel tank of almost 200 litres in the rear and was uprated to 265 bhp at a regime of slightly more than 8100 rpm.
With this reborn Ferrari car, Juan Manuel Fangio won three Grand Prixs (Argentina, Great Britain and Germany) and was crowned 1956 World Champion.

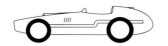
sentation of the programme for the following year, the man from Maranello solemnly announced: *"We will above all have the champion Fangio".*

The agreement was destined to be a triumph ... but it was also a marriage between highly-powered electrical poles. Things went well from a results point of view, with Fangio's fourth world title; the Argentinian also contributed to the conquest of another world title in the sport category. On a personal level however, the rapport was full of tension, and it could not have been otherwise. The driver and the constructor were two "primadonnas", and neither of them was prepared to accept second billing. Fangio was a bashful, apparently timid South American. His voice was small and rasping and he looked at people in the eye with great difficulty. In front of Ferrari, he felt ill-at-ease; moreover his personal entourage convinced him that the Maranello environment was not entirely clear-cut and that they would play dirty on him.

Fangio had begun his career a long way back. Born in 1911 in Balcarce from parents of Italian descent, he began racing in 1934 on the prehistoric and dangerous circuits of his country. National champion in 1940 and 1941, he was thirty years old when his fame reached President Peron, whose aspirations to make Argentina a great country ended up by involving the motor racing world. Peron immediately seized the opportunity to earn some easy popularity: he decided to set up a national squad of drivers and send it to race on the circuits of Europe with government financial support.

At the end of the 1940s Europe was already in awe of Fangio, but the driver chose to stay in Italy and lived in the villa in Galliate which belonged to Achille Varzi. Alfa Romeo, the undisputed champion of the time, had him under contract for 1950, the year of the debut of the modern-day Formula 1. Four more years and the South American champion reached the peak of the sport. As well as having an extraordinary driving ability, Fangio was a genius at evaluating the characteristics of the

car, the circuit and the race. This inborn skill helped him become an exceptional manager, to the point where he exploited the driver "transfer market" to the utmost, always managing to obtain the best possible car for the season to come. That was why by gaining the services of Fangio, Enzo Ferrari knew he now had the most competitive team of the day.

Maybe however the Argentinian driver did not realize he would find such an already well-established group at Maranello: drivers, engineers, collaborators, all bowing down to the undisputed authority of Ferrari. The 1956 season was a triumphant march for the flaming red cars. With a clear technical advantage, the team could enjoy the luxury of entering different cars in the races, in F1 and the Sport category. Different cars for different drivers, in turn depending on the needs and humour of the constructor. In this group of persons and personalities, Fangio himself found an environment which was a total contrast to what he had been seeking. In Ferrari, he was not a star: often his teammates were faster than he was. He immediately began to suspect that there were preferences in the cars and material. The difficulties in communication between the driver and the constructor, with the latter clearly holding the upper hand, only worsened the already turbulent situation. The Argentinian driver was 45 years old: the environment considered him "an old man", as well as the Number One. Everyone was full of respect for him and his opinion (as well as his whims) was never questioned. With Ferrari, things were different. The constructor was 58 years old and above all a

An engine change for the Lancia-Ferrari D50

self-made man. He had become "Ferrari" from nothing: the world, not only the racing world, gave him merit for this and he did not owe anything to anyone. Not even to Fangio.

In any case, Fangio won six of the fifteen races he disputed with the red cars in Grand Prixs and endurance events. His other results were six placings, and only three retirements. He was still fast and driving with extraordinary sharpness, despite his 45 years. On a couple of occasions, his teammates helped him to victory, as requested by the team. In particular at Monza, where the three times world champion had to stop because of mechanical problems and Peter Collins handed over the wheel to him, willingly abandoning his own hopes of winning the title. For the Argentinian, it was a fourth world championship crown; for the team, it was the third in six years of Formula 1: a success which became even more prestigious with triumph in the Mille Miglia, which was won by the Ferrari 290MM of Castellotti ahead of four more Prancing Horse cars. The rapport between the racing-driver and

Ferrari became even more complicated due to the personal problems of the constructor, who over the years had lost his son Alfredino, suffering from muscular dystrophy. Dino, as everyone in the company called him and as he will be remembered, lived an extraordinarily intense relationship with his father: they were not only linked by blood and anxiety over the

July 1956: Dino Ferrari's funeral at Modena.
The mortuary chapel was set up in Ferrari headquarters in via Trento e Trieste.
An advertising billboard (other page) for the 1957 Mille Miglia, the race in which De Portago was killed

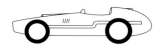

illness, but also by a common passion for engineering, for racing and everything else to do with the motor car. Dino studied mechanical engineering and collaborated with the production of a Formula 1 engine: the 2500cc six-cylinder unit powering the 246 which won the championship in 1958 with Mike Hawthorn. Later on a Prancing Horse car was named after him. After the death of his son, Ferrari was on his knees. His countless victories could not lessen the feeling of emptiness caused by the death of Dino, a death which was expected due to the advanced state of the illness. His anguish can be recalled in several of the letters written with difficulty by the constructor at the time: always worthy of attention, but particularly moving given the circumstances. Ferrari on his knees however was not the real Ferrari ... and a reaction was forthcoming; sudden, violent and not devoid of controversy. It was not surprising therefore that the divorce at the end of the year came as it did, falling at the end of the year like a mature fruit. *"We will no longer have Fangio* - confirmed Ferrari in the traditional end-of-year meeting - *We will no longer have him because we are not rich enough"*.

We will never know if the motives were financial or not. It was certain however that Maserati, where Fangio opted to move for 1957 to guarentee him a fifth world title, would pay him generously as well as give him total control over prize-money and retainers. A treatment which no Ferrari driver had ever had and no-one ever would. The split was clouded in controversy.

In the publication with which Ferrari celebrated its seasonal results, Fangio was only reserved a few lines of subtle insinuations:

"With the help of the other drivers of Scuderia Ferrari and all of Ferrari Automobili - he wrote or someone wrote for him - *he won the 1956 World F1 Drivers Championship"*.

Just that and no more. References to the other drivers came in abundance: Von Trips received a lot of space, Castellotti was described as "generous and daring", Gendebien "exceptional", fol-

lowed by kind words for Phil "Filippo" Hill and De Portago, for whom he predicted "a great future". And finally Musso, the most celebrated, whom Ferrari described as having "special driving skills". In any case, the news of the time reported that the constructor and Fangio harmoniously went their separate ways. A book published several years later in France by the driver - My Life at 300 kph - was therefore an underhand trick to play. The book's pages were littered with direct accusations and insinuations against Ferrari. The driver maintained that the Maranello manufacturer wanted to prove that even without Fangio his cars would have won anyway. He also wrote that an eventual victory in the world championship by Peter Collins would have given more satisfaction to Ferrari because of the beneficial effects it would have had on the British car market, which was, unlike in Argentina, not closed off to imports. To confirm these ideas, he even accused the team of attempted sabotage, leading to Ferrari, who wanted to sue him, harbouring a grudge. But things eventually turned out differently. In 1962 a book was published entitled "My Terrible Joys": a tale of drivers, emotions, races, cars and hopes. With a special section dedicated to the Argentinian driver ...

FROM CASTELLOTTI TO DE PORTAGO

Four dates written in blood: 14th March and 12th May 1957; 6th July and 3rd August 1958. In that order, in the terrible space of 1 year, 4 months and 20 days, Ferrari and motor sport lost Castellotti, De Portago, Musso and Collins. The causes, where they could be found, were different. The places and the details of the tragedies were all different. The consequences however were identical: terrible mounting charges levelled against Enzo Ferrari, his racing cars and his criminal logic of striving to win at any price, while sacrificing his drivers' lives.

Eugenio Castellotti lost his on the second lap of a test session organized at the Autodromo di Modena. His Ferrari went off the road at the chicane, flew into the air and landed on a grandstand, luckily empty. The constructor learnt of the accident by phone from Technical Director Amorotti. The incident was so incredible that hundreds of suppositions have been put forward. Ferrari denied mechanical failure; even a sudden illness could have been the reason. Castellotti, whose fiancée was the showbusiness star Delia Scala, seemed to be going through a difficult patch: continous, almost daily, journeys between Modena and Florence, where his girlfriend was on tour. Hours without sleep (the north-south Autostrada del Sole motorway had not yet been built), stress and tension. Fifty-nine days later, Alfonso Cabeza de Vaca, the Marquis De Portago, was killed in the final stages of the Mille Miglia. This was another mystery, which aroused the interest of the judicial authorities. They dragged Ferrari through a trial from which he only emerged when he was acquitted four years later on 27th July 1961. The events preceeding the incident are well-known. Five top Ferraris were entered for the race, dominated by Peter Collins, who however retired after more than 1000 kilometres. The Ferraris of Taruffi, Von Trips, De Por-

69

tago and Gendebien were still left, in that order. Ferrari, present as always at the Bologna halt, the last one before the finish in Brescia, imposed team orders: victory was to go to Taruffi, who had made a specific request and who with this victory wanted to wind up a long career. Von Trips argued against the team orders but was then persuaded. Nothing was heard from De Portago, but he was still out there racing. At Marmirolo, shortly after Mantua, his Ferrari 315S almost span off the road in a fast curve. His tyres left a rubber mark on the cat's eyes in the middle of the road. Ten kilometres later, at Guidizzolo, a tyre exploded and the car went off the road towards a row of trees and kerbstones, where De Portago and his co-driver Nelson were killed outright. Incited by the press, public opinion suddenly realized that motor racing was dangerous and this even gave rise to parliamentary lobbying and a series of accusations. The first result was that the Mille Miglia would no longer be held as a race. It would be held in '58, '59 and '61 as a time trial and then in its "historic" version many years later. The second outcome was that Enzo Ferrari was literally dragged up to the defendant's bench. His cars were seized: the accusation regarded the tyres, produced by the Belgian company Englebert, which were considered to be suitable for normal circulation but not for the performance of racing cars. The trial finished as expected, with the acquittal of Ferrari. But it was to be four years of accusa-

tions and insults to which the Modena constructor reacted with energy and firmness, not without many moments of grief, regrets and sense of guilt.

1957 drew to a close and Enzo Ferrari licked his wounds. The two racing-drivers who had been killed at the wheel of his cars filled his heart with anguish and there were also a number of other matters to be dealt with. To the attacks from those who called him the murderer of his "children" (i.e. his racing-drivers), he reacted without his usual verve. He was particularly moved by an article called "That's enough blood!", published in the Turin daily newspaper La Stampa: in the piece, he came under attack from a journalist who had always been a fan of motor sport as well as a personal friend of Ferrari. These were difficult days for the constructor: not only were there the attacks from the outside, but his conscience was weakening him from the inside. On top of this, results on the track were not particularly good either. The World Constructors title was won, thanks to victory by Taruffi in the Mille Miglia and two races in South America by Collins-Phil Hill and Musso-Castellotti. But in Formula 1, nothing could be done against the Maserati of Fangio, who became world champion for the fifth time: a result which no-one will be able to repeat, at least in this century.

But above all, the long list of disasters was yet to end. At Reims on 6th July, the French Grand Prix saw the death of Luigi Musso. The Italian driver had a chance of winning the world champion-

ship, together with Mike Hawthorn who had arrived in Ferrari mainly thanks to the support of the Prancing Horse distributor in Britain. Unlike Hawthorn, Musso had a warm and affectionate rapport with Enzo Ferrari. The blow for the Modena constructor was tremendous. Its impact deepened the grief which he had not managed to overcome after the tragedies of 1957: as well as Castellotti and De Portago, a young engineer - Fraschetti - who loved to try out his own cars, lost his life in a crash at the Autodromo di Modena in a Formula 2 single-seater. The list continued. On 3rd August at the Nurburgring, Peter Collins was killed while making up ground in second place on the Vanwall of his fellow-Englishman Brooks. For Enzo Ferrari this was another mortal blow. He was in no way consoled by the world title which was won by Hawthorn by one point from the competitive Vanwall of Stirling Moss. The string of losses was for Ferrari a sort of mortal embrace. Even Hawthorn, who retired from motor racing at the end of 1958, affected by the long series of deaths as well, lost his life on 22nd January 1958 in a road accident in his Jaguar. This happened following a duel organized between Hawthorn and Rob Walker, the owner of the team of the same name, on a bend in the English countryside near Guildford. Twenty-eight years later, near to that town not far from London, Ferrari's first "technical centre", built for John Barnard, was to have its headquarters ....

The 1957 Ferrari 801

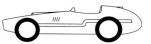

The tragedy of Le Mans

Tragedy struck Le Mans at 6.28 pm.
A few weeks after the death of Alberto Ascari, terror hit motor racing along the pits straight of the French circuit where the 1955 24 Hour race, one of the most exciting ever in its history, was taking place. Ferrari took part in grand style with five cars, driven by its top drivers, Phil Hill, Trintignant, Castellotti, Marzotto and Maglioli. On the eve of the race, no-one could have imagined that it would have been overshadowed by drama. It all happened by chance, the result of one of those banal incidents that happen at every race, on every circuit, in any conditions. The Jaguar driven by Hawthorn was about to enter the pits: before reaching the pit entry lane, he found Macklin's Austin Healey in his way, but overtook him anyway. Macklin was boxed in and made a sudden move into the path of the two Mercedes of Fangio and Levegh who were arriving at speed. Fangio managed to avoid the obstacle, Levegh didn't and ploughed into the Austin. The impact was tremendous. The Mercedes was hurled into the air, burst into flames and crashed into the crowd. The death toll was the worst ever in the history of the sport: 81 victims, including Levegh, with more than 300 spectators injured. The catastrophe clearly had worldwide repercussions. The fact that Mercedes was involved was a contributing factor to the German manufacturer's decision to abandon motor racing at the end of the season.

The 246 of the fourth title

In 1958 Mike Hawthorn won Ferrari's fourth world championship title with the Ferrari 246.
It derived from the F2 car of the previous year and was powered by a 2417cc V6 engine, designed and constructed using suggestions mode by the constructor's son, Dino, who died in 1956. The 246 had a 4-speed gearbox and its engine produced more than 280 bhp of power at approximately 8300 rpm.

THE REAR REVOLUTION

PULL OR PUSH?

At the end of the 1950s, Enzo Ferrari was rich and famous. But he was alone in his affections, battered by the loss of his much-loved son Dino. He was also alone in motor racing circles, which did not forgive him his fame, his authority, his power and the fact that he was an "awkward" personality. When Mike Hawthorn won the 1958 world title, Ferrari was more than 60 years old.

The memories of drivers who had lost their lives with his cars in rapid succession, made him seriously think about retiring. Maybe not a total retirement: the passion for racing, the will to win, never ceased to fill his dreams. But a measured and gradual absence from the spotlights was certainly a tempting idea. These were months of personal, unconfessable suffering for Ferrari. An internal grief which ended up by bringing him closer to religion: Ferrari had always been a believer, but also a bad example.

In brief, the challenge proposed by engineering technology and racing held the upper hand and Ferrari once again became "Ferrari". At the end of 1958, the Maranello constructor was the undisputed "King" of Formula 1: of the nine world championships held so far, the red cars had won four: Alfa Romeo and Mercedes two apiece and Maserati one. During 1958 Fangio said goodbye to motor racing: he would reappear in circuits occasionally for competitions here and there, but his age, his financial position, the fame and glory he had achieved with five titles, as well as the satisfaction of being still alive and well, convinced "El Chueco" to hang up his gloves and helmet. Even looking towards the future, Ferrari was still the "King" of motor racing, but on the horizon there were technical and sporting changes destined to revolutionize the history of Formula 1.

One step backwards. On 13th May 1957, twenty-four hours after the death of De Portago at the Mille Miglia, a Climax-engined Cooper made its debut at the Grand Prix of Montecarlo. It was driven by an unknown Australian, Jack Brabham. But the real sensation was that the single-seater - going against current technical trends - had its engine mounted at the rear. Small and nimble, Brabham's Cooper was based on a slender tubular chassis frame. The driver sat on this frame and was enveloped by the bodywork. The Cooper seemed like a metallic spider with its uncovered suspensions and wheels which held it anchored to the ground. For Formula 1 and motor racing, it was a revolution. With less weight, and smaller dimensions the rear-engined "spiders" swept away the engineering techniques of half-a-century.

Enzo Ferrari is reputed to have said something which went down in history:

"The horse is in front of the cart, it doesn't push it".

He is alleged to have said something like that, because there are thousands of different versions, as well as of the time and place he said it. Ferrari himself (in his splendid autobiography "Ferrari 80") however denies ever having said these words.

"I have been accused of having stub-

bornly underestimated the true worth of a rear-engined car - he wrote in his book - *In fact, some time earlier I had prepared designs for a rear-engined car, but I feared commercial repercussions on my Granturismo production, which was at its initial stages and which was based on a rear engine".*
True? It is undeniable however that in 1958 the rear-engined Coopers began to seriously trouble Ferrari, who lost out to Vanwall in the Constructors' championship, but won the Drivers' with Hawthorn. The situation deteriorated the following year. The line-up for the start of the Montecarlo GP, the opening round of the championship, saw eight rear-engined cars. One of these, the Cooper-Climax of Jack Brabham, won the race, 20 seconds ahead of Brooks' Ferrari and began its march towards the world title. The red cars won two Grand Prixs that year: France and Germany, both with Brooks, the "Flying Dentist". The British "spider" cars won five races: two for Brabham, who won the world title; two for the eternal runner-up Stirling Moss and one for Bruce McLaren. The latter victory was in the final round of the championship: on the Sebring circuit in Florida, Brabham finished fourth after pushing his Cooper over the line because it had run out of petrol.
In 1960, the situation began to get really difficult, embarassing even. The Coopers won six of the ten world championship rounds: five with Brabham who won his second successive title, and one with Bruce McLaren. Ferrari had to settle for one victory: at the Italian GP with Phil Hill, a race which was deserted by the British constructors because they refused to race on the banked high-speed curves of the Autodromo di Monza. Two victories went to Stirling Moss' Lotus, which was also

The Ferrari Dino 412Mi "posing" for photographers at Monza and (other page) in the pits at the 1958 Italian GP with Hawthorn, who was to become World Champion. The rear-engined Cooper of Moss (alongside) sets the pace in the 1959 Italian GP

powered by the Coventry Climax engine. The remaining race in the calendar, the third chronologically, was the Indianapolis 500 for American cars and drivers, which was won by Jim Rathmann.

A REAR REVOLUTION: THE 156

At this point, faced with the spectacle of his 246 losing from the start against the Coopers, Enzo Ferrari decided to make a move. His policy of having the most powerful engines, something which he had always been proud of, no longer guarenteed success. The greater equilibrium from this new weight division, thanks to the engine located at the rear, made the British cars unbeatable, not only on medium-fast twisty circuits, but also on fast ones. According to Ferrari, in 1957 the newly-appointed engineer Chiti had already been given a brief to design a future rear-engined car. The project slowed down in 1958, but was then resurrected in 1959, despite not being satisfactory at a technical level, thus causing further delays.

In the late spring of 1960, the first rear-engined Ferrari Formula 1 carried out lengthy testing at the Autodromo di Modena. On 29th May, it made its debut at the Monaco GP: Richie Ginther, a 30-year-old American, finished sixth. But he was also fourth last in an elimination race and the gap between him and the Lotus of the winner Moss (30 laps!) made it clear that the Ferrari needed a long period of preparation.

For the next Grand Prixs the old front-engined 246 was dusted off.

For 1961, the Ferrari 156 was ready and immediately competitive. At the opening GP in Montecarlo, Moss won again with the Lotus-Climax, but Ginther's Ferrari was second, just 3.6" behind and third was another Ferrari driven by Germany's Wolfgang von Trips. At the next GP in Holland, von Trips won in a dash to the line ahead of his teammate Phil Hill, who took his Ferrari to victory in the next race on the Belgian circuit of Spa-Francorchamps. It was clear to everyone that the music had changed: Ferrari was back. France and Great Britain brought another two victories for Ferrari: the first with the young Baghetti, who ama-

zed everyone by winning on his GP debut in France; the second with von Trips. Moss won at the Nurburgring but at Monza, the seventh and penultimate round of the championship, Phil Hill won the race and the championship. Celebrations were dampened however by the tragedy which befell Wolfgang von Trips, who died after a terrible crash in which he was hit by a Lotus on the second lap. These were again hours of high feelings. The German driver, who started from pole position and who had a good chance of winning the title (in the end he was second, one point behind Hill), was thrown out of the cockpit of his 156 which went up the bank and crashed into the crowd. Once again, the death toll was appalling: 13 spectators and von Trips lost their lives. The Prancing Horse was back at the top of Formula 1, but mourning inside the team left no room for celebrations.

The Ferrari 256P F1 from 1960. On the other page (below), last-minute modifications to the 156 under the watchful eyes of Enzo Ferrari, on the wall, and engineer Chiti

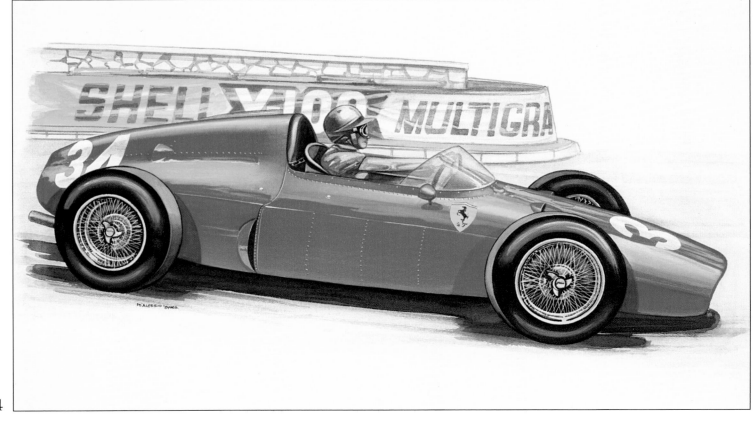

MAKE WAY FOR THE YOUNG

The end of 1961 marked a new phase in the legend of Ferrari. Almost 64 years of age, the bastion of the old guard in a sport whose lead was being challenged by younger, more dynamic and revolutionary men, the Engineer took home a number of triumphs in one fell swoop. He wiped out three years of late Ferrari development by convincingly winning the 1961 World Championship with his first real rear-engined single-seater racing car. He took Phil Hill to the title, the first American to succeed at this level. He won a fifth world title (in 12 championship seasons!), levelling the score, in a certain sense, with Juan Manuel Fangio. Above all he realized that Ferrari had to undergo a renovation, in order to continue to win in this world which was increasingly characterized by the innovations brought about by the British constructors.

Alongside, from top to bottom: 1961 Dutch GP, von Trips took the Ferrari 156 to its first victory in F1; testing at the Modena circuit; the car in the version which would take Phil Hill to victory in the 1961 World Championship

There was just enough time to recover from Monza. The tragedy of von Trips could not fail to dampen the day of joy for Phil Hill's title. From Germany, Countess von Trips, the mother of Wolfgang, asked for her son to be brought back the day of the race. She wanted to receive him in a coffin "... with a glass window, to see him". The request was granted by the team, which in the agitated post-race atmosphere managed to organize this unusual and sad funeral journey.

Once the team had returned to Maranello (Ferrari had already been there since Saturday evening, as per tradition), the constructor began to tackle the problem. His ideas were clear. He realized that the world of

THE REAR REVOLUTION

Monza 1961: triumph and tragedy. Two Ferrari 156s, driven by Ricardo Rodriguez (8) and Wolfgang von Trips (4), started from the front row of the grid. Von Trips' Ferrari (below), hit by Clark's Lotus, goes off the road and into the crowd. Thirteen spectators, in addition to von Trips, were killed and the tragedy left a mark on Phil Hill, the new World Champion. Enzo Ferrari at the wheel of a 250 SWB (other page) at the Modena circuit

motor racing, especially Formula 1, had changed more rapidly than Ferrari. Formula 1 was moving into its second decade. The heroic years, drivers already themselves in part legend, races organized on a wave of enthusiasm, had all given way to new teams, new men and new technology. The switch to rear-mounted engines was only the first step towards a new type of car. The search for smaller-sized cars and engines and more refined aerodynamics had begun. As

well as the Cooper phenomenon, the Grand Prix world was already familiar with future legends such as the designer (and ex-driver) Colin Chapman with his Lotus; Graham Hill, the BRM driver and future constructor; Jim Clark who became a track hero with his Lotus; Jack Brabham and Bruce McLaren, successful drivers who would also become successful constructors. These were the men of the future. In one word: the generation had changed. Ferrari, at an age

which made him resemble a pensioner rather than a dynamic engineer, could not change his birth certificate ... but he could change the men around him. At the end of the day, the skills he needed to "motivate" men and ideas - a definition which was dear to him - were still intact.

As for the drivers, the operation had already begun. On 2nd July of the year which had just concluded, Giancarlo Baghetti made his debut in the French Grand Prix at Reims. A young man of 27 years old, Baghetti will forever go down in history as the first (and the only!) driver who managed to win his debut race. The previous March, a test had been organized at Monza to evaluate the most interesting new Italian drivers. Amongst these was Eugenio Monti, a bobsleigh champion who set some interesting times. But there was also Lorenzo Bandini, who was destined for a great career. With Richie Ginther moving to BRM, it was Bandini and Baghetti, as well as the reconfirmed Phil Hill, the Mexican Ricardo Rodriguez and Willy Mairesse, who made up Ferrari's 1962 F1 driving squad. Before concentrating on the new championship however, the team had to be revamped. At the end of the year, Enzo Ferrari simultaneously said goodbye to eight of the top men in the team and the company. Some of them came from the commercial and administrative areas, but others were closely linked to activities on the track. Carlo Chiti left the company for which he had designed the 156 which won the world championship with Hill, its V6 1500cc engine, the 246 which won the 1958 title with Mike Hawthorn, as well as the cars which won five titles for the Prancing Horse in the World Manufacturers' Championship for Sports Cars. Others to go were the engineer Giotto Bizzarrini, who was responsible for prototypes, Sporting Director Romolo Tavoni and Director of Production Federico Giberti.

A similar "purge" (even though Ferrari commented on it by saying *"I've lost my generals ..."*) could not have taken place without the men to step into the various roles. Half-way between courage and irresponsibility, and maybe to satisfy that need for youth which he, as a 64 year-old man could have no longer, Ferrari promoted a number of young men to the most sensitive positions. One of them was the engineer, Mauro Forghieri, who joined Maranello in 1959 immediately after graduating and who was appointed Technical Director of the team at the age of 26. A task which he would perform brilliantly and which would lead him to become one of the most important figures in the history of motor racing right up to 1987.

FORD WANTS THE PRANCING HORSE

At this point, it is impossible to continue the story without touching on the subject of Ford and Ferrari. The 1962 and '63 Formula 1 seasons were unsuccessful for the Italian manufacturers. As predicted by Ferrari, the new generation of British constructors had revolutionary ideas. The 1962 championship ended with just one second place for Phil Hill and Ferrari at Montecarlo. The Ferrari 156, which had dominated 1961, suddenly looked old. The more agile and modern BRMs and Lotuses had things easy and divided the spoils of the Grand Prix victories between them. In the end, it was Graham Hill with the BRM who won, but the Lotus and its genial owner-designer Colin Chapman took revenge in 1963, which was dominated by Jim Clark and the revolutionary "25", the first single-seater in history to be constructed on a monocoque chassis, designed around the driver. This was the new frontier in motor racing. With the Lotus 25, Jim Clark was forced to drive on the straight with his head leaning to the left, to improve the aerodynamics. Ferrari considered these cars dangerous, as they were too narrow

around the body of the driver. But he was soon to adapt to the new situation. Meanwhile Ferrari continued to win in the Sport category, picking up world titles in 1962 and 1963. On the horizon however, there was a gigantic deal looming.

On 10th April 1963 the Director of Ford Italia telephoned Maranello. His name was Filmer M. Paradise ... and he wanted a meeting with the Engineer. This happened two days later in the Prancing Horse offices in Modena. The proposal was simple: an industrial agreement, extended to racing activity. Ferrari was immediately interested.

"I replied that I was interested - he wrote in his autobiography, Ferrari 80 - I had never thought of myself as an industrialist, just a constructor. The production of my company interested me only as long as it was run by others. I was interested in only one thing: being able to devote myself entirely to prototypes and racing cars, but only by being totally independent and with an abundance of technical and financial means which were not at my disposal. I remember that in 1962 I spent 450 million lire (US$ 281,250 - about 7.5 billion lire of today's money - US$ 4,687,000 - Ed.): total madness for such a small company. A visit to Maranello followed: we parted by agreeing that he and his colleagues would have returned to have a look at each sector".

Business was brief and frenetic. For a month a task-force from the US manufacturer had free access to every division of the Prancing Horse. It carried

out checks, estimates, controls, counts and made lists. Ford was serious about the deal. Ferrari was calm about it: if it deal went through, the future of the company would be in good hands, and he could continue to enjoy himself in racing as his structure would have been strengthened. The Modena constructor would later say that he had also, out of scruple, spoken to all the leading Italian car companies to see if they were interested in competing with Ford in the deal. But to no avail.

They arrived at the meeting of 15th May. Three top management representatives of Ford and Enzo Ferrari signed an agreement at Maranello to set up two new companies: Ford-Ferrari, which would manufacture Granturismo cars for the Italian and Euro-

pean market; Ferrari-Ford for the construction and running of racing cars. For Ferrari, the position of Vice-President in the former company and that of plenipotentiary President (and 90% of the shares) in the latter. The Italian and international press had managed to "sniff" out what was brewing and had written about it without prompting any denial or approval from Ferrari. The deal was nearly completed, but the meeting for the signature spoiled everything.

On the evening of 20th May, a swarm of translators were hard at work to make every comma for the two different sides comprehensible ... and then it was time for the signature. The Americans telephoned Detroit before every signature, for authorization from

1962: a difficult year for Ferrari. Phil Hill drove the 156 to second place at Montecarlo. At the Targa Florio Vaccarella left his car in this state. Celebrations for Colin Chapman (above) at Monza in 1963 for the victory of Jim Clark, who became World Champion

Henry Ford II, the grandson of the founder and boss of the American manufacturer. Everything was going smoothly, until they arrived at the file marked "GS" (Gestione Sportiva), which stood for Sporting Administration.
"It had strangely been kept for last", remembered Ferrari.

There was something wrong. At the crucial moment, the Modena constructor read the passage regarding his independence of action as plenipotentiary president. He discovered that he would not have full powers at all, and that the programmes would have to be submitted for the consensus of the partner. Ferrari didn't understand. He tried and tried again: the formula of "consensus of the partner" irritated him, but he just could not believe that the Americans were "taking him for a ride". Racing and associated decisions had to be his responsibility, and only his alone. It was all too clear...

To cut things short, amidst the growing irritation of Ferrari and his entourage, it was clear that neither side was going to back down. The agreement stalled. The first to realize this were the Ford representatives, who left the room with a few abrupt words for the Modena constructor:
"Mr. Ferrari, you are selling your company and you expect to continue to do what you want with it?".

One of the representatives of the American manufacturer appeared to be the most interested in finding a way out of the impossible situation. Ferrari turned to him, for one last attempt. He explained that the demands of racing required immediate action, agility and the specific knowledge of certain problems: they were not compatible with the organization of a large company. The American hesitated. Finally Ferrari asked him:
"What is the limit you can commit yourself to without prior authorization from Detroit?". The reply filled him with disappointment: *"Up to 10,000 dollars"*. Ten thousand dollars: less than seven million lire at the time, about one hundred million in today's money (US$ 62,500) ...

It was all over. In five minutes, the agreement between Ford and Ferrari, the detailed preparation of which had required forty days of exploratory talks, projects, alternatives and variants, was in tatters. It was all over. But Ferrari, in a certain sense, was saved.

*1963 Italian GP: Hill (BRM)
ahead of Surtees (Ferrari)
Surtees with Mike Parkes (above).
The 8-cylinder Ferrari (top)*

The comfort of religion

"I believe in God, not the beyond", were the words of Enzo Ferrari, replying to the numerous questions asked over the years about his relationship with religion. They provide only a small clue about the constructor and his faith.

On one occasion, Ferrari admitted he had not been a good Catholic. On another occasion, he said he had prayed with these words: *"God, help me to be a better man"*. At a certain moment, he would admit his lack of belief in the existence of "something" up there after death. Reports from the last few years depict Ferrari not only as a believer, but also an observer of the sacraments. This was maintained by Don Erio Belloi, the parish priest of Maranello, with whom the constructor had a deep and warm relationship in last few years of his life and from whom in 1988, with death just around the corner, Ferrari expressely chose to receive the Last Rites.

In any case, Enzo Ferrari asked for and got help from religion. In the dock after the death of his drivers in 1957 and 1958, religion came to the rescue of the besieged man.

In particular, in the Catholic publication "Horizons", Father Giacomo Perico, a Jesuit, wrote an article which was a sort of panacea for all of Ferrari's troubles.

"In the chance cases which characterize motor racing - it could be read - the integrity of man can not be attributed to anyone in particular, if everyone involved has done his utmost to guarentee safety and protection. The unexpected is the inevitable result of progress". He continued by praising the quest for progress which is inherent in every intelligent human being, concluding: *"In the face of these deaths, (Catholic) morals do not condemn"*.

Don Erio Belloi, parish priest of Maranello

All-rear one-and-a-half litres

The first rear-engined Ferrari, which enabled Phil Hill to win the 1961 World Championship, was the 156. The first two numbers stood for 1500cc, the cubic capacity of the engines imposed by the new regulations which fixed maximum cylinder size at that limit.

The final "6" indicated the number of cylinders. The design of the car dated back to early 1960 and was the work of the engineer Carlo Chiti, who had arrived at Maranello three years before and who penned the first designs of the rear-mounted 6-cylinder engine.

The single-seater, a total innovation for the Maranello constructor, was designed after lengthy studies in a small wind-tunnel for models, and its development required the angle between the two banks of 3 cylinders to be changed from 65° to 120° in order to lower the centre of gravity.

The maximum power output of the engine was slightly less than 200 bhp at approx. 9500 rpm. The car had a 5-speed gearbox.

Honorary Engineer

It was in the middle of a disappointing patch, resulting from failure to match the technical evolution of the British rear-engined competition that Enzo Ferrari was awarded an honorary degree in Engineering at the University of Bologna. The ceremony, on 7th July 1960, came just after the victory at the Le Mans 24 Hours and was emotional for the "new" engineering graduate, who could not hold back a few tears. His father Alfredo had insisted, unsuccessfully, that Enzo finish his studies. In the years to come, Ferrari regretted over and over again that he had not had a real education and a diploma.

A report by Enzo Ferrari, entitled "How to construct a Racing Car" is the memory which lingers of that emotional day in 1960. Twenty-eight years later, on 11th February 1988, he received a second degree: this time in Physics, which was awarded by the University of Modena. But on that occasion Ferrari, a sick-old man (he died just over six months later), did not give him the same amount of pleasure.

in the world

1961 - On 12th April, Soviet cosmonaut Yuri Gagarin became the first man to travel in space on board the satellite Vostok 1.

1961 - The Communist East German government constructed the Berlin Wall in August to divide the city into two parts.

1963 - On 22nd November in Dallas, Kennedy was assassinated in circumstances which still today remain unclear; Vice-President L.B. Johnson took over as President.

in motor sport

1961 - In the French GP, Giancarlo Baghetti, driving a Ferrari, became the first man to win his first F1 Grand Prix.

1962 - Jim Clark won his first F1 GP in Belgium in a Lotus. The following year, he went on to win the World Championship and Lotus the Constructors' title.

1963 - Jack Brabham, in a Brabham-Climax, won a non-championship F1 race in Stuttgart. It was the first time that a driver had won in a car of his own construction.

THE 8-CYLINDER EPISODE

At the end of 1963, Enzo Ferrari was the undisputed "star" of international motor sport. His presence went far beyond the results achieved by his scarlet red cars. As well as Ferrari the constructor, there was also Ferrari the writer. His book "My Terrible Joys", a clear-headed response to the "j'accuse" of Fangio a few years before, was extremely successful, and led to a series of other books. At the traditional end-of-year press conference, the Engineer came out with all guns blazing. He didn't have much to say about Formula 1, which was monopolized by Jim Clark and Lotus, but he did have a few words about the new Grand Prix car, to be presented on the 7th April the following year. The 158 had the ambitious task of bringing back the world title to Ferrari. In the Sportscar category, they were celebrating yet another victory in the Le Mans 24 Hours. This time however, it was for the all-Italian triumph of Lorenzo Bandini and Ludovico Scarfiotti with a Ferrari 250P, the first prototype of a long series characterized by the letter "P" and which in the years to come would have great success. But that wasn't all. The end-of-year "meeting", held in the presence of Italian and international journalists, whose numbers multiplied year after year, also saw the presentation of the Dino Ferrari Journalism Award. Officially the aim was to honour the best press article of the season. As the years went by, the award would be given for personal relations, because of the enormous quantity and quality of positive articles about the Prancing Horse, and would end up by ignoring anything other than just that.

Back on the motor sport scene, 1963, which was drawing to a close, was a special year for Ferrari. Apart from the victories (and defeats) in races, the road cars the Maranello factory was producing began to really come into their own. The numbers were plain for all to see. Road-going Ferraris were being sold in Italy, in almost all European countries, in North America, thanks to the sales network of Luigi Chinetti, but also in South America, in the Far East (especially Japan, which was starting to become a major market) and in Australia and New Zealand. At the start of 1964, there were more than 400 Ferrari employees. Enzo Ferrari used to maintain that the ideal number of manufactured road cars was the same as the number of employees in the company.

Graham Hill in a BRM. A group of drivers (alongside) before the start of the 1963 Italian GP. From left to right, Hailwood and Brabham (from behind), Clark, Surtees, Hill and Ginther

Over the year, the company increased that number of cars to more than 650 ... and every single one of them was sold. With the growing success and prestige of the road division, racing remained the Engineer's number one passion. In Formula 1, the "offensive" by British constructors (the famous "garage-owners"), who with Graham Hill (BRM) in 1962 and Jim Clark (Lotus) in 1963 had kicked GP racing (and Ferrari) in the face - had to be wiped out. The reaction of the Modena constructor was immediate.

Initially viewed with scepticism, the first Ferrari monocoque single-seater was created at the end of 1963. It was called 158: design work was by Angelo Bellei with the elderly Vittorio Jano as consultant. Jano was also behind the choice of the 8-cylinder engine, inherited from the Jano-designed V8 used almost ten years beforehand for the Lancia D50 which was then entered by Maranello and which had taken Fangio to the 1956 title.

Depite his 66 years of age, Ferrari continued to be the incarnation of the role he liked the most: "motivator" of men and ideas. On a technical level, the Prancing Horse was a reality acknowledged the world over. Its innovative capacity was renowned and feared by its rivals. Going back to the 158, winter tests between the end of 1963 and the start of 1964 showed that the ex-Lancia engine needed "freshening up" a little. Carburettor feed was abandoned and replaced with direct fuel injection. The results were immediate and plain for all to see: around 210 bhp at more than 11,000 rpm, not bad for a 1500cc engine ...

With the Ferrari 158, John Surtees and local hero Lorenzo Bandini competed in the 1964 World Championship. The constructor had a lot of

faith in the ability, both on the track and as a tester, of the seven-times British ex-World Motorbike Champion, Surtees. His origins on two wheels evoked memories of a past era for Ferrari: Nuvolari and Varzi, but also Ascari and Serafini ...

The ability to race and win on two wheels proved the existence of two overriding qualities: boldness and aggression - two natural gifts which the Engineer, despite having total respect for the mechanical side, admired and would always admire in some of his drivers. Alongside Surtees, Bandini underlined the impor-

tance for Ferrari of having an Italian driver in the team. The grief of half-a-decade ago, with the tragic deaths of Castellotti and Musso as well as De Portago and Collins, had by now almost disappeared. The Surtees-Bandini pairing worked well. The World Championship got underway with the British teams in evidence: Graham Hill won in Montecarlo for BRM and Jim Clark took Lotus to victory in Holland and Belgium. At the Rouen circuit in France, Dan Gurney won with a Coventry-Climax engined Brabham. In Great Britain Clark returned to the top of

Ferrari 1964: make way for the youngsters! Drivers Bandini and Scarfiotti together with engineer Forghieri. (Above) Hill (BRM), Gurney (Brabham) and Surtees (Ferrari) on the front row of the grid for the 1964 Italian GP

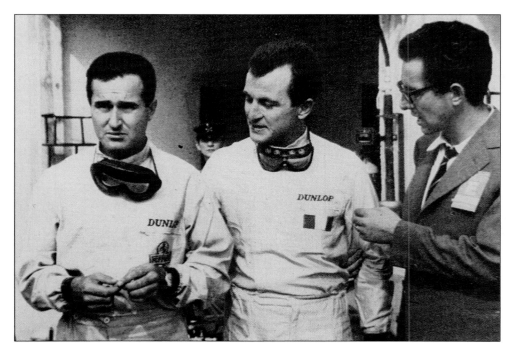

the podium. For the Scottish ace, the championship was downhill all the way. At Maranello, Enzo Ferrari was nervous: constant hard work and testing, yet the British continued to win. Surtees only managed a second place in Holland and third in Britain, where Bandini was fifth, picking up his first championship points. But the recovery was just around the corner.

In Germany, on the thousand curves of the legendary Nurburgring circuit, where he had won the previous year, Surtees triumphed ahead of Graham Hill and Bandini. In Austria, Bandini won his first GP. It would be his only victory. At Monza Surtees was back at the top, with his young Italian teammate again on the podium in third place behind Bruce McLaren in a Cooper. The World Championship would be decided in a sprint finish. The next round was the US GP at Watkins Glen. Clark set pole position and fastest lap in the race, but victory went to Graham Hill who took the lead in the championship in front of Surtees, who finished second. On to the final round, the Mexican GP. Here Clark was a steamroller: he dominated qualifying, set fastest lap and led for 64 laps. The Grand Prix however was made up of 65 and the last lap saw Dan Gurney's Brabham take the flag ahead of the Ferrari of Surtees. The British driver became World Champion after Hill retired from the race after a clash with Bandini, who then let his teammate through. Surtees finished just two points ahead of Clark, who pulled out one lap from the end with a broken engine and who was classified fifth.

For Ferrari, this was total glorification. Three years after the first title won by his rear-engined car, the constructor had left his mark with a victory worth its weight in gold. The British "garage-owners" had been defeated, Ferrari technique and technological superiority had been confirmed and his first monocoque single-seater was immediately victorious against the very people (Chapman and Clark) who had been responsible for bringing it into into the Grand Prix world. It was also a triumph for the 8-cylinder engine against the identical technology of the British constructors. As if that wasn't enough, Ferrari also had the pleasure of taking a former motorcycle champion to the F1 title. The year concluded with victory in the World Championship for Makes, dominated by the Prancing Horse cars against the massive Ford works team, which was also defeated by the Ferrari 330P of Vaccarella-Guichet in the Le Mans 24 Hours.

Monza 1964: the Honda F1 of Bucknum. (Above) Fooling around at the Modena circuit. From left to right, Scarfiotti, Surtees, Parkes, Vaccarella and Ferrari

THE ONLY NON-RED FERRARIS

It happened about half-way through 1964, the year of triumph in Formula 1 with Surtees. Ferrari was involved in a number of different categories: the World Championship for Makes and the Granturismo Championship as well as Formula 1. It was in the GT series that the problems arrived. In this category, the red cars were racing (and winning) against the Porsches with the Ferrari 250 LM, but they ran up against a bureaucratic hitch. The regulations in fact stipulated that to obtain homologation for a car in this category, 100 models had to be produced. The Maranello factory failed to do this and the International Federation immediately decided to disqualify Ferrari, handing the GT title to Porsche. Enzo Ferrari exploded in rage. Not so much against the Federation and the regulations, but against their total lack of flexibility: all that was needed was to consider Ferrari different to a large constructor, because it did not have the material capacity to construct 100 cars in a year. According to Ferrari therefore, the regulations were intollerable and his anger was directed above all against the Italian Motor Sport Federation, that failed to come to the defence of

*The Ferrari in the white and blue
colours of NART at the final two
Grand Prixs of the 1964 season.
Below, the 4 litre Ferrari at
Le Mans on the cover of a French
newspaper. Centre page,
a technical meeting between the
drivers and Forghieri*

Ferrari in the international body.
He protested ... and in a sensational
way. With a clamorous gesture, Ferrari resigned from his position as
member of the national federation
and renounced his Italian competition licence in international races.
This was, to all appearances, suicide:
without a licence, Ferrari couldn't
race; especially in Formula 1 where
Surtees was in with a chance of the title with the 158. But the constructor
clearly had an ace up his sleeve. He
contacted his friend Luigi Chinetti,
the American Ferrari distributor,
and asked if he could "borrow"
his competition licence. He removed
the national red colour from the cars
(something which has never been
missing from the company's origins
to the present day), painted them
the blue and white of the American
national colours and sent them across
the Atlantic for the final rounds of the
championship.
So at the Mexican and US Grand
Prixs, decisive for the outcome of the
championship, the F1 Ferraris raced
in the colours of the North American
Racing Team of Chinetti, who couldn't
believe his eyes at the publicity
he was getting for his commercial
and sporting activities. This publicity
continued in 1965, with a blue
and white Ferrari 250LM at the
Le Mans 24 Hours. This was the last-
ever victory of the Prancing Horse
at Le Mans, with future World
Champion Jochen Rindt and Masten
Gregory.

THE ENTRY
OF FIAT

The failure to obtain homologation for
the Gran Turismo 250LM would not
be the last obstacle for Ferrari. It was
followed by the problem of the
275GTB, a car which won on the
track but was thrown out for irregularities by the international federation
which didn't really care much about
Ferrari's protest and decision to abandon his competition licence. When it
was time to construct a Prancing Horse single-seater for Formula 2, Ferrari
had to find another idea, possibly less
controversial and blatant but just as
strong. The regulations for the F2 category stipulated that the engines of
the cars taking part had to come from
a production model, produced in at
least 500 examples. Once again this
was an impossible figure for Ferrari
and his limited production means.
At this point, Fiat entered the stage.
March saw the signing of an innovative agreement between the Turin
manufacturer and the Prancing Horse

for the production of road cars which
would take the very name which was
so dear to the Modena constructor -
Dino. It was a two-way agreement.
Ferrari gave to Fiat the 6-cylinder
engine which would equip the spyder
and coupé Dinos, with bodywork designed respectively by the constructor's
old friend Pininfarina and by Bertone.
With more than the required 500
examples produced, this engine
ended up by powering the Ferrari Formula 2 cars, to be piloted by numerous drivers: Bandini, Andrea de Adamich, Brian Redman, Clay Regazzoni,
Jackie Ickx and Chris Amon. To all appearances, this deal was a great success: an innovative and important partnership. But it was only the prelude to
a future, much more important agreement between Ferrari and Fiat. This
would be finalized four years later
after the elimination of the famous
Ferrari Sefac company (Società Esercizio Fabbriche Automobili e Corse)
and the creation of Ferrari SpA (Società per Azioni/Joint-stock company).
50% of the shares belonged to Ferrari,
40% to Fiat and the remaining 10% con-

NO TO FORD, YES TO FIAT

trolled - according to the official communication - by "a person very close". At least this was the official version. To a well-known Italian journalist and very close friend, Ferrari confided that he himself had 49% and the rest was split between Fiat (40%), his son Piero (10%) and Pininfarina (1%). The other part of the agreement was that on the constructor's death, his 49% would go to the Turin manufacturer. True? False? Utter fantasy? One thing is however certain: Pininfarina has never possessed shares in Ferrari SpA. The answer to the mystery, as this book goes to print, remains a secret. Whatever the share division, the Ferrari company for the end of the century was created: a company ready to take on the sporting and market challenges of the early 1970s right up to the present day. For Enzo Ferrari, the agreement meant everything .... but it was also without limitations.

"On 18th June 1969, I went up to the eighth floor of Corso Marconi in Turin and I was shown into the office of Gianni Agnelli - recalled Ferrari in one of his books - *It was the concluding act of a story which had come about through a number of different situations".*

He continued:

"I left Turin late in the evening to go back to Modena. I felt happy after finally having found the right future for my company; and calm because I had ensured continuity and development at work for my collaborators".

This is most probably one of the thousand different truths mixed with "convenient" versions that are in the tradition of the history of the man and the constructor himself. But there is certainly one element of truth: in 1969 Ferrari was more than 71 years of age. On the international markets, as well as in motor racing circles, almost all the competition rested on the shoulders of men who were a lot younger than him. Most of them had worked, constructed and developed on an already-existing industrial and entrepreneurial basis. Enzo Ferrari was different. In 71 years he had built from nothing a splendid, sensational and sound reality. He had built it up one brick at a time, one drop of sweat after another, tackling one problem after a-

nother. He had given life to it by sacrificing an entire life for the aim, to reach his dream, to satisfy an ambition. He had not even taken one day's holiday, because living in that way, in total control of himself and his creature, was probably already a holiday for him.

The end of the 1960s was approaching and Ferrari was virtually alone. He was without Dino, his much-loved son who had been taken away from him 13 years before by a terrible destiny. That was 30th June 1956: the next day at Reims, a Ferrari driven by Collins won the French GP, a major step towards the world title which in the end went to Fangio. Life went on.

He was without his much-loved drivers: Nuvolari, Moll, Ascari, Castellotti, Musso. And with them many others. Life went on.

He was without Vittorio Jano, his technical alter ego of the early days, from the heroic days of the Ferrari adventure, when the cars were also scarlet red but were called Alfa Romeos. Jano departed from this world in 1965, together with his friend Giovan Battista Pininfarina.

Life went on.

He was without his mother, signora Adalgisa, who died in October of the same year at 93 years of age.

Even after this, life went on.

A constant point of reference for her son, a "spiritual guide" as he himself called her, Adalgisa left in her will the desire to have her much-loved grandson Piero at her funeral. Piero was the son of Enzo Ferrari and Lina Lardi and had for a long time had been kept away from the eyes of those who were not close family. This was the moment when Piero Ferrari "entered the company".

He was young and had always been attracted by cars, drivers and racing and was to earn his place in the shadows of the Prancing Horse before taking up important roles after a lengthy and not entirely tranquil apprenticeship.

Cautious and modest, bashful even, at first the heir to the "motivator" of men was present only for a close circle of people.

But he was there.

Life went on.

The first monocoque

Enzo Ferrari had looked upon the Lotus 25 with which Jim Clark dominated the 1963 F1 championship with dread. The first single-seater constructed on a monocoque frame which virtually enveloped the driver, the "25" evoked danger. In fact, the biggest threat was for its opponents, which were totally outclassed by Clark thanks to this genial idea by Colin Chapman, a man who was to come up with many others over the years.

In any case, the Ferrari 158 was created - at least on paper - in autumn 1963, when Lotus domination was total and had pushed aside any thought of danger.

With Mauro Forghieri concentrating on sportscars, Ferrari entrusted the design of his new F1 car to Angelo Bellei. He was flanked by engineer Vittorio Jano, who had remained at Ferrari's side. Jano was also the designer of the 8-cylinder engine, first mounted on the Lancia D50 (called Ferrari in the year of Fangio's title in 1956), which was then remodernized to power the F1 car for the 1964 championship. Powered by a 1500cc V8 engine with a 90° head angle, the Ferrari 158 developed more than 210 bhp.

In addition it was successful from a weight balance and aerodynamics point of view, as the results in the races demonstrated. For 1965 a new 12-cylinder engine was constructed.

in the world

1964 - In October, Khruschev was deposed as premier of the USSR, accused, like Stalin, of fostering a "cult of personality". Leonid Brezhnev was elected new Soviet Communist Party Secretary.

in motor sport

1964 - Honda arrived in Formula 1 with a car entirely constructed by the Japanese manufacturer. The driver was Ronnie Bucknum.

1965 - Vittorio Jano, the man who created the first great Alfa Romeo racing cars, died.

*The Ferrari 158:
the first F1 car from
the Prancing Horse manufacturer
with a monocoque chassis won
the 1964 title with John Surtees*

THE MOTOR-CYCLISTS

John Surtees used to say over and over again that had it not been for his friends in British motor racing circles, he would have abandoned competition for good. Seven times World Champion on two wheels (3 in the 350cc and 4 in the 500cc class, always on MV Agustas), Big John had no intention of making the move to four wheels, but he was persuaded by Mike Hawthorn and Tony Vandervell.

From that moment on, it was all too easy: tests with Vanwall (as well as Aston Martin); a debut in the 1961 World Championship with Lotus, and an offer from Ferrari. The offer was first refused, then accepted in 1963, the year of his first GP victory in Germany with the Prancing Horse.

Surtees was the first driver to win world titles on both two wheels and four. Others had tried before him. Nuvolari himself, before the Second World War, began to win in cars only after triumphing on bikes.

Varzi was the same. Even Ascari managed to win in both disciplines.

In the second half of the century, several other riders tried to be successful with racing cars: pluri-titled Giacomo Agostini was never entirely convincing behind the wheel; his eternal rival Johnny Cecotto reached F1 (the first and probably only competitive teammate of Ayrton Senna) but had to lower his aims after a terrible accident in a race.

For all these drivers, Enzo Ferrari had always had special admiration, probably similar to that reserved for forms of extra-terrestrial life landing on our planet. Boldness and aggression: these were the main characteristics of riders who switched disciplines in the eyes of the Modena constructor.

They were not totally essential in a driver because one can even win by calculating better, by adopting a better strategy or just by being in perfect tune with your car. But they had always been admired in a special way by Ferrari, as in acrobats or jugglers.

He would one day have the same feeling for another driver, not from the world of motorbikes, but from motor-sleds. His name was Gilles Villeneuve ....

Images of Umberto Masetti: below with the MV Agusta in 1955; on the other page the celebratory postcard of his two motorcycle racing world titles. Above, the trophy won at Monza by the motorcycle racer before he switched to four wheels

Masetti
from World Championship to Ferrari

It was no secret that Enzo Ferrari had always held special admiration for motorcycle racers, and more than one ended up driving the scarlet red cars. Tazio Nuvolari was the best example in the early years. Ferrari adored the superior balance, the capacity to drive like an acrobat and the confidence when going to the limit which "il Mantovano Volante" and two-wheeled riders in particular possessed.

Ferrari had a similar infatuation in 1953 for Umberto Masetti. Twenty-seven years old, born in Parma and world champion (with Gilera) in 1950 and 1952, Masetti caught the attention of the Modena constructor at the new Imola circuit, where he was testing bikes.

Alberto Ascari and Gigi Villoresi were trying out the 250.

The request came out of the blue:
"Would you like to test the 250?", Enzo Ferrari asked the rider.

The answer was clearly yes. Masetti, after a few laps of the circuit alongside Ascari and then Villoresi, took the wheel of the Ferrari and soon managed to set some interesting times. The logical consequence was that he was invited to Maranello.

In 1953 Umberto Masetti signed a contract to drive sportscars: he was the first two-wheeled champion to drive a Ferrari racing car. His first race was the Tour of Sicily, better known as the Targa Florio.

"They put a boy alongside me - remembered Masetti - and as soon as he arrived in Sicily, he was overwhelmed by the natural beauty of the place. In the race we had a few problems. We stopped after brushing against a bridge parapet: there was no real damage, but the radiator tap was broken and we had to stop".

That was the start of the four-wheeled career of Umberto Masetti, who went on to drive with Osca and Alfa Romeo. It was also the start of Ferrari's fascination with motorcycle racers which continued with John Surtees who became Formula 1 World Champion in 1964 ...

UMBERTO MASETTI
Campione del mondo assoluto
1950 · 52

SURTEES, THEN THE FLOOD

It has been said that in 1965 Enzo Ferrari was no longer the man he used to be. Certain rough edges of the past had disappeared; certain essential traits had changed, leaving room for him to enjoy life, friends, success and solid economic security. Maybe they were all just stories, because it was the world which had changed: the poverty of post-war Italy had given way to the economic "boom". Financial security had never left Ferrari since the end of the First World War. People "who know him well" say that Ferrari half-way through the 1960s no longer put on a black tie, which he wore as a continuous sign of mourning after the death of his son Dino. Maybe the new ties and suits in lighter colours were a sign of a renewed spirit. Or maybe not. What had not changed however was the will to win ... in races, in competitions and in confrontations. Victory was the pretext for this will.

"The best victory - he used to say - *is the one that is still to come".*

Having turned seventy some time before, Enzo Ferrari now only had eyes for success. As his personal life had stabilized some time ago, his life in racing now became a unique and total mission. Most men in their 70s begin to enjoy old age. Not necessarily slumped in an armchair, but certainly without worries, no timetable to respect, no fixed obligations.

This was not the case with Ferrari. Every morning, he repeated the same habits over and over again: a quick visit to the barber's shop in the centre of Modena, then off to Maranello in the car of his loyal driver Peppino. On Saturday and often Sunday as well. He wore the same dark sunglasses, even in the midst of winter, on the top of a nose which appeared to separate "him" from "everybody else". So he could see, observe, scrutinize and take mental notes without being seen, observed or scrutinized. He had the typical expression of a person who is absorbed in things: his chin resting on an upturned hand, thumb under his throat and little finger between his lips. A key expression both in the Thirties and at the

Ferrari at the table, wearing one of his typical expressions. Below, Mike Parkes in the 1966 Italian GP won by Scarfiotti. Alongside, Jackie Stewart

start of the Seventies. It meant concentration, meditation and balance in weighing up the elements.

The man, even though he was old, had not changed.

John Surtees realized this in 1966. The year before, Big John had been unable to, or did not know how to, repeat the triumphs of 1964. The season was marked by Clark and his Lotus dominating again, followed in vain by the BRM of Graham Hill. For the record, third was a certain Jackie Stewart, who won at Monza with a BRM. Luckily a title came in the World Championship for Makes. The curtain was drawn on the 1965 season, and 1966 got underway with what could be said to be fraught relations within the team. Especially between Surtees and the Sporting Director, Dragoni, who lost no opportunity to show up the driver in a bad way. Moreover, the idyllic rapport between Big John and the team appeared to be over. The driver stood his ground: he wanted to race with the 6-cylinder engine instead of the V12 unit which the team entered and which enabled Bandini to finish second at Montecarlo.

Graham Hill ahead
of a Ferrari at Montecarlo,
from the cover of a 1965
French magazine. Below,
a close-up of the 12 cylinder
Ferrari engine at Monza 1966

Things reached boiling point with Sportscars. Under pressure from Ford which was launching a massive technical and economic offensive on the category, Ferrari looked towards the World Championship for Makes with particular interest. From 1953 to the start of 1966, the red cars had won the title every year apart from two: in 1955 when Mercedes won and in 1959 with the turn of Aston Martin. Now there was Ford ...

Surtees however started off well. He competed in a Grand Prix not valid for the World Championship at Siracusa, taking the 312 to victory. Then he won at the 1000 kms of Monza, driving a P3 together with Mike Parkes. The situation deteriorated after a stormy Montecarlo GP, the scene of numerous arguments between the British driver and Dragoni who returned to Maranello and said that he had seen *"... a Lola sportscar (in England) which was virtually identical to our Ferraris"*.

For the Engineer, this accusation - if proved - would be sufficient to get rid of Surtees, a partner in Lola with its owner Eric Broadley. At the end of 1965, Surtees even managed to escape unhurt from a massive accident in Canada, testing the famous Lola Sport. It was decided to announce the separation between Surtees and Ferrari at the end of the next GP in Belgium. But at Spa,

The Ferrari 312, driven by Scarfiotti, which won the 1966 Italian GP: F1 is gaining a wider TV audience. Below, the 1965 Ferrari 512

Brabham and his Repco-powered car of the same name. There was another win for Surtees in 1967: at Monza, giving Honda their second (the first was Richie Ginther in Mexico 1965) and final victory in Formula 1. Afterwards, there was nothing, or almost.

The same could also be said of the scarlet red cars, which would not see another world title until 1975 with Niki Lauda.

to everyone's surprise, Surtees won and the order from Maranello was "Let's wait".

A few days later, qualifying got underway for the Le Mans 24 Hours. Here Dragoni used the first excuse he could think of to get rid of the driver, whom he prevented from taking part in the race. This was just the first step: on 22nd June Surtees came out of Ferrari headquarters at Maranello for the final time. The real reasons for the divorce remain a secret: both for the team and the driver. What is certain is that an unresolvable personal split had emerged between Big John and Dragoni. Fer-

rari's decision to get rid of Surtees was amazing: in these cases, it is usually the Sporting Director who packs his bags. In any case Dragoni didn't have long to go either: the following year he was replaced by Franco Lini.

A photo remains of John Surtees on that day: the driver with an unfathomable look, impeccable in jacket and tie, his left arm holding what appears to be a heavy leather briefcase. Surtees returned to the victory rostrum that very same year: in Mexico with a Maserati-engined Cooper, and he finished second in the World Championship behind

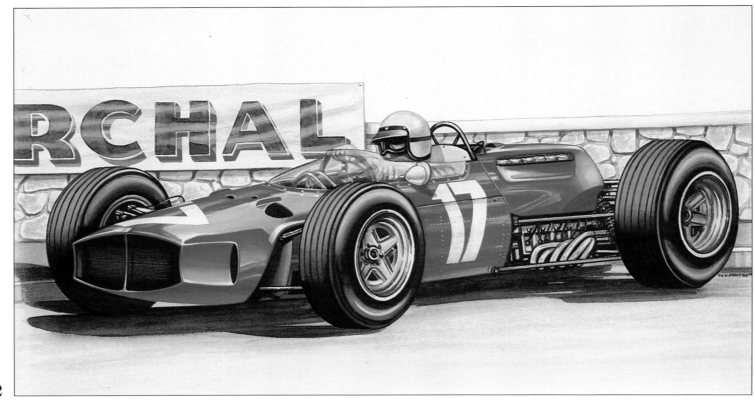

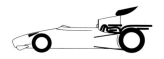

FROM DEFEAT TO TRAGEDY

Ferrari in the post-Surtees period was a team searching for its own identity. From a number of quarters, even within, accusations were levelled at the 312; if Surtees had not left and his rapport with the team had continued to be positive, maybe the car could have challenged for the 1966 title which instead easily went to Jack Brabham. As an immediate consequence of the split with the British driver, Ferrari had to pin most of his hopes on the fast, yet fragile Lorenzo Bandini. The Italian driver was under a great deal of stress, as he was number one Ferrari driver. In addition, he had a dual commitment: Formula 1 and World Championship for Makes, the latter in the midst of a tremendous battle with the American giant, Ford.
The US manufacturer had geared up its industry, to what seemed like a wartime level, to win the World Championship for Makes.
The small but agile and powerful MkIIs were rapidly improving and causing problems for the scarlet cars which in the meantime were also facing a challenge from the powerful American Chaparrals: a car powered by a 5700cc engine with an automatic gearbox, which won the Nurburgring 1000 kms after a long duel with the Ferrari P3 of Bandini and Scarfiotti. The title however would be fought out between Ford and Ferrari and the last round - the Le Mans 24 Hours - would be decisive.
The 1966 edition of the Sarthe marathon was a classic. Three Ferrari 330 P3s were entered to be driven by Bandini-Guichet, Scarfiotti-Parkes and Rodriguez-Ginther. Ford had a massive entry of thirteen cars, split between the MkII prototype and the GT40 Sport. Above all in the pits, it had put together a task-force which was destined to revolutionize the spirit of competition. Where Ferrari counted on a staff of a few selected engineers and mechanics who had to stay awake for two days on the run, the American manufacturer turned up with field kitchens and a quantity

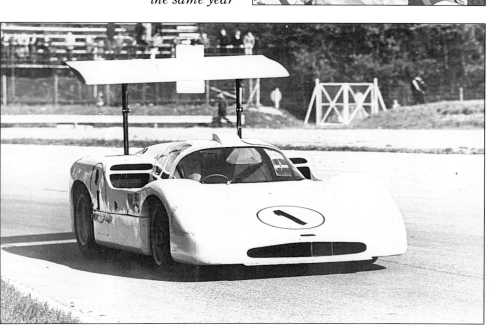

Chris Amon at the 1967 Italian GP. Below, the fast Chaparral ZF of Hill-Spence at the 1000 Kms of Monza sportscar race the same year

THE LEAN YEARS

of men and means to enable six-hour shifts per person to be organized. During the night, it was strange to see fresh and well-rested Ford mechanics in the pits, which were usually populated by tired, sleepy personnel, ready to wake with a surge of energy when their car arrived for refuelling or a tyre change. In brief, all the Ferraris had mechanical problems and all except the two 275 GTB Granturismos retired.

The Fords ran like clockwork.

The French press churned out comparisons of biblical proportions. In the annual publication "Année Automobile", a cartoon portrayed the titanic battle between David and Goliath. The logical conclusion was that the Fords took the flag in parade formation, even though not in the agreed order. The top podium slot went to the New Zealanders Chris Amon and Bruce McLaren, who crossed the line with the sister car of Denis Hulme and John Miles alongside. The Kiwi pairing only won because they had started 12 metres behind Hulme-Miles on the grid and had therefore covered a greater distance over the 24 hours. The immortal photographs of those days show Henry Ford II on the podium together with McLaren and Amon. Three years after the failure to buy Ferrari, revenge was total. Thirteen years later however, a letter full of respect was sent by the American tycoon to Ferrari for his eightieth birthday.

The year concluded for Ferrari without even the traditional victory in the World Championship for Makes. Although things looked promising in the Sport category for the following year thanks to the almost-ready 330 P4 (the legendary P4), in Formula 1 the situation was bleak. As mentioned before, Bandini was nervous about being the team's leading driver. As a replacement for Surtees, Ferrari had called upon Mike Parkes: not a great individual driver, but a good finisher to obtain points for the red cars and above a good teammate, who helped Ludovico Scarfiotti to win the Italian GP at Monza on 4th September. Still today this remains the last victory of

an Italian driver (Switzerland's Regazzoni scored two in 1970 and 1975 and Italo-American Mario Andretti one in 1978) at the Autodromo. The red cars' season more or less ended here. Ferrari finished second in the World Manufacturers' Championship, one point ahead of Cooper, but eleven behind Brabham. The Australian driver-constructor won the Drivers' title, Surtees, the ex-Ferrari driver was second, Bandini and Parkes eighth equal ahead of Scarfiotti.

At this point Maranello decided to sign Chris Amon. The New Zealander had been victorious with sportscars, but remained an unknown factor in Formula 1. In the 17 Grand Prixs he disputed between his debut in 1963 up until the end of 1966, he had raced for three teams (Lola, Lotus and Cooper, all with different engines) and scored 2 points with a Lotus-BRM at the Dutch GP in 1964. The story of Amon and Ferrari was a strange one. Three years together, but no victories. Undisputed class behind the wheel, maybe lacking in aggression, Amon had a few problems when the track was wet. The partnership between the two was destined to end amidst mutual reproaches:

"I lost three years with Ferrari", he declared at the end of 1969 as soon as he signed for March.

"Amon? - thundered Enzo Ferrari - *We supported him and tollerated him, because we were convinced we were on to something good. If he thinks he made a mistake, then we all made a mistake ...".*

Let's go back in time to 1967. The year began with two important and in a certain sense historical victories. Bandini and Amon won both the Daytona 24 Hours and the Monza 1000 kms. They were a strong and well-sorted pairing, but Bandini had other aims in sight: he wanted to prove he could be number one in Grand Prixs as well. With these premises, they arrived at the GP of Montecarlo, the first European round of a championship which began in far off South Africa.

Monza 1967: the Ferrari 330 P4 of Bandini-Amon at the 1000 Kms sportscar race. For the Prancing Horse it was a difficult moment and the Italian weekly magazine Autosprint summed up the situation in this way ...

Ferrari did not take part in the South African race, but on the curves of the street circuit Bandini started from the front row, seven tenths of a second off the pole position of three-times World Champion Jack Brabham. *"What's the difference between Bandini and Baghetti?"*, it was asked at Ferrari in 1962 when both were at the wheel of Ferraris.

"Bandini, unlike Baghetti, would agree to die for Ferrari", was the blunt answer.

These words were prophetic on the eve of the 1967 Montecarlo GP.

The Italian driver wanted to win at all costs. After an accident in Friday qualifying, when the car was almost totally destroyed, Lorenzo beat everyone off the line at the start. Behind, Brabham had a broken engine and dumped oil all over the track. The group had difficulty in passing after the marshalls had waved the oil flags. Bandini came round, unaware of what had happened behind him. He arrived on the scene flat-out, slid on Brabham's oil, span and was overtaken by Denny Hulme's Brabham and Jackie Stewart's BRM. The Scot retired, leaving second to the Ferrari driver, who began a furious fight-back. He got close to Hulme, but then the gap widened again.

On lap 82, there was drama. The race was an exhausting one: the following year, it would be reduced from 100 to 80 laps. Bandini was probably tired and made a mistake entering the chicane after the tunnel on the waterfront. The Ferrari crashed in fifth gear (it was a third-gear curve) into one of the bollards used for mooring the boats in the port. The car overturned and caught fire. Bandini was stuck inside: several minutes passed before the fire was under control. Ferrari was watching the race from home on television. When the cameras picked up the column of smoke down in the port from a distance, he exclaimed:

"Oh God, it's Bandini!".

The Grand Prix finished with victory for Hulme, who took the championship lead and stayed there right until the end. Second was the Lotus of Graham Hill, third Amon in the Ferra-

ri. When the chequered flag fell, Bandini was in an ambulance, heading at full speed towards the hospital where three days later he was to die of incurable burns. No-one knew at the time, but the death of Bandini took Ferrari back to the time when he was on trial, not only in court, but following the death in rapid succession of some of his drivers in the 1950s. The fear of having to account for the injury or the death of one of his drivers began to spread again at Maranello. In the following years, apart from the brief appearances of de Adamich and Giunti, the Prancing Horse manufacturer would only have one other Italian driver in F1 - in 1972 when Arturo Mer-

zario joined the team. Then nothing for 11 seasons, until the arrival of Alboreto in 1984 ... and he was the last Italian to drive the scarlet cars full-time until the present day.

A disastrous 1967 Italian GP: Surtees (14) won in a Honda, Amon (2) was only seventh for Ferrari

The legendary P4

The Ferrari 330 P4 only disputed one season in the Sportscar category. The car will simply be remembered as the P4, with admiration for the fantastic results obtained in 1967.

Born as a development of the P3, the first Sportscar built on a semi-monocoque chassis, the P4 repeated this technical solution but it was more powerful. The power output of the 12-cylinder 60° engine (at 3989.5 cc, not quite 4 litres) was almost 450 bhp and it was positioned at the centre of the car, immediately behind the driver's back. The characteristics of the

chassis and the suspension, as well as its refined aerodynamics, virtually made the P4 a covered-wheel Formula 1 car: nimble and easy-to-drive on every type of circuit and in every condition. It also had a massive amount of power and an efficient Ferrari-made 5-speed gearbox.

The brief life of the legendary P4 can be explained by the change in the Sportscar regulations, which from 1968 onwards limited engines to a maximum 3000cc cylinder-size. The P4s, which had already been constructed, were then transformed for use in the North-American Can-Am sportscar championship.

Revenge at Daytona

The finish of the 1967 Daytona 24 Hours will have a permanent place in history. Three 330 P4 Ferraris in perfect side-by-side formation at the chequered flag which marked the end of the 24 Hour race. Bandini and Amon won with the number 23 car, ahead of Scarfiotti-Parkes (24) and the 412P in the white and blue colours of the North American Racing Team driven by Rodriguez-Guichet. For the Prancing Horse, badly beaten the year before at Le Mans and in the World Championship for Makes by Ford, the triumph at Daytona assumed a particular significance because it was achieved on the home turf of the American

giant. It was also the first step along the road towards recapturing the Makes title at the end of the season. During the race, the significance of the event was growing hour by hour. The newly-appointed team manager, Franco Lini, organized the parade finish: then he repeated it with a static photo after the flag and this image was also sent around the world. The local press celebrated the event: the Daytona Beach Morning Journal dedicated a full-page headline to the victory ... in Italian: "Ferrari: Primo, Secondo, Terzo".

A 1-2-3 which would go down in history: three Ferrari P4s win the Daytona 24 Hours in a parade finish. Below, the 312 F1 of the 1967 World Championship

A 312 for four years

Three victories in four seasons: Surtees in Belgium 1966, Scarfiotti at Monza in the same year and Ickx in France 1968. This was the roll of honour in Formula 1 by the Ferrari 312, the precursor of the series which, with a transversal gearbox, would become successful in the 1970s but which was disappointing in terms of results in the second half of the 1960s.

The 312 was put together in the winter between 1965 and 1966. The choice of the 3000cc 12-cylinder engine (not yet flat but with a 60° cylinder head angle) was the cornerstone of Maranello's technical thinking. It would generate more than 410 bhp of power at around 11,000 rpm: a lot more than the 8-cylinder Ford Cosworth engine which scored its first victory at the 1967 Dutch GP (Clark with a Lotus) and which immediately became the technical leitmotif of almost all the British teams until the arrival of the turbo engines at the end of the 1970s.

But even without the hoped-for results, the Ferrari 312 will remain in the annals of F1 thanks to the continuous flow of technical innovations

presented during its time in Formula 1. The first version of the engine was in fact two valves per cylinder (Surtees' victory in Belgium 1966), but the 36-valve version, capable of more than 370 bhp of power, made its debut at Monza (Scarfiotti's win). The engine was further developed at Monza 1967, with the 4-valve per cylinder version capable of producing more than 410 bhp. In 1968, starting from the Belgian GP, the fourth round of the championship, the 312 was the first single-seater to adopt wings and this was the main innovation four weeks later in Ickx's victory in the French GP at Rouen.

End of the 1960s:
Mauro Forghieri was by now
the main engineering brains
of the F1 Ferraris.
From top to bottom, the F1 312
respectively in its 1966,
1968 and 1969 versions

AMON AND ICKX

Chris Amon and Jacky Ickx were two faces of the same Ferrari, a Ferrari in the midst of a driver crisis. The New Zealander has already been mentioned. Signed at the end of 1966 on the strength of his performances in Sportscars, he ended up by being a disappointment. Not a single victory: a record in the history of Formula 1, given the often technically outstanding material he had available and given the number of races he dominated during his three years with Ferrari from 1967 to 1969. The words "bad luck" have often been used to describe the phenomenon of Chris Amon, but the driver himself was not convinced:
"Bad luck does not exist - he tried to persuade his colleagues - *It's our conviction, an excuse. In reality, we call bad luck that negative run of events we are not prepared for and which we are unable to predict".*
Nice words, but the suspicion remains. Amon's class, his brilliant and elegant driving style, came as a shock. To someone who appeared an artist on the track, his chronic inability to win can even be pardoned.
A few drops of rain were all that was needed for Amon the Stylist to turn into Amon the Beginner. At this point, even Enzo Ferrari's sturdy pa-

tience began to run out: his trust in the driver wavered, a great relationship gave way to the traumatic divorce at the end of 1969, as mentioned before. Amon was above all a human being, and was therefore prone to mistakes: professional mistakes, as well as personal, business and family ones. Ferrari was not going to go back on his decision.
Jacky Ickx's period in Ferrari was different. He came to Maranello at the end of 1967, when the marriage between the Prancing Horse and Amon appeared still to have a few more surprises up its sleeve. A young man at 22 years of age, Belgian, from a wealthy family, good-looking and brilliant, Ickx had a difficult character, soon to come to the fore: he entered the Engineer's office and immediately caught Ferrari's eye with his impudence. His career was, until then, almost embarassing: four F1 races, just one point in 1967 with a not particularly competitive Cooper-Maserati. Despite this, Ferrari judged him to be the right man for the job of taking the team back to the top ... immediately. For his part, Ickx was certainly a man who feared no-one: his strong self-confidence was a weapon which would turn out to be double-edged, but it was too early to realize that. He stayed with Ferrari five seasons, from 1968 to 1973, with one at Brabham in between

(1969) and won a total of six races in Formula 1, numerous rounds of the Sportscar championship and ... hundreds of arguments, small and large. The period was full of obstinacies, whims, about-turns, vitriolic declarations and rapid denials, small and big lies. Not for nothing were his six years with Ferrari to be remembered as "terrible" years.
At the moment when Amon was picked, as well as when Ickx arrived, Formula 1 was a totally different world to what Ferrari had been used to in the past. Until the end of the 1950s, Ferrari could do and undo things as he pleased, pick and choose the best drivers, force them to adopt his strategies and his policies. From the 1960s the increase in the number of British teams (the famous assemblers or, even worse, "garage-owners" who were not "creators" like Ferrari, but who in any case raced and won with single-seaters) revolutionized Grand Prixs and motor racing in general. Ten years before, leaving aside the Fangio phenomenon, drivers would have paid out of their own pockets to race for Ferrari. At the end of the 1960s they knew they could race and win with other cars, irrespective of the fact that the engines were all the same or that their allure was not as fascinating as Ferrari's. Above all, they knew that racing without earning money in this new market was unthinkable ...
Ferrari found himself unprepared for this new reality.
"Drivers have never had to pay to race for us - the Modena constructor used to say - *On the contrary, they have always been paid: maybe not very much, but certainly regularly. We are a small company: we don't have money to burn".*
This was the truth: Ferrari did not have money to burn by following the market trends. Or in any case it did not want to. The situation changed much later, when Jody Scheckter came to Maranello in 1979 with a contract which was in tune with the

(8) and Villoresi (2) in the first two rows. Below, Enzo Ferrari discusses 312 F1 with mechanic Sergio Vezzali in 1968.

Monza 1968:
Enzo Ferrari together with
the mechanic, Sergio Vezzali

market. Before him, a long list of drivers either said no or left, even (for some it would be better to say only) for financial reasons. One name stands out above everyone: Jackie Stewart. He was signed to race for Ferrari in the World Championship for Makes in the final round of the 1967 championship, but the future three-times World Formula 1 Champion never drove a Grand Prix Ferrari. Financial reasons played a major part in this. Another was Emerson Fittipaldi. 1972 World Champion with Lotus and in 1974 with McLaren, the Brasilian driver was often to be seen at Maranello, but nothing ever came of it. Niki Lauda himself left at the end of 1977, officially because he no longer had any motivation, but the massive sum of money offered to him by Brabham at the time was certainly one of the reasons.

The barrier between Ferrari and the British teams in 1968 was not only financial. The 1967 Dutch GP saw the debut of the Ford Cosworth engine (from a combination of the names of its two designers: Mike Costin and Keith Duckworth). The debut was a

Monza 1968: wing fever hits Formula 1. From top to bottom, Derek Bell's Ferrari, Jack Brabham's "Biplane" Brabham and Jackie Oliver's Lotus

positive one: Jim Clark took pole position, victory and fastest race lap with a Cosworth-engined Lotus 49. The title went to the Brabham-Repco of Denis "Denny" Hulme, a New Zealander like Amon and McLaren. The Cosworth era had begun: it was to last all through the 1970s and even longer, before the invasion of the turbo engine. In 1968 Graham Hill, who had already been World Champion in 1962, returned to the top driving a Lotus-Cosworth. 1969 saw the first of three world titles for Jackie Stewart at the wheel of a Matra-Cosworth MS80. 1970 saw the return of Lotus with the 72, with Jochen Rindt and with the Cosworth engine once again. Exactly the same engine as the Tyrrell 003 of 1971 champion Stewart, the Lotus 72D of the 1972 champion Emerson Fittipaldi and the Tyrrell 006 of Jackie Stewart who was champion for the third time in 1973.

What had happened to the famed engine superiority of Ferrari? Where was the general technical superiority of scarlet red cars? The number of British cars increased. During this astounding string of defeats, the cars from Maranello suffered in 1968 (one victory with Ickx in France on the wing-car debut) and were non-existent the year after without a single victory, pole position or even one fastest lap. They returned to the forefront in 1970, when the brand-new 312B showed to the world the competitivity of the 12-cylinder Boxer engine, with opposing cylinder heads and a flat 180° angle. Four victories were notched up that year: Austria, Italy, Canada and Mexico, all thanks to Ickx, except for the race at Monza which saw a win for the young and brilliant Italo-Swiss driver, Clay Regazzoni, from the canton of Ticino.

Circuito di Modena - 1969
Chris Amon - Sergio Vezzali Sergio Vezzali

Testing at Monza for Amon's Ferrari 312. Below, the 312 in "Biplane" version

*The 1970 Ferrari 312B:
below, the car driven
to victory by Clay Regazzoni
in the Italian GP at Monza
that year. Saturday's qualifying
session saw the tragic death
of Jochen Rindt, killed in
a terrible crash (below)
in his Lotus*

Ickx and Ferrari finished second respectively in both the Drivers' and Manufacturers' championships, beaten only by Lotus and the Austrian, Jochen Rindt who lost his life at Monza and won the title posthumously.
The illusion didn't last long. Starting from 1971 the Prancing Horse entered the fray with the 312B2 and then again with the 312B which was more competitive. The number of races won was rather meagre: only two in 1971, in South Africa with the newcomer, Mario Andretti, and in Holland with Ickx.

THE END OF THE SPORTSCARS

Things were worse in 1972, when Ickx the Terrible triumphed at the Nurburgring where he had already won before in 1969 with a Brabham. On to 1973, another "annus horribilis". Ickx and his new teammate Merzario could only score a fourth place in Germany and two thirds in Brazil and South Africa. On the horizon, 1974 would be the year when Ferrari bounced back, but no-one at Maranello could have imagined it at the time.

In the six years between 1968 and 1973, Formula 1 had completely changed and Ferrari had passed through an extraordinarily lacklustre period. In 1968 Jim Clark lost his life in a Formula 2 race after winning the opening round of the season in South Africa and setting the new record for GP victories: 25, one more than Fangio, who with 24, had held the record since 1957. That same race in South Africa saw the debut of Andrea de Adamich: he stopped after just twenty minutes of the race and would never drive a Ferrari again in the World Championship. A Ferrari was involved in Regazzoni's splendid victory at Monza in 1970, but also in the tragic death of Ignazio Giunti who was killed in the 1971 Buenos Aires Sportscar race.

It was Jean-Pierre Beltoise's fault, after the Frenchman pushed his Matra along the curve leading to the pits and was hit head-on by the 312PB of the Italian driver.

In the same year, Pedro Rodriguez also lost his life at the wheel of a

Clay Regazzoni in the Ferrari pits at Monza in 1971. Below, Enzo Ferrari at the tests of the 312 B2 at the Modena circuit. At the foot of the page, the revolutionary refuelling system for the Alfa Romeo Sport at the 1971 Monza 1000 Kms

Ferrari 512 Sport in the 200 Miles of Nuremburg.

At Maranello, Enzo Ferrari was licking his wounds. His absence from the race-tracks was now a matter of course: his future appearances at a circuit would only be on special occasions. But his attention and will to win were just the same as ten, twenty, forty years ago. The passage from the 1960s to the 1970s had brought him further success in the World Championship for Makes, victories which further strengthened a company which had become one of the most prestigious in the world, even though its production numbers were limited. But in Formula 1, things were not so rosy. At the end of 1973, the constructor was 75 years of age. The desire to get back on top was more important than his age. And he was ready for a new, even more splendid challenge ...

THE LAST WORLD CHAMPIONSHIP FOR MAKES

First however we have to go back to 1972, the year of the last victory of the scarlet cars in the World Championship for Makes. Although Ferrari was in the midst of its blackest crisis in Formula 1, in endurance racing it entered the field with the 312PB: the sportscar was the work of Mauro Forghieri, whose technical importance within the company had grown year by year and was now at its peak, to the point where the Modena engineer would soon be moved onto the Formula 1 cars.

The 312PB steamrollered the opposition. The Prancing Horse entered at least three cars in almost all of the ten rounds of the Sportscar championship: one singleton entry, driven by Arturo Merzario and rally-driver Sandro Munari at the Targa Florio, which they also won; four cars at the Zeltweg 1000 kms which finished in the first four places: the red cars won all the races on the calendar and brought back the World Championship for Makes to Maranello for the first time since 1967.

The 1972 World Championship for Makes was also important for the quality of the drivers who alternated behind the wheel of the 312PB in that particular series. In four races (Daytona 6 Hours, Sebring 12 Hours, Brands Hatch 1000 Kms and the Watkins Glen 6 Hours), success went to the pairing of Mario Andretti and Jacky Ickx; the Buenos Aires 1000 Kms, the opening round of the season, to Sweden's Ronnie Peterson (another driver who came very close to driving a F1 Ferrari) together with Tim Schenken, and they repeated the feat at the Nurburgring 1000 Kms. Ickx and Regazzoni won the 1000 Kms of Monza, Merzario triumphed in the 1000 Kms of Spa and at the Kyalami 9 Hours, together respectively with Brian Redman and Regazzoni, as well as in the Targa Florio with Munari. The Zeltweg 1000 Kms in Austria saw victory go to Ickx and Redman. The 1972 triumph was followed by confirmation of the Prancing Horse's involvement in the World Sportscar Championship the following year. The 312PB won at Monza and the Nurburgring, with Ickx and Redman, but overall victory went to Matra and the reduced prestige of endurance racing convinced Ferrari to pull out of the category. For 1974, a new and more competitive version of the 312PB had already been designed by the incredibly creative Mauro Forghieri, but the new year would mark Ferrari's exclusive commitment in Formula 1, where there had been no victories for a very long time.

1971 Italian GP: Pratt & Witney turbine-engined Lotus T56B driven by Emerson Fittipaldi

THE END OF THE SPORTSCARS

The 312 B2: with Ickx at the wheel and with Peter Schetty during tests with a curious "snow-plough" nose. Ferraris in endurance racing. Arturo Merzario reading Autosprint together with Ickx and Redman. Fiorano, April 1972: the presentation of the 312P with the sportscar drivers. From left to right, Regazzoni, Ickx, Munari, Peterson and Schenken. 1970 Monza 1000 Kms: a pitstop for the 512S of Giunti-Vaccarella. Below, during the 1968 Monza 1000 Kms race

FIORANO AND THE MEMORY OF DINO

It was 1972. Amongst the many signs of Enzo Ferrari's total commitment to return to the top, was one which had a particular significance: the inauguration of the Fiorano test-track. It was a figure-of-8 circuit, with a bridge passing over the main straight alongside which there was a small pit garage for the cars. There was also a data-processing room, with monitors covering every part of the track and a sophisticated time-keeping system. But the most important feature of Fiorano was that it had curves extremely similar to some of those on Europe's Formula 1 circuits. There was a hairpin bend similar to the "Rascasse" at Montecarlo, a jump which resembled the "Brunnchen" at the Nurburgring, a wide corner which was like the "Tarzan" at Zandvoort. On the side of the track there was a modern steering-pad for the study of lateral acceleration and centrifugal force. The circuit was located in front of Ferrari headquarters: to reach it, the car transporters only had to cross the Abetone state road. An agricultural area of the Municipality of Fiora-

no, bordering on Maranello and obviously Ferrari property, was used for its construction.

For Formula 1 and motor racing in general, Fiorano was of outstanding value. Never before had any manufacturer had its own circuit to test racing cars and the Autodromo di Modena, built years before thanks also to funding from Ferrari, could not be said to be as convenient and useful. The true worth of Fiorano was immediately evident, with long, detailed test sessions taking place in its first year. It also had the advantage that the cars and the squad could be back in the factory in just a few minutes, the technical changes suggested by the test programme could be carried out quickly and the cars could be back out on the track again without wasting time with flights, cargo travel and the availability and cost of other circuits. Amongst the drivers to benefit the most from Fiorano was Niki Lauda, who between winter 1973 and the end of 1977, carried out endless test sessions to make the scarlet cars unbea-

table. Gilles Villeneuve, between '77 and '82, also used Fiorano on an almost daily basis, putting in tens of thousands of kilometres of tests.

In 1972 Fiorano completed the series of buildings near Ferrari headquarters, which also included the 1972 extension to the main building used for the production line.

There was also the Dino Ferrari Technical Institute with sports equipment for students. Furthermore, the Old Man promoted a campaign informing the public about muscular dystrophy, the genetic disease which killed Dino and which for Ferrari himself became the subject of study and philanthropic initiatives,

THE END OF THE SPORTSCARS

such as the donation of a high-tech machine for preventative diagnosis to Modena Hospital. All these activities would be continued by Piero Ferrari, the son who was destined to become the constructor's sole heir.

Monza 1972: the Ferraris of Ickx-Regazzoni (1) and Peterson-Schenken (2) in a downpour at the 1000 Kms race. Alongside, Peterson together with Fittipaldi, his 1973 Lotus F1 teammate

Above, testing at Modena: from left to right, Enzo Ferrari, the engineer Caliri and the reporter of the Italian magazine Autosprint,

Giancarlo Cevenini. On the other page: the 312P of Reutemann-Schenken at the 1973 Monza 1000 Kms

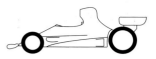

The arrival of the boxer !

The first F1 Ferrari powered by a 12-cylinder boxer engine, with a flat 180° angle between the two banks of cylinders, was called 312B. The car was designed in 1969 to race in the 1970 World Championship. The idea to use this type of engine came from the Ferrari 212E "barchetta", which won the European Championship of the Mountains in 1969 with Peter Schetty and which had a 2000 cc 12-cylinder boxer engine. Its transformation into a circuit-racing engine was immediately successful: 1970 will be remembered for Ferrari's second place in the Constructors' championship, along with Ickx finishing second in the Drivers' championship. Twelve-cylinder boxer Ferrari engines continued to race until the end of 1980, and from 1975 onwards were fitted with the revolutionary transversal gearbox. The list of victories was impressive: three World Drivers' titles (Lauda in 1975 and 1977, Scheckter in 1979) helped make the flat-12 boxer the Prancing Horse's most successful engine, as well as a unique reference point for the other types of engines used by Grand Prix constructors.

*Autodromo di Modena 1970:
the Austrian GP version
of the Ferrari 312B*

World Championship for Makes: 13 out of 20!

From 1953 to 1972: twenty years of the World Championship for Makes, every one of which disputed by Ferrari, and 13 world titles. These are the details of the title winners over the twenty years:

1953	**Ferrari**
1954	**Ferrari**
1955	**Mercedes**
1956	**Ferrari**
1957	**Ferrari**
1958	**Ferrari**
1959	**Aston Martin**
1960	**Ferrari**
1961	**Ferrari**
1962	**Ferrari**
1963	**Ferrari**
1964	**Ferrari**
1965	**Ferrari**
1966	**Ford**
1967	**Ferrari**
1968	**Ford**
1969	**Porsche**
1970	**Porsche**
1971	**Porsche**
1972	**Ferrari**

Scenes from the World Sportscar Championship at the end of the 1960s. From above: the Ford GT40 of Hawkins-Hobbs, winners of the 1968 Monza 1000 Kms; the Porsche 908 SP of Scarfiotti-Mitter in the same race; the Ferrari of Merzario-Amon at Monza in 1970

THE ANDRETTI PHENOMENON

Mario Andretti was the biggest and best surprise for Ferrari early in the 1970s. In South Africa, the opening round of the 1971 World Formula 1 Championship, Mario made his debut with a Ferrari Grand Prix car and won a race packed with excitement. It began with Regazzoni in the other Ferrari powering into a commanding lead and it concluded with the retirement of Hulme's McLaren, handing victory to Andretti with the 312B1. In 1970 however Mario had already been the star of an amazing race in the World Championship for Makes. At the Sebring 12 Hours, Andretti and Merzario in the Ferrari 512S dominated the race, but rolled to a halt with mechanical failure just a couple of hours before the chequered flag. There was still the other car of Vaccarella-Giunti, the latter in trouble with the local Florida police after being arrested the day before for speeding. At this point, Franco Gozzi, Enzo Ferrari's famous press officer, but at the ti-

me also sportscar team manager, had a great idea. He put Andretti in Vaccarella's car ... and this move made an incredible impact. Thanks to a storming finish, Andretti won the race virtually in a final sprint from the Porsche 908 driven by Peter Revson and film star Steve McQueen.

Mario Andretti at the wheel of the Ferrari 312B2 in 1972 and, below, together with the mechanic Gisberto Leopardi in an endurance race with the Ferrari sportscar team

THE PERIOD OF MONTEZEMOLO

Well into 1973, there were signs that an era was coming to an end. The main language of Formula 1 was now English. Lotus wasted a great opportunity: Colin Chapman's single-seater, the 72, held all the right cards but confusion in running two top drivers, Emerson Fittipaldi and Ronnie Peterson, ended up by the points being ridiculously divided. In the end, victory went to Jackie Stewart: it was his third world title, and his second with a Tyrrell. At the end of the season, Stewart had competed in 99 Grand Prixs and won 27 of them. The last few victories were the result of superior class, guarenteed not necessarily by extraordinary performance, but by a level of concentration and an ability to get the best out of the car in driving every single stage of the race, which none of his rivals could match. Someone once said that Stewart killed off the poetry of driving a racing car. When the lights turned to green, his Tyrrell powered straight into the lead. If there were no mechanical problems, it was impossible to catch him. It seemed that for Jackie Stewart everything came easily. In fact the opposite was probably true.

The start of 1976: Niki Lauda and Clay Regazzoni present the 312T2 at Fiorano

In his interesting biography "Faster", Stewart wrote that if a driver tried with all his force to set a fast time, he would never do it: something, either in him or in the car, would go wrong. He could only really go fast when things were done in the most natural way possible: when speed was absorbed and when a lap of the track became long and musical like a film in slow-motion.

But in the long run, this pleasure gave way to something else. To fame and glory, and to the money paid generously by the sponsors who were gradually becoming the major players in Grand Prixs. Sponsors names were appearing everywhere, and sometimes replacing the names of the cars. Except for Ferrari. When Jackie Stewart decided to stop racing, he left Formula 1 without a true heir. This unfortunately was not going to be Francois Cévert, his teammate at Tyrrell who had had a fantastic season, picking up six second places, three of which could easily have been victories if Stewart had retired from the races. Cévert lost his life at the Watkins Glen circuit in America, decapitated by a guard-rail in Saturday qualifying for the final GP of the year.

With Stewart gone and no-one ready to take his place, something new was about to happen in Formula 1. It had to happen.

That something new was called Ferrari. At Maranello, the historic centre of motor racing which was gradually transferring its central base to Great Britain, a 75 year-old man was continuing to live and hope with the energy of a 30 year-old. The year for Ferrari was a terrible one. No victories, no pole positions, no fastest laps. The driver pairing was Italo-Belgian: alongside the 312B3 for Jacky Ickx, there was also one for Arturo Merzario, who arrived in Formula 1 after good results over the years in Sportscars. But the situation was desperate. Two fourth places - in Brazil and South Africa - for Merzario, who in South America finished ahead of Ickx. The victories however went the way of cars whose names ended in consonants: Lotus, Lotus, Tyrrell; Lotus, Tyrrell, Tyrrell; McLaren, Lotus again; McLaren, Tyrrell, Tyrrell, Lotus ...

It was futile to continue. Ignoring accusations of anti-sporting behaviour, Enzo Ferrari decided not to enter his cars in the Dutch and German Grand Prixs. The rumours maintained that the decision was also taken in order to offer a golden opportunity to Ickx to break his contract, something which in fact immediately happened. At the Nurburgring, Ickx appeared (and was immediately competitive!) in a McLaren. At the next round in Austria, there was only one red car for Merzario. At Monza the two drivers were back together again, but in the last two Grand Prixs, Canada and United States, there was only one car driven by the Italian at the back of the grid.

It had been a long time since Ferrari was in such a difficult situation and there was not even a ray of hope. Despite the good performance of the 12 cylinder Boxer engine, the 312B3 could do absolutely nothing against the British competition which continued to notch up victory after victory, launching itself into frenetic race-by-race development. It was rumoured that Ferrari was close to collapse: that the Engineer could not carry on any more and that Fiat no longer had any desire to continue spending hundreds of millions of lire in this way, without any returns, either technically or image-wise. It was not true ... or at least it was true only in part. The Prancing Horse was in fact going round in circles, despite a major effort. On the technical side of things, Mauro Forghieri was the point of reference, but doubts surrounding team management meant

NIKI LAUDA

"At first Niki Lauda reminded me of a young Enzo Ferrari: silent, reserved, maybe a little shy, but blessed with exceptional self-confidence".

These words came from Ferrari himself. At the end of 1973, Lauda arrived at Maranello like a breath of fresh air. He was not yet 25 years of age: rather young to inherit the "mission" of taking Ferrari back to the top. He did have an ally however: Clay Regazzoni, his 1973 teammate at BRM. Clay was summoned by Ferrari: he proposed Lauda as second driver, defining him as "... inexperienced, but fast and very, very bright".

Maybe Ferrari believed these words. Or instead - and this is easier to accept - three-quarters of a century of a great, insuppressible instinct led him to believe that beneath Lauda and his apparent coolness, his "boy-next-door from a good family" appearance, there lied unimaginable skills.

One thing is certain. With the BRM, Lauda stood out in 1973 thanks to a couple of incredible performances. The first was qualifying for the German GP at the Nurburgring, where he was just two seconds off the

The 312B3 with Regazzoni in 1974. The Politoys-sponsored ISO F1 with which the British constructor Frank Williams made his Grand Prix debut the previous year. Henri Pescarolo in the cockpit of the car together with Williams, sitting on the wheel

zemolo - a young and brilliant lawyer, who had no experience of Formula 1, but who was clearly backed by the Agnelli family and therefore by Fiat - appeared on the horizon, Ferrari realized that he had to get his man. Not because he was forced to, but because in this rampant, open-minded and above all fresh figure, there was maybe the revolutionary force which would take everyone by surprise and would end up by rewriting history.

that he too was involved and was therefore unable to devote much attention to his two specialist fields: tactics and relations with the drivers. Confined to his lair in Maranello, tied increasingly by an umbilical cord to the Grand Prixs which were his only real outlet of activity, and which he followed when he could on television or at the end of the phone, Enzo Ferrari was desperate for success. This was his burning desire. When a certain Luca de Monte-

In the other photos, the CSAI licence of Niki Lauda and the driving licence of ... Elvis Presley

pole of the incomparable Stewart, but also eight seconds faster than his teammate Regazzoni. Or Canada, where in the pouring rain, Niki had the satisfaction of leading the race for twenty laps (after overtaking Peterson in the Lotus by sheer force!) before retiring with transmission failure amidst the cheers of spectators. Clay's suggestion might have been true; but it would be nice to think that on that 23rd September, while watching television images from the Canadian circuit at Mosport, Ferrari realized that something special lay behind the beaver-like teeth of the young Austrian driver. Back to the racing. In 1974, the Ferrari line-up was Regazzoni and Lauda. The strictly non-alphabetical order is motivated by the fact that the highest hopes were on Regazzoni. Instead, thanks to the feeling which emerged between the Austrian and Luca di Montezemolo, who was almost the same age, it was Niki who shone. Small, thin and not very talkative, the Austrian driver, heir of an industrial dynasty which had done everything in its power to prevent him from becoming a racing-driver, had an iron will but he did not show it. Gone were the days when in order to race he had to pledge to a bank his life insurance policy, underwritten in his name by his paternal grandfather who adored him but who saw him exclusively in the role of future magnate. The contract offered by Ferrari was not a lucrative one - the Engineer's tradition was still intact - but it was good enough for Lauda to be satisfied, thus allowing him to concentrate exclusively on the team, the testing work, and the car which he got to know curve after curve and which he improved day after day. Lauda had no half measures. Alongside the Austrian, Clay Regazzoni also yearned for success and glory, but the Swiss driver was a lover of the pleasures of life. Niki wasn't: for him there was only racing and Ferrari ... and that was all. He took up residence at Modena, at the Canal Grande Hotel in the centre just a few minutes walk away from Enzo Ferrari's own house. Luca di Montezemolo took care of him at the track. Outside of Fiorano, where the driver spent endless days testing and asking to test even more, he was

Lauda at Fiorano: together with the Prancing Horse's PR man, Franco Gozzi and mechanic, Borsari; next to the Ferrari BB of Luca di Montezemolo and posing for photographers on the 1976 312T2

looked after by Sante Ghedini, who in the future would leave Ferrari to follow Lauda to Brabham and who would become his right-hand man.

It didn't seem that way, but Lauda was a man in a hurry. With the much-improved but still far from perfect Ferrari 312B3, he set pole position in his third race in South Africa. In the next race in Spain, Ferrari returned to the winner's rostrum - victory number 50 in the World Championship - with an extraordinary 1-2. It was not a lucky victory either, because Lauda was ahead of Regazzoni. At the end of the season, Lauda had set 9 pole positions out of 15, a massive total. He scored two wins: Spain and Holland (another Ferrari 1-2). At the half-way point, Niki was second in the points table, one point behind Emerson Fittipaldi, who would

become champion at the end of the year; he had a two-point lead over Regazzoni, seven over the boisterous, but very fast, Jody Scheckter who had moved to Tyrrell to replace Stewart. But in the second half of the championship, the Austrian made a few mistakes and there were also some mechanical failures to contend with. He scored few points - eight in seven races - and only finished third overall. On the other hand, Regazzoni won at the Nurburgring and was in with a chance of the title until the final round in the United States, where he retired and handed a second championship victory to Fittipaldi. Behind his ever-present dark sunglasses, Enzo Ferrari was smiling. Ferrari's return to the big time was complete: all that was needed now was to continue along that path. He had some kind words for Regazzoni:

" ... he has proved himself to be an accomplished driver and his standard is now very high".

With Niki Lauda, he was more abrupt but did not hide a certain affection:

"Niki often obtains fastest laps - he declared - *and knows how to set his own pace".*

Shortly the harmony within the team gave way to tension and jealousy. Towards the end of 1974, no-one could deny that Lauda was the darling of the team and that Regazzoni was overshadowed. At the final GP at Watkins Glen, Niki was out of the title race, Clay wasn't. Yet two Ferrari 312B3s were reserved for Niki, one of which almost brand-new; "Rega" only had one, and

The Team Everest Ferrari 312T at Silverstone in 1976. Below, the press conference for the world title won by Lauda in 1975. From left to right, Luca di Montezemolo, Piero Fusaro, Enzo Ferrari and Franco Gozzi

THE LAUDA ERA

that was the previous year's model. Public opinion was also divided. Lauda, with his extraordinary ability to be quick almost immediately and apparently without effort, was a fascinating driver but did not stir the emotions. Clay aroused a wave of affection because of his personality and his exciting performances on the track. But the important factors, the consideration of Ferrari and Montezemolo, were clearly in favour of the Austrian.

This was the situation at the start of 1975. In motor racing circles, Niki was recognized as a brilliant tester, but was not considered to be number one driver. Above all his colleagues and rivals envied his Ferrari, particularly his unbeatable 312T.

They asked him what his secret was. The response was icy:
"I always wonder what I have to do to finish first".
Someone maligned that at least another five drivers were as good as he was, that he was unable to arouse enthusiasm, and so on.
"Patience! - he replied - On the track I work to win, not to put on a show".
Asked for his opinion about Lauda, Ronnie Peterson lost his patience: *"He should remember the Formula 2 days when he could never overtake me ...".*
Lauda shrugged his shoulders ... and won in 1975. Again and again. When he tested the Ferrari 312T, with its 12-cylinder Boxer engine and transversal gearbox which improved weight distribution at the rear, he did not have a shadow of doubt:
"You drive it like a bicycle", he exclaimed to the delight of Forghieri who had designed it. *"We will win a lot with this car".*
It was an easy prediction to make. Niki picked up win after win: Montecarlo (Ferrari had not won there for twenty years!), Belgium, Sweden. Then onto Holland, where he was second behind the Hesketh of James Hunt, a rival who would cross his path again, in a dramatic fashion, one year later. Another victory in France. The world title was almost won and it became a mathematical certainty at Monza, where Regazzoni won the race. A Ferrari driver became world champion for the first time in

eleven years, since the time of John Surtees. Lauda ended the season on a high note, winning the Watkins Glen round and confirming the first world title for a 12-cylinder engine.

THE FIRE THAT CHANGED HISTORY

At the end of 1975 Niki Lauda was not only World Champion for Ferrari: he was its ambassador, its triumphant face and its credit card for the motor racing world. In a certain sense he was also a star. Success began to bother him: the search for privacy became more important than the benefits of fame. Maybe it was in those months after the conquest of the '75 title that something in his rapport with the Prancing Horse began to go wrong.
The results on the track however were no different. Lauda began the championship with a series of wins: first in Brazil, then in South Africa. Regazzoni won the third GP of the season at Long Beach. Niki was second and turned against the new Sporting Director of the Prancing Horse, Daniele Audetto, accusing him of wanting victory for

Clay at all costs and for who knows what reason. Then he got back into the cockpit of the 312T2 and started to win again: Spain (but only after the disqualification of the McLaren of Hunt, who was then reinstated as winner by the sporting tribunal months after), Belgium, Montecarlo. Then came Great Britain, again won by Hunt, who was disqualified for sporting irregularities. After nine of the sixteen races on the calendar, the Austrian had what seemed like an unassailable lead: Niki 61 points, Scheckter 30, Hunt and Depailler 26. Neither Hunt nor McLaren, not even the revolutionary and immediately competitive six-wheel Tyrrell (four at the front) of Scheckter and Depailler could touch him.

And so the German Grand Prix, which would dramatically mark the turning-point of the season and also an era.

Back in July however, the rapport between Lauda and Ferrari was no longer the same as the previous year. The driver continued to concentrate on the cars and the races, but his mind was occupied with other things such as lucrative advertising contracts and the house he was building on the hills of Hof near Salzburg. During building work, Niki overturned a tractor and cracked a rib. Nevertheless he took part in the Spanish Grand Prix, which marked the debut of the 312T2, but it was clear that his skill behind the wheel had suffered and ill-feeling began to spread throughout the team. So-

mething also changed in the private life of the driver whose only real family seemed to be Ferrari. During a party at the house of the actor Curt Jurgens, Niki got to know the beautiful Chilean model Marlene Knaus. It was love at first sight, an impetuous and uncontrollable relationship, which led him to suddenly break off with Mariella von Reininghaus, the woman who had been at his side, in silence and in the background, since he first arrived in the sport.

From Maranello, Enzo Ferrari was watching, controlling and taking notes. But he refrained from any official comments.

"Niki has discovered the joys of life - he joked - *but I am sure he will still be the great driver he has always been".*

He was wrong. Lauda had something to reproach Ferrari with: first of all the lower pay he was getting, at least with respect to the British teams. Rumours began to spread about offers from other teams; prompting increasingly embarassed rejections by the driver. Furthermore the climate within the team was deteriorating: despite his massive lead, Niki started to criticise the team and its sporting director. From the Brazilian GP onwards, the Brabhams were powered by the 12-cylinder Alfa Romeo Boxer, which soon Niki accredited with greater performance than the similar Ferrari engine. The technical scene also presented the powerful 12-cylinder

Ferrari through the lens

The best photographs of Ferrari road or racing cars of the 1960s and 1970s bear the name of Peter C. Coltrin. They covered the era when the scarlet red cars dominated world-wide, but before that, they captured some unforgettable days of testing, dialog and interesting meetings at Modena, Maranello and nearby.

Today, more than 15 years after his death, the memories of Peter Coltrin and his intense love for Ferrari live on in the unique photographic archives he left behind.

The American photographer (but with an Italian heart) Peter Coltrin together with his wife Gabriella and their much-loved dog

THE LAUDA ERA

Matra, demonstrating that Prancing Horse supremacy in the engine field would not last much longer.

Volumes have been written about that fateful day of 1st August 1976 at the Nurburgring; Lauda's Ferrari way over the limit of grip on the wet surface on lap 3 and the crash against the Bergwerk rock. The 312T2 bounced back onto the track in a crumpled state. The rest of the group arrived: Brett Lunger's Surtees and Harald Ertl's Hesketh hit the Ferrari which cannoned around like a billiard-ball and caught fire. Inside the cockpit, Niki lost consciousness: without the assistance of several drivers - above all Arturo Merzario who pulled him out - he would have died amidst the flames. The rest is history. The first images, shot by a spectator, show Niki on a stretcher: he was looking at his hands, but he didn't know his face had been destroyed by the flames. He asked his helpers:

"What's my face like?"

What a difference to the Lauda of one and a half months later, when he was blinded by the desire to return to the track and defend his title.

"I prefer to have my right foot than a pretty face".

Niki was taken to hospital. The consequences, which seemed slight at first, soon turned out to be much more serious. The smoke Lauda had inhaled during the fire caused major respiratory complications. Late in the evening he was given the Last Rites: he was unlikely to see through the night.

The world learnt about Lauda's fate the morning after in the newspapers, especially in Italy, where the GP was not shown on television either live or delayed. Slowly the alarming news on the health of Niki began to fade away, but no-one could say when (and if) he would return to the track. Meanwhile, after his victory at the Nurburgring, Hunt had begun an incredible fight-back, edging him closer and closer to the no longer uncatchable Lauda. The British driver, Niki's friend, was in superb form and his McLaren M23 was becoming increasingly competitive. As if that wasn't enough, nervousness also began to play its part within Ferrari. The International Federation restored the points and victory in Spain to Hunt: Ferrari, instead of attempting to defend Lauda's lead in the championship, decided as a protest not to take part in the Austrian GP on 15th August. The team returned to the track two weeks later in Holland with a sole T2 for Regazzoni, who finished second behind Hunt. The British driver celebrated his 29th birthday in the best possible way by closing the gap on Lauda to just 14 points.

Niki returned to the track on Friday 10th September during first practice for the Italian GP. Forty days had passed since the inferno at Bergwerk. He tried to reassure everyone but he was in a terrible state: due to the constant vibrations, his helmet rubbed against the healing burns, causing them to bleed. The rest forms part of the history of Formula 1 and racing. Lauda finished a

miraculous fourth at Monza. Hunt retired, but went on to win in Canada and the United States, closing the gap to just three points. Then onto the pouring rain of Fuji for the final Grand Prix; Lauda abandoned the race, fourth place went to Hunt's McLaren and the championship went to the British driver by just one point.

The divorce between Lauda and Ferrari, which was officially recorded as taking place in October 1977, actually began in the pits of the Japanese circuit. Niki only completed two laps in the pouring rain. He was almost driving blind because of the bleeding from his wounds. Then he decided to retire. When he abandoned the circuit in a Rolls-Royce, controversy was already brewing in Italy even though dawn had just broken.

At first, Ferrari defended him.

"I also decided not to race in the Lyon GP in 1924 because I didn't feel like it. I wasn't feeling well, I was exhausted. I can understand Lauda: he did the right thing".

Strong words, destined to change after a few hours of criticism. Once again the motor racing world was divided over Lauda: there were those who supported *"the courage to be afraid"*, while others spoke about *"the fear of having courage"*.

Lauda tried not to let it bother him, but it was difficult.

A six-wheeled revolution: the Tyrrell P34 of Jody Scheckter at Monza in 1976 and the scale model of the experimental 1977 Ferrari with twin rear wheels

For 1977, Ferrari flanked Lauda with Carlos Reutemann, after Regazzoni had been fired without notice, comment or explanation. Reutemann had already been put on stand-by at the end of summer 1976, in case Lauda couldn't make it back on the track, and he drove a third 312T2 in the Italian GP. In fact, contacts were also made with Ronnie Peterson, who was summoned to Maranello in secret by team manager Daniele Audetto and sent back home again as soon as he landed at Milan airport, because Ferrari was not interested.

For Niki Lauda the start of 1977 was an uphill battle. It seemed that the team was betting everything on Reutemann. Fiat had to intervene to give Lauda some help. The Austrian didn't waste any time. Three victories in South Africa, Germany and Holland. Not many but enough to see off the challenge of Mario Andretti's Lotus, the brand-new Wolf of Jody Scheckter and the McLaren of Hunt, who was victim of "world champion" syndrome with a season of mixed fortunes.

These three victories would be enough to guarentee Lauda his second world title. But he was not to finish the season: in open dispute with Ferrari - and attracted by the multi-millionaire offer from Brabham which waved a two-year contract for 1978-79 in front of his nose - Niki did not take part in the final two Grand Prixs of the season in Canada and Japan. That was the end of Lauda's wonderful story at Ferrari. A story which marked an era in motor racing and sport in general. Enzo Ferrari, critical towards Lauda and openly hostile when he replied to Niki's harsh anti-Maranello book "Protokoll", final-

Monza 1977:
Reutemann at the Italian GP.
The race was won by Andretti in
a Lotus and Lauda, second at the
flag, took his second world title
with Ferrari. He left at the end
of the season, giving rise
to controversy not only
in the specialist magazines

ly concluded the story two years later with affectionate words.

"Lauda sent me a telegram to congratulate me on the title won by Scheckter - he said at the end of 1979 - I replied with this message: If you had not decided to leave at the end of 1977, today you would have equalled Fangio's record".

Ferrari's appraisal was too kind: even if he had won the title with Ferrari in 1978 and 1979, Niki would have taken his total to 4, whereas Fangio won 5 titles. Unless Ferrari wanted to give an even more contorted and hidden meaning to the period of ill-feeling between the team and the driver.

"Our interpretation is that if at the end of 1976 Niki had kept his faith of Ferrari when he wanted to defend the Austrian's leadership by using Reutemann in the third car for the rest of the championship, he would also have won that title which eventually went to Hunt".

Too complicated and "Macchiavellian"? Maybe so. But the Engineer would certainly have been capable of such an interpretation ...

VILLENEUVE FEVER

The world discovered Villeneuve fever in 1979. It first came to Italy, the centre of Ferrari. Gilles Villeneuve arrived at Maranello with a travelling bag: a telephone call to his house in Canada, which at first he considered a joke, had convinced him to come for a talk with Enzo Ferrari. For Gilles the call came out of the the blue, just like the decision of Lauda to move to Brabham-Alfa Romeo, despite the fact that with the second title almost certain, the team had tried to reach an agreement for the following year.

Many different stories survive from that obtained meeting which was destined to end in divorce. What is certain however is that Niki was totally outspoken.

"Ferrari no longer gives me any more motivation".

What was just as certain was that the Engineer was very disappointed: deep down, despite the various recent misunderstandings, he was close to Lauda. He had created him from nothing ... and now he was leaving.

The Engineer also tried to tempt Lauda with the financial card:

"How much do you want to stay?", he shouted to him in his Maranello office. Lauda's reply was in Austrian Schillings and after getting the company accountant to convert the sum into lire, Ferrari spluttered. It was way beyond Ferrari's means and possibilities. Lauda was lost. He let him go, however not before calling him a name which would remain in history: *"Jew!"*.

The news of the divorce broke on Monday 29th August, the day after Lauda's third win of the season in Holland which gave him a lead of 21 points over Scheckter and 28 over his teammate Reutemann with four Grand Prixs left to run.

Talks immediately began over Niki's replacement in Ferrari. First with Mario Andretti, who was blocked by a contract with the Lotus of Colin Chapman, who in 1978 was building his fortune around the Italo-American. Then Scheckter, who also could not move because of an agreement with the team of multi-millionaire, Walter Wolf. Thoughts also turned to Patrick Tambay, but he was in the McLaren orbit. Who knows why no-one contacted Ronnie Peterson, one of Ferrari's old favourites and free even. Maybe something clicked in the mind of the almost eighty year-old from Maranello: nothing and no-one could take the place of Lauda in the scarlet red cars better than Villeneuve ... The world of Formula 1 knew little about Gilles Villeneuve. A 27-year-old Canadian who for many years pretended to be two years younger for fear of being too old for Grand Prixs, Gilles Villeneuve came from motor-sled racing. He had some interesting results in Formula Atlantic, a sort of overseas Formula 2. He made a quiet F1 debut in a McLaren on 16th July: tenth in qualifying with an old M23, 27/100ths of a second faster than Jochen Mass who had a new M26, identical to polesitter James Hunt's. He finished eleventh in the race, but was ahead of everyone in the Sunday morning warm-up in race trim.

Villeneuve arrived at Malpensa airport one sunny morning in September. He was met by Ennio Mortara, the Ferrari translator, who took him to Maranello by car. As soon as he got in, Gilles asked how long the journey would take, then fell asleep.

When they introduced him to the living legend of motor racing, Villeneuve didn't seem all that impressed. When they asked him if he would like to drive the Ferrari which belonged to Lauda, he replied that it would probably be a good idea to talk with McLaren, with whom he had a sort of contract. After Ferrari's calm response, they moved on to financial matters.

"How much would you like to earn to be happy?", said the Legend. *"Enough to give my family a decent life".*

His family: his wife Joanne, a woman who lived in the shadow of her husband's overriding passion for the sport, their son, six and a half year old Jacques, and Melanie who was younger. They all moved together from one Grand Prix to another in a motorhome.

A few words and a handshake. On 7th October, Gilles made his official debut in a Ferrari during practice for the Canadian GP. He had not had much time to get to know the 312T2 and qualified in 17th position, slightly more than half-a-second slower than teammate Reutemann. In the race he finished twelfth, 4 laps behind the winner Scheckter (Wolf). Two weeks later it was the Japanese GP at Fuji. The circuit, situated under the sacred mountain of Japan, is a difficult one: its long pit straight takes the cars up to over 300 kph. In qualifying, Gilles was no higher than the third row from the back of the grid. On the sixth lap of the race, he braked hard and ran into the rear of the six-wheeled Tyrrell of Peterson at the end of the straight. It was later rumoured that his brakes had faded. What is certain is that the Ferrari took off and then landed in an

area which was banned for the public, leaving two people dead and ten injured. Villeneuve's fame as an "aviator" started here, as the 1978 championship was to confirm.

1978 was a strange year. The Ferrari 312T3 was not the T2, but without a couple of disastrous starts (Montecarlo and Belgium) Reutemann could have fought for the title with the Lotus of Andretti, who became world champion. Alongside the Argentinian driver, Villeneuve was maturing. His times were rapidly approaching his teammate's, but at a high cost: off road excursions, crashes, jumps. The "Aviator" was on everyone's lips. On 26th July, after three victories by Reutemann but with the title virtually in the hands of Andretti, Ferrari signed Jody Scheckter for 1979. It seemed that Villeneuve would have to give up his place to the South African. In-

Two versions of Gilles Villeneuve: in the cockpit of his 1979 Ferrari 312T4, and relaxing alongside an unusually smiling Enzo Ferrari

stead it was Reutemann who left, and had no alternative but to go to Lotus. Gilles won his first race at the final round of the season, the fifth for the Prancing Horse after four with Carlos. But above all he began to hold a place in Enzo Ferrari's heart.

The 1979 World Championship saw the debut of the ugly but victorious Ferrari 312T4. Scheckter took it to victory in the championship, which was clinched with victory in front of a delirious crowd at Monza. Villeneuve obeyed orders: he was the Number 2 driver and gave way to Jody. He did however take three wins, the same number as his teammate. But above all 1979 was the year when Villeneuve Fever became white-hot. Gilles was no longer an "aviator". On the track he won, convincingly. He guaranteed non-stop excitement. The wheel-to-wheel duel with Arnoux's Renault in the final stages of the French GP at Dijon will remain in the memories of those who follow motor sport. Not for the win, which went to Jabouille's Renault, the first in the new turbo era in Formula 1, but for

second place, which went to Villeneuve by just 64 hundredths of a second from Arnoux. The fans celebrated the world title of Scheckter, but went wild over Villeneuve's victory in the final round of the championship, putting him in pole position for the title fight the following year.

1980 failed to fulfil its promise. Ferrari, which had moved on to the pretty but out-dated 312T5, could do nothing against the ground-effect Williams which gave the title to Alan Jones, as well as Piquet's Brabham and Reutemann's Lotus, second and third overall. Gilles was out of luck: 6 points and tenth overall. Scheckter, 2 points and nineteenth overall, was even more disappointing, and at the end of the year left his place to Didier Pironi. The same could be said for 1981, even though it did come with some added excitement. The Formula 1 cars were as rigid as go-karts, ground-effect dominated, and so did turbos with their more than 600 bhp. Ferrari switched to turbo power. With the 126C, Villeneuve won two memorable Grand Prixs: in Monte-

carlo, he overtook the Williams of an incredulous Jones with a final dash to the line; in Spain, at Jarama, where Gilles had problems in curves because the car was undriveable, but thanks to the power of the 6-cylinder turbo he managed to keep ahead on the straights with sheer horsepower.

"Gilles, you are wild!" was the full-page headline in the Italian weekly magazine Autosprint after the victory at Montecarlo. But it was all an illusion: Williams and Brabham dominated F1. In the end the title went to the young Brazilian Nelson Piquet, who was fresher and more lucid at the end of the absurd car-park Grand Prix around the Caesars' Palace Hotel in Los Angeles, where Reutemann said goodbye to yet another title.

At the end of 1981 Gilles Villeneuve was tired. He had worked so hard and tested the Ferrari turbo for tens of thousands of kilometres in an attempt to make it competitive and reliable. He had excited crowds all over the world, as in the 1980 Canadian GP where he scored a legendary third place without a front wing (after a col-

lision) in the rain. He was 31 years old however and saw the possibility of becoming world champion slip further and further away. He listened to offers from other teams but Enzo Ferrari loved him and knew how to make him understand. He would remain with the Prancing Horse for 1982.

That year was to be the end for Villeneuve. On Saturday 8th May at Zolder, Gilles Villeneuve lost his life in a stupid accident during qualifying for the Belgian GP. At Imola, thirteen days before, he had lost control in a bid for victory which was "snatched" from him by his teammate Pironi after orders came from the pits to hold positions with Villeneuve in the lead, seeing as the two Ferraris were uncatchable. In the Terlamen Forest, shortly before 2 o'clock on that terrible afternoon in Belgium, the world's favourite driver said goodbye to Formula 1 for ever. For the medical record, the time of death was the evening at Leuwen hospital.

Enzo Ferrari and Ferrari were filled with grief. The 126C2 Turbo was without a doubt the fastest and most

competitive car of the season, and Didier Pironi could not fail to take the title. The Frenchman went on to win in Holland: on the eve of the German GP, the 12th of the 16 rounds on the calendar, he had a nine-point lead over Watson (McLaren) and 14 over Prost (Renault). But on 7th August, the final day of qualifying at Hockenheim, Pironi crashed into Prost at 300 kph in the pouring rain and broke both his legs. His career was over. The 7th August was a Saturday, the same day of the week as Gilles' accident.

At the end of the year, Ferrari won the Constructors' title, thanks also to the victory of Patrick Tambay who won that fateful race in Germany. However it is the memories of Gilles which put the seal on perhaps the most heart-rendering season in the history of Ferrari.

Monza 1978: flames and smoke at the start of the Italian GP in which Swedish driver Ronnie Peterson lost his life

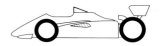

Villeneuve Fever also led to several "fakes". The memorabilia of ex-Ferrari mechanic Gisberto Leopardi also included this picture dedicated to Gilles and to his famous incident during testing at Imola in 1979.

But look closely and the photo has obviously been touched up.

Below, Lauda's 312T at the Paul Ricard circuit in France in 1975. In the background, Graham Hill and his driver Tony Brise, who shortly after were to perish in an air crash

in the world

1978 - In Italy, the Red Brigades kidnapped the Christian Democratic Party Secretary Aldo Moro in March and murdered him on 9th May after holding him hostage for several weeks.

1978 - On 16th October, after the brief papacy of John Paul I (August-September), Polish Archbishop Karol Wojtyla became Pope under the name of John Paul II.

1979 - Margaret Thatcher of the Conservative party became British Prime Minister.

in motor sport

1978 - At Monza, Swedish driver Ronnie Peterson was involved in an incident at the start of the race and was trapped in his burning car. He died in hospital later that night.

1979 - At Kyalami, Gilles Villeneuve won the South African GP with the new Ferrari 312 T4 designed by Mauro Forghieri.

1979 - Two great drivers of the seventies, Niki Lauda and James Hunt, both retired from motor racing.

Call Montezemolo 3131

Maybe not everyone knows how Luca di Montezemolo, an amateur rally-driver with bright hopes but little specific experience of motor racing or even F1, came to be in charge of the Ferrari F1 racing team. Montezemolo was a young lawyer, closely connected to the family of Gianni Agnelli - who at that time, it should be said, was a partner of Ferrari as he was the owner of Fiat. In 1972, Luca di Montezemolo was a guest on the famous radio programme at the time "Call Rome 3131".

The subject of the radio conversation soon moved onto Ferrari and its current bad patch. At this point, Montezemolo replied by defending Ferrari and its work and was so convincing on the air that the Modena constructor got in touch with the young lawyer.

"What are your future plans?", Ferrari asked Montezemolo.

"I'm about to leave for the United States to do a masters degree".

"If you like, when you come back - concluded Ferrari - I would be happy to offer you a position within our sporting activities".

This almost fairy-tale story was how Ferrari offered a contract to Montezemolo, who at the end of 1973 took over the F1 team. It won a total of 9 Grand Prixs over the next two years, the last of which was crowned by Lauda's world title.

Monza 1979: with a 1-2 for Scheckter and Villeneuve at the Italian GP, Ferrari and the South African driver wrapped up the world title.
This was also a triumph for the 312T4, the ugly but very competitive Ferrari single-seater car which won six races during the season

THE LAST WORLD TITLE

The 1979 World Championship began with Ligier and Jacques Laffite winning in Argentina and Brazil. It continued with a remarkable performance by Williams which began to win with Clay Regazzoni and then dominated the second half of the season with Alan Jones. But 1979 will go down in the annals of motor sport as the year of the world title of Ferrari and Jody Scheckter, who was signed at the end of 1978 to replace the *"troubled and troublesome"* (another label thought up by Enzo Ferrari) Carlos Reutemann.

The days of a fast and over-the-limit Scheckter were long gone. James Hunt used to call him "Fletcher", the name of the seagull who in the famous book by Jonathan Livingstone had ambitions which were way beyond his possibilities. The 1979 version of Jody Scheckter was very different to the

young South African driver who made his debut in 1972 with incredibly fast times and some hair-raising overtaking. The Ferrari version of Scheckter was a fast, consistent, regular driver who had one aim: win the world title with the Ferrari 312T4. The T4 was so ugly that at the official presentation on 19th January it was renamed rather unkindly "the Slipper" or "Hippo-nose". Enzo Ferrari however wasn't in the least worried about the comments: *"Let's hope* - he said - *that the ugly T4 becomes pretty on the track"*.

And that is exactly what did happen. With the T4, Scheckter and Villeneuve won three victories apiece. The title went to Jody, who scored more placings. No-one could have imagined it at the time, but that world championship victory was the last one for Ferrari until the present day.

in the world

1981 - On 13th May, the Turkish terrorist Ali Agca made an aborted assassination attempt on Pope John Paul II in St. Peter's Square, Rome.

1982 - The Falklands War between Britain and Argentina lasted from April to June and ended with Argentina renouncing any claims to the islands.

in motor sport

1981 - The Spanish GP at Jarama on 21st June saw one of the most exciting Grand Prixs in the history of Formula 1. Villeneuve won from Laffitte, Watson, Reutemann and De Angelis, all separated by one second at the flag.

1982 - On 8th May, Gilles Villeneuve was killed during qualifying for the Belgian GP, when he crashed into the car driven by Jochen Mass.

1982 - Colin Chapman, one of F1's great innovators and owner of Lotus, died of a heart attack in mysterious circumstances on 16th December at the age of 51.

T for three,
T for title

From the 312T to the 312T5: from 1975 to 1980 the history of Ferrari cars has only been written with the letter "T". It stands for transversal, the tytpe of gearbox fitted on all the production models, which guarenteed a better balance in the distribution of weight behind the cockpit and therefo-re better handling despite the considerable bulk of the 12-cylinder boxer engine. The six years of the "T" Ferraris brought an incredible series of results for Ferrari: three world titles in 1975 (Lauda with the 312T), 1977 (Lauda with the T2) and 1979 (Scheckter with the T4). The cars won a total of 27 victories, with 19 pole positions and 25 fastest laps. It was an exceptional performance, and deserves admiration when bearing in mind that all these results were achieved between 1975 and 1979. In 1980 in fact, Scheckter and Villeneuve failed to win a race, set a pole or even one fastest lap.

A "poker" of Ferrari "T" cars. Clockwise from left: the 312T (12) of Lauda's 1975 title; the T2 of Niki's second title in 1977; the T3 with Reutemann in 1978; the T5 here with Villeneuve in the unlucky 1980 season

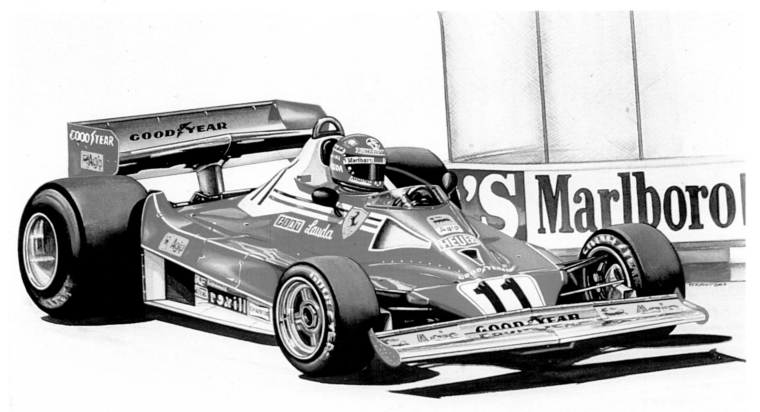

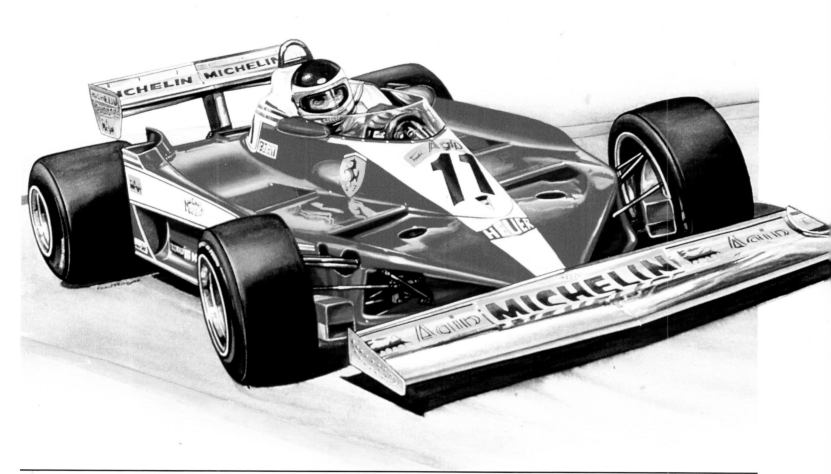

ALBORETO

After the death of Gilles Villeneuve, Enzo Ferrari found that he was 84 years of age. Not in the sense that before he had been unaware of his age: but now the tiredness and pressure were starting to make themselves felt. He was the most famous car constructor in the world, in motor racing and road production. His name and his symbol, the Prancing Horse, were one thing only and told the same story whichever way you look at it: the dream which turned into a legend, glory, enterprise, innovation, success. But with the death of Gilles Villeneuve, he had to say goodbye to what had remained his personal dream. An unexpressed dream, which he never told to anyone or which he probably only confessed to a few close friends: create a new Nuvolari. There was no doubt that Villeneuve

was a creature of Ferrari in the true meaning of the term. Who amongst Ferrari drivers could, in the past, have been the cause of so many incidents, invent so many incredible spins, destroy so many cars and play so many tricks? No-one. Gilles on the other hand could do this and a lot more. Without risking anything.
"I was very fond of him", said Ferrari on the death of Gilles Villeneuve. That expression said it all: from the dream of Gilles as a "total driver" of the end of the century, to the affection of a father towards his son, without taking into consideration his pros or cons.
It is difficult to imagine whether and how much the great rapport between Gilles and the Engineer derived from the behaviour of the driver at the wheel of Formula 1 cars. Certainly fearlessness, indifference to risk and reckless courage were dominant

characteristics in Gilles Villeneuve. Enzo Ferrari liked this in a driver, as he had with Tazio Nuvolari, Guy Moll and with very few other champions behind the wheel.
On the death of Villeneuve, Ferrari was a dual industrial and sporting reality. On the one hand, striving for success in the most professional way, using more modern and refined technology and administrative methods; on the other, the almost family-like cohesion linking the protagonists. A tightly-knit staff, on a human and professional level, has always been a special feature of the Prancing Horse. Enzo Ferrari was now more than just old. The problems of asthma which at the end of the 1970s became serious, requiring innovative surgery by a Turin specialist with the use of human placenta, were a thing of the past. But the high doses of cortisone which at the time were neces-

sary to combat the asthma had their effects on Ferrari's kidney functions which got worse year after year, weakening the constructor, subjecting him to daily analysis and making him follow a strict diet. In this situation, the family ties between Ferrari and his closest collaborators were as deep and solid as ever.

Here are just a few examples:

Franco Gozzi, who entered Ferrari in the 1950s after being recommended by Ferrari's barber, was for more than a quarter of a century the Prancing Horse spokesman. Born and bred in the Ferrari school (i.e. only say the things which Ferrari wants everyone to know, deny the rest), Gozzi was an integral part of the "family". Ferrari trusted him blindly, to the point of making him "master of ceremonies" at public occasions and in press conferences, but also in everyday contacts with Italian and foreign journalists.

From 1968 to 1970 Gozzi was also team manager and this experience helped him to get to know every minor detail of how a racing team worked. This characteristic also helped him to become a vital, irreplaceable piece of the Ferrari jigsaw, and the situation would not change until 1988, the year of the Engineer's death. Mauro Forghieri was the technical "soul" of the Prancing Horse. He arrived at Maranello immediately after graduating in 1959 and a few years later took over the difficult role of Prancing Horse technical director, putting his name to many of the Sport and Formula 1 cars which from then until the 1980s scored some of Ferrari's greatest victories. Forghieri's influence on the "T" series of single-seaters was considerable and he designed and constructed the successful 12-cylinder boxer, as well as the 312T which gave Lauda his

The Ferrari 126C2. With this car, Ferrari enjoyed total technical superiority, but failed to win the Drivers' title following the tragedy of Villeneuve at Zolder and Pironi's crash at Hockenheim

first title and the T4 of Scheckter's triumph in 1979. At the start of the 1980s, Forghieri was involved in the lengthy development work which would take the 6-cylinder turbo to victory in 1982 and 1983, a car which then suffered in the technological battle against foreign manufacturers such as Porsche, Renault and Honda. Marco Piccinini was manager of the Formula 1 team from 1978 onwards. No-one held or would hold this post longer than him and he continued to run the Grand Prix team and drivers until the death of Ferrari in 1988. He would also represent the Prancing Horse in the International Motorsport Federation with an authority which no-one, except for the Engineer himself, had ever had. Piccinini, like Gozzi and Forghieri, was tied to the Prancing Horse and Ferrari above all by total loyalty, almost a blood tie, forming a bond that no external threat or pressure could change. The last name on this list, but not the least important, was Piero Lardi. At the start of the 1980s, the son of Ferrari was one of the cornerstones of

The presentation of the 126C2 at Maranello. From left to right, Dario Calzavara, Marco Piccinini, Piero Ferrari, Harvey Postlethwaite and Franco Gozzi can be recognized. With the 126C3, in the drawing, Renè Arnoux just missed out on the 1983 title

the company and the team. He grew up in the shadows, away from all the official dealings but always where it mattered in the company and he had always had a passion for racing, for cars and drivers. He played a key role in the signing of Jody Scheckter in 1978: the driver had also attracted the attention of the Engineer, but it was not easy to persuade him to pay the one million dollars (more than one-and-a-half billion lire at the time, around seven billion today) necessary to make him refuse the offers from the British competition. Now Piero was ready to inherit the work of his father, who in 1978 lost his wife Laura with muscular dystrophy, the same disease which had taken away his son Dino many years before. This was the Prancing Horse family which lost Gilles Villeneuve, the adopted son, in such traumatic circumstances. It was clear that it was Enzo Ferrari, the patriarch, who suffered the most. As well as mourning the death of the Canadian driver, Ferrari was passing through a moment which was to say the least, unfortunate. Gilles' place was taken over by the Parisian, Patrick Tambay: a driver whom Ferrari had always liked, Tambay was now available, despite it being late in the season. When Pironi, seriously injured in qualifying for the German GP, was removed from the title race, the superiority of Ferrari's technical "package" was evident. The early days of the Ferrari turbo, power-

ful yet almost undriveable because it had such a harsh and brutal power distribution, were a memory of the past. Whereas that turbo could only be controlled by Villeneuve, who took two extraordinary victories in 1981 at Montecarlo and Jarama, good results could be obtained by almost anyone with the 1982 edition of the 126C2 V6 turbo. This was demonstrated by Tambay, who won in Germany a few hours after Pironi's crash, but who due to his late arrival on the scene had no chance of going for the title, which went to the Williams-Ford driver Keke Rosberg. It was also confirmed by Mario Andretti, who was called upon by Ferrari to drive in the final two Grand Prixs and who set an extraordinary pole position on his debut at Monza for the Italian GP. He eventually finished third behind Tambay, who lost out to the winner Arnoux in a Renault. Ferrari was left with success - or rather domination - in the World Constructors' Champion-

ship, but it was bitter consolation. When the 1982 season was drawing to a close, the Ferrari "family" had to chose the driver to race alongside Tambay the following year. The choice fell upon René Arnoux: the young and fast French driver of the Renault team who Ferrari immediately took a liking to, due to the determination he had shown in a year when he fought against (and twice beat) his teammate Alain Prost, a driver tipped to be tomorrow's champion.

But Ferrari also liked another driver. He was Italian, and this was surprising because after the last episode with a home-grown driver, Merzario in 1973, it seemed that the Prancing Horse did not want to repeat this experience, which would clearly have negative repercussions on the press and public opinion, in the event of bad results.

The Italian in question was Michele Alboreto; he was 26 and since 1981 had been driving for the Tyrrell team for whom he had won his first Grand Prix in the final round of the 1982 championship in the bizarre car-park race at Caesar's Palace in Las Vegas. It was a great moment for Italian drivers in Formula 1: during the 1982 season, before Michele's victory, Riccardo Patrese (at Montecarlo with Brabham) and Elio De Angelis (at Zeltweg with Lotus after a historic 125/1000ths of a second photo-finish with Rosberg's Williams) had also scored wins. However this was not the reason why Alboreto earned Ferrari's favour. Between the young Milan driver and the Grand Old Man of Maranello, there was in fact the start of a personal friendship, at first kind and affectionate and then increasingly intense. At the end of 1982 Ken Tyrrell, who had a keen eye for drivers, put the brakes on the mutual courtship:

"Michele is a good driver - he declared - *but he still needs more experience. Another season with us and he'll be ready to race with Ferrari".*

The story, it seemed, had already been written ...

In 1983 Ferrari raced with Tambay and Arnoux. It was a great season, totally concentrated on the race for the title. Only McLaren, amongst the top teams, was still tied to the old normally-aspirated Cosworth engine, but it still managed to win at Long Beach with Watson. For the rest, the red cars fought an incredible battle with the turbocharged Renaults of Prost and Cheever and the Brabham-BMWs of Piquest and Patrese. The Prancing Horse won four races: one with Tambay at Imola and three with Arnoux in Canada, Germany and Holland. But it wasn't enough. Ferrari again won the World Constructors' Championship, but the Drivers' title - clearly the most important - went for the second time to Piquet and his Brabham. The disappointment at the South African circuit of Kyalami was plain for all to see. The Ferrari cars returned to Maranello without the title they had chased in vain since 1979 and no-one could imagine how long this "fasting" was going to go on for. At the ritual end-of-year press conference the Engineer was totally outspoken:

"On Saturday evening they telephoned me from South Africa to tell me that Tambay on pole position had requested a bonus to guarantee his support for Arnoux in the final assault on the title", he told the massive numbers of journalists present at Maranello. *"Promise him the moon if you want",* I replied to Piccinini, *"because with our Michelin tyres we've got no chance of winning anyway. I was right".*

He continued with the presentation of Alboreto for the next season:

"One year ago I said to Alboreto that when his contract had expired, there would be a Ferrari available for him. This moment has arrived and I am happy to have him with us starting from the 1984 World Championship".

Just a few words therefore to confirm that the "family" was again complete. René Arnoux, a fast driver whom Ferrari liked, was not the right man however to become part of the family. This was confirmed after the first GP of the 1985 season in Brazil

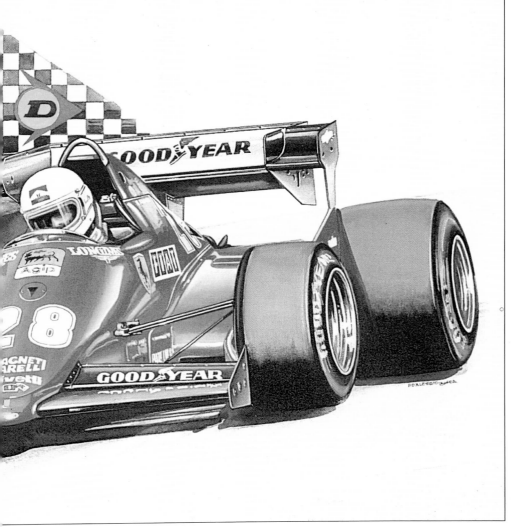

when he was abruptly sacked in a no-nonsense way by the team for reasons never made official, but which certainly had nothing to do with his performance behind the wheel. This was followed punctually by the arrival of Michele Alboreto, who even before taking to the track for his first race with a Ferrari (Brazil 1984, second fastest time on the grid alongside the Lotus-Renault of De Angelis) had been perfectly integrated into the Maranello environment. He wasn't on first name terms with Enzo Ferrari, unlike Villeneuve, but Michele was without a doubt the "son" Ferrari had found again.

Michele Alboreto and the 126C4, in the drawing, with which he won in Belgium in 1984. With the 156/85 (below), the Italian driver scored two wins in Canada and Germany and was in with a shot at the world title which eventually went to Prost

DEFEAT AT THE HANDS OF GERMANY AND JAPAN

Alboreto began well in Ferrari. As well as the front row in his first GP in Brazil, the first season with the scarlet red cars stood out for his victory in Belgium. At the end of the season, the record was however disappointing: second place in the Constructors Championship, fourth and sixth in the Drivers' with Alboreto and Arnoux. But the year belonged to McLaren with the Tag Porsche turbo engine, which won 12 of the 16 Grand Prixs, sharing the victories between its two drivers who, from a certain point in the season onwards launched themselves into a sensational head-to-head battle. The two drivers were Alain Prost, who had joined McLaren from Renault, after the French manufacturer abandoned F1

because of lack of results and never-ending investments without any success, and Niki Lauda. The Austrian was back on the track in 1982, tempted by offers from both McLaren under the new management of Ron Dennis - a former mechanic of the team - and Arab tycoon Mansour Ojjieh. It was Lauda himself, at the end of a hard-fought season, who took the 1984 title and his third championship by just half-a-point from teammate Prost.

After much promise, the Ferrari 126C4 was pensioned off in the wake of a sudden technical and technological disadvantage against the rival cars and engines. The man who came off worse was Mauro Forghieri, who was switched to other responsibilities - to use a symptomatic yet very significant expression. It meant he was removed from his position during 1984. He eventually left Maranello in 1987 for Lamborghini when the Bologna manufacturer entered F1 as engine-supplier. The technical

BITTER TURBO

squad of the Prancing Horse remained in the hands of the British engineer Harvey Postlethwaite, who came to Maranello in 1981 and who was the first of a long and still unfinished wave of foreign engineers. Track management was in the hands of team manager Marco Piccinini as well as the engineer Tomaini, and it was already clear by autumn that for the following season the destiny of the Prancing Horse would be entrusted to a new car.

The Ferrari 156/85 was created for the following year. On the face of things, it was a simple evolution of the 126C4, but it had numerous major changes, starting with the engine, the

1985 Italian GP at Monza:
a group photograph confirming the
links between Ferrari and Fiat.
From left to right: Piero Ferrari,
Gianni Agnelli, Vittorio Ghidella,
at the time President of Fiat Auto,
and the future President
of Ferrari, Luca di Montezemolo
can all be recognized

design of which was the same (120° 6-cylinder V with turbocompressor) but which bore important modifications to the cylinder heads, the timing and the exhausts. Hopes were high for this car. Alboreto set pole position in its first race at Brazil's Jacarapegua circuit and finished second behind Prost's McLaren. It was the same story in Portugal, this time behind a certain Ayrton Senna who notched up the first victory of his glorious career with a Lotus-Renault. Another second place at Montecarlo and victory in Canada took Michele to the top of the world championship, a position he maintained with another win in Germany. Now he was level on 50 points with Prost after 10 of the 16 races in the calendar.

At Maranello, they were getting ready to celebrate. But it was at this point, after the Austrian Grand Prix half-way through August, that the scarlet cars' progress ground to a halt. The V6 turbo engine, pushed over the limit in the search for greater power, began to show signs of yiel-

ding. The 156/85 had a series of problems, the McLaren could no longer be caught and a first long-awaited title went to Prost.

Ferrari was now on a downhill slide. Alboreto and his teammate Stefan Johansson, the only Swede to drive a Ferrari Formula 1 car, were the drivers in the 1986 world championship, which turned out to be very disappointing: no victories, no pole positions and no fastest laps; fifth and eighth place overall in the Drivers' championship with Johansson and Alboreto in that order, a long way behind Prost who won his second title; fourth in the Constructors' table behind Williams, McLaren and Lotus. It was at this point that Enzo Ferrari, having reached 90 years of age, realized that the time had come to change once again. At Williams there was a top-class driver whom he liked a lot: Nigel Mansell. At the end of July he invited him to Maranello. The British driver landed at Bologna airport with a private flight from the Isle of Man, where he lived.

He was welcomed and taken to Maranello where he signed a pre-contract for the 1987 season. He returned home that same evening, a Ferrari driver. Afterwards however Mansell changed his mind, thanks also to a "veto" by Frank Williams who had helped him mature within the team and had no desire to see him move to Ferrari. Williams had admired Ferrari right from his early days as constructor, and in 1986 managed to equal the number of F1 Constructors' titles (8) won by the Engineer from Maranello. Mansell was required to pay a penalty for his refusal to go ahead with an already-signed contract: 100,000 dollars at the time (more than 160,000 at the current rate, the equivalent of 260 million lire) which was donated in charity to the Association for the Study of Muscular Dystrophy.

But the Mansell deal was not the only weapon in Ferrari's armour. With perfect timing, Ferrari managed to convince the British engineer John Barnard to leave McLaren, for whom he had designed and constructed every world championship car from 1984 to 1986. The story of Barnard and Ferrari was to be a brilliant one, although full of ups and downs. He left the team in 1989, but came back again in 1992, only to leave Ferrari again in spring 1997 after twice creating a research and development centre for the Prancing Horse in Great Britain. On the driver front, it was Enzo Ferrari who chose the Austrian Gerhard Berger in 1987 as teammate to Alboreto after Johansson had left.

27-year-old Berger came to Maranello at the end of 1986. The following year, in perfect technical and personal consonance with John Barnard, he took two wins for Ferrari in the final two Grand Prixs in Japan and Australia, after spinning away another certain victory in Portugal. 1987 however was the year when Williams and the Honda turbo dominated. Against competition from Honda and before that Porsche and BMW, the once unbeatable Ferrari engines had lost the battle of performance, reliability, fuel consumption and electro-

nic management. Ferrari's disadvantage would also be evident in the years to come, when because of new international regulations turbos gave way to normally-aspirated engines. This period was characterized first by the continuing domination of Honda and then the entry of new manufacturers such as Renault and Peugeot. The final season of turbo power in 1988 was marked by both a historic victory at Monza but a lot of disappointment for Ferrari ...

Above and below:
the Ferrari F1/86 and the
F1/87. In the two years they
raced, the cars scored totally
different results: in 1986,
no wins, no pole positions and
no fastest laps; the following year,
two wins for Berger
(Japan and Australia), three
poles and three fastest laps

MANSELL, BUT ONLY "AFTERWARDS"

Enzo Ferrari died on Sunday 14th August 1988. It was a Sunday without Formula 1 and a day which was even more quiet than usual because it was the day before the August 15th Bank Holiday when the whole of Italy was virtually at a standstill. As for the racing, Ferrari left without seeing all his work and the money spent rewarded by the scarlet cars' return to the top, where they had not been since 1982. Until his kidney problems deteriorated, and despite

his 90 years, Ferrari had continued to follow Formula 1 race after race, day after day. He lived to see the definitive consacration of Honda as engine-builder, its preference for McLaren instead of Williams, despite the title conquered by the latter in 1987: both Constructors' and Drivers' titles with Nelson Piquet winning his third world championship after a season-long duel with his teammate and number 1 rival, Mansell, who was injured in the final GP of the year in Japan. But both the F1/87 and the F1/87-88 were only competitive on occasions.

On the industrial production side, thanks to the popularity

of the marque and its commercial success, Ferrari was a world leader. From 1982, the year of its institution, Ferrari's office was within the new Sporting Management Division building and this enabled him to follow every aspect and every detail of the industrial activity of the Prancing Horse. The Engineer retired almost full-time, Saturday and often Sunday included, in this new building, which was totally independent for all racing car activity. Here he was able to celebrate the creation of the Ferrari F40: virtually a F1 car with bodywork which was destined to break a whole string of production records. The car, which cost almost 400 million lire in 1987-88 (US$ 250,000), equivalent to 600 million lire in 1997 (US$ 375,000) had a market price of more than one and a half billion lire (almost US$ 1m) and created an unprecedented demand throughout the world.

On 4th June 1988 in the vast area inside the Fiorano circuit, the Ferrari company was visited by Pope John Paul II, an event captured by photographers and broadcast world-wide. The Pontiff made a lap of the track in a Mondial 8, with the "blessing" of all those present. Unfortunately that day, Ferrari himself was only able to greet the Pope by phone, given the gravity of his condition.

71 days later in fact, Enzo Ferrari departed from this life. On his specific request, news of his death was given the following day. As the daily newspapers in Italy do not come out on the day after August Bank Holiday, the news was only published on Wednesday 17th August.

This was yet another "lie" in an entire life, spent hiding news from jour-

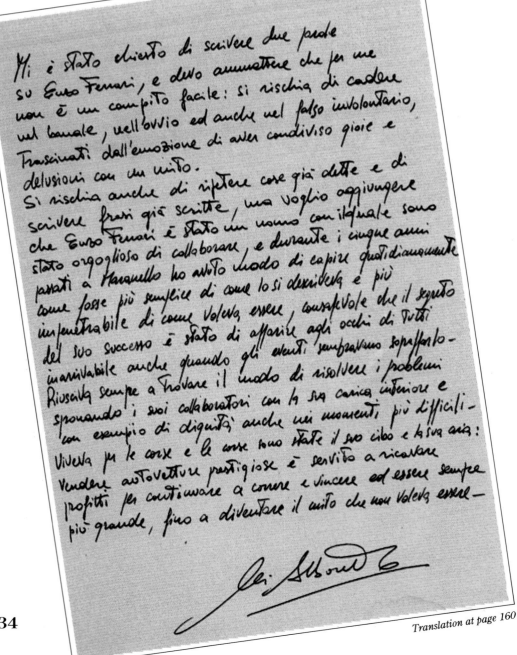

Translation at page 160

nalists, to whom Ferrari was linked by equal measures of love and hate, respect and dislike, solidarity and, at times, competition.

The world appeared to come to a brief standstill on being told of the news of the death of Enzo Ferrari. The man, a living legend who had constantly modernized the world of the car and of competition, who had changed the balance of world automobile power with his influence, was no longer with us. Afterwards everything resumed as before - work, progress, invention - as if out of respect for the dictates of this man from Modena, whose life had covered almost a century, the first 100 years in the history of the car and motor racing.

On 11th September at Monza, exactly four weeks after the death of the Engineer, Gerhard Berger won the Italian Grand Prix. The victory was purely down to luck: Ayrton Senna,

the almost certain winner, was pushed off the track in his McLaren by Jo Schlesser in a Williams with just a few corners to go before the chequered flag: that triumph would go down in history as a "lap of honour" for the Grand Old Man who died on the field of battle.

Furthermore the news that Nigel Mansell, in place of the outgoing Alboreto, was to drive the 1989 Ferrari alongside Gerhard Berger, assumed a special significance. It was the very same Mansell whom Ferrari had wanted in his cars two years before.

The final days of Enzo Ferrari. The company lunch for his 90th birthday (on 18th February 1988) and, on the other page, the notice of death posted up by the local Communist Party and a moving message written by his last Italian driver, Alboreto

The visit of the Pope

On Saturday 4th June 1988, something akin to a miracle happened at Fiorano. It had already been visited over the years by a series of presidents and kings, actors and politicians, sportsmen and show-business personalities, but this time the doors of Ferrari headquarters were opened for a special guest: Pope John Paul II. The visit, organized by way of team manager Marco Piccinini's excellent relations with the Vatican, had a purely pastoral purpose, with the blessing of the factory and a Holy Mass at the Fiorano circuit. But even before the day began, the implications of the event for the mass media had far exceeded every expectation.

When the Pope arrived at Ferrari, the only person missing was Enzo Ferrari himself. His increasingly grave health condition had confined the constructor to his Modena house: only a telephone call connected the two Grand Old Men, the

Pope taking Ferrari's call inside the headquarters at the Ferrari circuit.

A few hours later, a sudden idea presented the world with a totally unprecedented image. When the Pope was just about to get into his bullet-proof Land Rover for the blessing during a lap of the track, someone objected, in all good faith, that at Fiorano a similar moment "must" take place in a Ferrari car. And John Paul, far from being embarassed, immediately got into a Mondial 8 driven

by Piero Ferrari. He remained standing up, holding on to the upper part of the windscreen for an entire lap, blessing an enthusiastic crowd of Ferrari workers and employees, guests, journalists and photographers from all over the world, thrilled by what was happening right before their very eyes.

Pictures of the Pontiff in the Ferrari Mondial 8 went all around the world and were published in every newspaper and magazine.

THE ARRIVAL OF PROST

Mansell's rapport with Ferrari couldn't have got off to a better start: with a win. It happened on 26th March 1989 at the Jacarepagua circuit south of Rio de Janeiro. It was a "first" for many reasons: for Mansell at the wheel of a Ferrari; for the semi-automatic gearbox constructed by Barnard; and for Cesare Fiorio at the helm of the Maranello team. Although it was true that Nigel should have driven for Ferrari back in 1987 as the Engineer had wanted, it was also true that without the death of the Modena constructor Fiorio would probably never have been put in charge of the team.

Cesare Fiorio was from Turin and had been a brilliant team manager for Fiat and Lancia in rallies and endurance racing. He was without a doubt the most highly-qualified and successful team manager in the history of Italian motor sport. For some time, the appointment of Fiorio as team manager of Ferrari had been one of the mysteries of the sport, especially considering the frequent turnover of managerial staff inside the Scuderia. Maybe it was a lack of genuine feeling between Fiorio and the Engineer or maybe because at Maranello there was no intention of handing over control to a man - despite his clear professional and sporting capacity - who was the incarnation of Fiat power. Once Ferrari had left this world, the Competitions Director of

Alain Prost: in close-up on the podium of the Spanish GP he won at Jerez in 1990 and together with Mansell, then in the company of Cesare Fiorio and current president of FIA, Jean-Marie Balestre. The French driver only lost all chances of winning the 1990 title at the penultimate round

Lancia and Alfa Romeo was put directly in charge of the Prancing Horse's sporting activities. The month of March had just begun and in a few days time the team was due to leave for the first GP of the 1989 season in Brazil. With Fiorio and the car which was officially called "640" but unofficially bapti-

zed "the duck" due to its strange nose, Mansell won in Brazil and Hungary. Berger also gave a hand to its success, winning in Portugal in September, when he was officially McLaren-bound for the next season. Half-way through July in fact, on the Friday before the British Grand Prix, Alain Prost announced that he would be leaving McLaren. There had been too many rows with his teammate Ayrton Senna, 1988 world champion and the favourite of the British team, despite an open battle for the 1989 championship.

"I'm leaving McLaren - said Prost - *even if I win the championship at the end of the year. I don't know if or who I will be driving for in 1990".*

That was all: a cold and concise declaration. Rumours went around that his place, alongside Senna, would be taken by Berger, who was now second-string driver behind Mansell at Ferrari, and who had a close personal friendship with Ron Dennis, the McLaren owner. Even without thinking of the future of his driver, Cesare Fiorio was the first to welcome Prost's decision, and he approached him in the Silverstone paddock.

"Are you interested in the possibility of an agreement?", he asked him point-blank. *"Yes - went the reply - but give me a few more races".*

When the Japanese Grand Prix on 22nd October saw Senna disqualified in the race and Prost obtain mathematical certainty of the world title, the three-times winner was already officially with Ferrari for the next two seasons. In 1990, with Prost behind the

wheel of a scarlet red car which had the number 1 on its nose for the first time since Jody Scheckter's title, Ferrari went very close to winning the much sought-after world championship. It came about with the F1 90 car, better known as the 641 from its design project number. Without John Barnard in the team following the engineer's transfer to Benetton the previous autumn after refusing to move to Maranello, the 641 was an evolution of the successful but unreliable car of the previous year. The problems were all gradually corrected by the vast experience of Prost, who won five Grand Prixs in the year - including France, the 100th victory for Ferrari in Formu-

la 1 - and who was still in with a chance at the final round, the Japanese GP at Suzuka. In Japan however, Senna with the McLaren-Honda did not hesitate to knock Prost's Ferrari off the track at the first turn after the start. By taking revenge (as he would officially admit one year later) for the collision which gave a third title to Prost at Suzuka '89, Senna was crowned world champion for the second time.

The dream did not come true and all eyes were on 1991. At this point however the rapport between Prost and Fiorio was strained to breaking-point. During the summer, the team manager had come to a sort of agreement with Ayrton Senna for the Brazilian to drive a Ferrari from 1991 onwards. The news alarmed Prost, who was not prepared to have Senna in his team once again and who turned to the support of Fiat for appropriate guarentees. Alain was also defended by the President of Ferrari, Piero Fusaro, who, by assuming this stance, embarked on a collision course with Fiorio. The outcome of this intricate web of friendships and rivalries is still fresh in the memory. Jean Alesi arrived in place of Senna in 1991, Fiorio was fired in May the same year, Prost left one race before the end of his contract and later Fusaro abandoned the presidency of Ferrari. In between however there was the 1991 world championship which once again saw Ferrari in deep trouble. And that was only the beginning ...

Seventy years of team managers

Team manager of the Prancing Horse is undoubtedly one of the most difficult jobs in motor sport. As well as representing the scarlet red cars at circuits and road races throughout the world, the Ferrari team manager (or sporting director, to use Italian terminology), also had to be aware that the day after the race he was required to carry out an even more difficult task: brief Enzo Ferrari in person at Maranello. Ferrari had never been soft with his representatives at the races, as demonstrated by the long list of names who held the job from 1930, shortly after the constitution of Scuderia Ferrari, to the present day. From 1989 onwards, immediately after the death of Ferrari, the figure of team manager was modified into responsable for Sporting Management (Italian terminology again), clearly maintaining the previous role. Frenchman Jean Todt is the latest Ferrari sporting director to hold the job. Former rally co-driver (he was 1981 World Rally Championship runner-up with Guy Fréquelin), from 1983 to half-way through 1993 Todt was responsable for Peugeot's sporting activities, winning in world rallies, rally-raids and endurance racing. He was called to Ferrari by President Montezemolo in spring 1993. He took charge of the Ferrari F1 team on 1st July that year, immediately after winning the Le Mans 24 Hours race with the Group C Peugeot 905.

1930-'31	Saracco Ferrari	1971-'72	Peter Schetty
1932-'33	Mario Lolli	1973	Sandro Colombo
1934	Federico Giberti	1974-'75	Luca di Montezemolo
1935-'40	Nello Ugolini	1976	Guido Rosani e
1947-'51	Federico Giberti		Daniele Audetto
1952-'55	Nello Ugolini	1977	Roberto Nosetto
1956	Eraldo Sculati	1978-'88	Marco Piccinini
1957	Mino Amorotti	1989-May '91	Cesare Fiorio
1958-'61	Romolo Tavoni	May-end '91	Claudio Lombardi
1962-'66	Eugenio Dragoni	1992-June '93	Sante Ghedini
1967	Franco Lini	June 1993	Jean Todt
1968-'70	Franco Gozzi		

Thirty years of presidency at Maranello

1978 was the year in which the first Prancing Horse president other than Ferrari himself was appointed. Already in 1970, as soon as the purchase of the majority of Ferrari shares by Fiat was made official, the founder of Ferrari decided to leave the presidency of the company, opening the door to a series of new presidents, who clearly had to come from Fiat. Here is the list year by year:

Until 1977	Enzo Ferrari
1978 - '80	Nicola Tufarelli
1980 - '84	Giovanni Sguazzini
1984 - '88	Vittorio Ghidella
1988 - '91	Piero Fusaro
Since November 1991	Luca di Montezemolo

Sixteen years after the triumphs of Niki Lauda, when he was team manager, Luca di Montezemolo returned to Maranello as President of Ferrari. It was November 1991 and the date coincided with the start of the commercial and sporting recovery of Ferrari

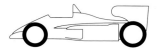
The technological centre

Almost everything that can be said, has been said about John Barnard, his merits and his defects as designer. What is certain however is that his arrival at Maranello as technical director at the end of 1986 will forever remain unique in the history of Ferrari. As soon as he began work at Ferrari, the British engineer clashed with the ways of doing things of the Italian factory. The ban on the mechanics from having their customary bottle of wine at lunchtime in 1987 virtually said it all, and it caused such a violent uproar that a quick about-turn was necessary to allow the staff to resume their habits, which in any case had never had any ill effects on how they worked. Barnard will also be remembered for the good things he did. The semi-automatic gearbox, introduced on the 1989 Ferrari 640, paved the way for its use by all the major Formula 1 teams. The aerodynamic solutions, which gave form to the 1989-90 and the 1993-97 Ferraris, were also valuable, even though not to the same degree as those with McLaren in the first half of the 1980s.

The same can be said for the plate suspension mounts, which no longer used mechanical joints, an innovation by Barnard in 1993, to be copied by other designers.

Another success was the creation of a Ferrari R&D centre in Shalford, England, in what was called the Formula 1 "Silicon Valley", due to the high technological concentration of teams and technical suppliers in the area. Without a doubt the Technological Centre gave positive results, but it is also true that its distance from the Ferrari factory and the production departments had a negative impact. This included the scarce harmonization of the various phases of design and construction, making the work of Barnard and his British team go way over the time scale.

This had a negative effect on the construction of the cars, which were never ready on time and which, as in 1996, prevented an adequate test programme from being carried out.

Almost the last Ferrari World Champion

The Ferrari which came close to taking the 1990 world title with Prost was called F1 90. Better known as 641, from its project number, the car, which was initially designed by John Barnard and then taken over by Enrique Scalabroni and Steve Nichols, won a total of 6 Grand Prixs in the 1990 World Championship: 5 with Prost and 1 with Mansell, and it only said goodbye to the title at the penultimate round of the series.

Powered by a normally-aspirated 65° 12-cylinder Vee engine with 5 valves per cylinder (maximum power was around 710 bhp at almost 14,000 rpm), the Ferrari F1 90 had a longitudinal, electronically-controlled 7-speed gearbox.

This semi-automatic box worked by means of a balance-lever located behind the steering-wheel, and was an evolution of the first system of this kind ever seen in Grand Prixs which was mounted on the previous year's Ferrari 640.

The Ferrari F1-90 on the track with Mansell in the 1990 World Championship. With this car, Prost almost took victory in the championship

ALESI

Prost liked him, Fiorio was interested in him and the same could be said for the rest of the Formula 1 world, impressed by his ability to drive fast almost immediately and in any conditions, irrespective of whether he was familiar with the circuit or not. The man in question was Jean Alesi, who made his Grand Prix debut half-way through 1989 and who immediately became the New Man in F1. Ferrari was also secretly impressed by the Frenchman and it was clear that sometime in the future he would become part of the Prancing Horse team, completing the plans which had first

his ability behind the wheel could still be a benefit for the red cars. Furthermore there was the question of the "offence" perpetrated the year before at the Portuguese GP, when Nigel (involuntarily?) damaged Prost's Ferrari at the start, thus preventing him from winning a crucial race in his championship battle against Senna.

With Mansell gone therefore, fresh air was required within the team. The choice of Alesi was perfect: a youngster full of hopes; happy to come to Maranello, something which a few months ago was seen as an impossible dream. Above all he was liked by Prost, who couldn't wait to have by his side a non-competitive

beginning of the story) the young, future Ferrari driver. Alesi's tendency to talk too much was already in evidence: in total good faith of course, but often ending up by complicating the situation. In a moment of difficulty, with Ferrari involved in negotiating far away from the spotlights, Jean burst out with *"I'd rather retire than drive for Williams"*, something which pretty much sums up the impetuosity of the man. The agreement was only reached after considerable delay and Alesi eventually ended up at Maranello. This was the start of a marriage which was to last five seasons. A marriage of love, without a shadow of doubt, but also one full of arguments and

Prost signs an autograph for a French policeman. In 1991 Alain wanted the rising star Jean Alesi as his team-mate. He was to remain with Ferrari until the end of 1995. His team-mate from 1993 to 1995 was Gerhard Berger (below, other page)

started with the successes of 1989 and 1990 and were destined to form an all-French pairing for a new cycle of victories. All this happened in summer 1990, a season of growing enthusiasm, of incredible results with Prost, who as mentioned above, only said goodbye to the title at the penultimate round of the championship. 1990 was a year which absorbed all the team's energies, but Ferrari was looking ahead. They had to replace Mansell, who pulled out after being suffocated by the presence of Prost in the team. With Nigel, the laws of Ferrari - but also F1 in general - were implacable. In a team increasingly dominated by the natural charisma of Prost and by his "political" capacities, the British driver was slowly but surely overshadowed. It didn't matter that

teammate who wasn't anxious to beat him. Basically, a driver who was not a threat.

And so it was: Cesare Fiorio's offer convinced the young French driver of Italian origin (his father was from Alcamo in Sicily). It was a pity that Alesi's enthusiasm in the face of this sudden surge in popularity led him to exaggerate things. Jean still had an option with the Tyrrell team, with whom he had made his F1 debut at the 1989 French GP and with whom he had competed in his first full season in 1990. He signed an agreement with Ferrari; a few weeks later however it was discovered that he had already signed one with Williams as well. There followed a long period of uncertainty which ended up by unsettling (and we are only at the

moments of great tension. The only negative factor in Alesi's period at Ferrari was to be the almost total lack of race victories: just one, in Canada '95. Too few to prevent a divorce which was not entirely devoid of controversy. This part of the story however belongs to the future, let's go back to the start of the relationship. Alesi arrived at Ferrari and the driver and the team already had high expectations for the 1991 world championship. Unfortunately for both of them, the situation was no longer the same as the year before. Hopes for a crisis of the McLaren-Hondas in the face of a Ferrari onslaught, soon vanished with the victory of Senna in the first four rounds of the championship. The situation in Ferrari was close to boiling-point and exploded with the sacking

Jean Alesi

Born in France on 11th June 1964 from a family of Italian origin, Jean Alesi made his Formula 1 debut for Tyrrell at the French GP in 1989, the season in which he disputed a total of 8 Grand Prixs and at the same time won the International F3000 Championship. He also took part in the 1990 F1 season with Tyrrell, obtaining two splendid second places at the United States GP (Phoenix) and at Montecarlo, results which opened the door at Ferrari.

With the red cars he raced five full seasons, scoring numerous remarkable results including dozens of podium positions. His last season at Maranello in 1995 saw Alesi's only victory with Ferrari, at the Notre Dame circuit in Montreal. The long period of Jean without a victory was over and all signs were that from this moment onwards things would be different. But his Ferrari career brought no more wins: the closest he came was at Monza when he was robbed of certain victory by mechanical failure. Three races later the rapport between Alesi and Ferrari was over: the Frenchman ended up in the Benetton team where he took the place of newly-signed Ferrari driver Schumacher and where he is also driving this year.

of Fiorio as team manager. The results clearly went some way to explaining the decision but weren't the whole reason. Divorce between Ferrari and Fiorio, which came on 15th May like a bolt from the sky, was the final episode in a rapport of growing disagreement between the team manager and Prost, who had already been shocked the previous summer by negotiations to bring Senna to Ferrari in 1991. News reports from that summer 1990, which have however never been officially confirmed by the people involved, spoke of a meeting between Fiorio and Senna off the "Costa Smeralda" coast in Sardinia, on the yacht of the team manager who was taking his summer holidays there. On that occasion, Ayrton is reported to have even signed a draft agreement. But plans were destined to fail. The President of Ferrari Piero Fusaro brought it to an end, assuring Prost that no-one would force him to be teammates with the Brazilian champion, his much-disliked teammate in McLaren in the 1988/89

1992 - In February, the Maastricht Treaty, signed by EEC countries, laid down the conditions for the process of European political and monetary integration, to be implemented by January 1999.

in motor sport

1992 - Ferrari celebrated its 500th GP in Hungary.

1992 - Michael Schumacher, driving a Benetton-Ford, won his first F1 GP at Spa, Belgium.

1993 - Ayrton Senna won his fifth successive Monaco GP. With his first win in the Principality in 1987, Senna's total of 6 was a record for the race.

1993 - Damon Hill won his first GP on 15th August in Hungary.

period. On top of this, Fusaro also guarenteed Alain a key role on a political and decision-making level.

The departure of Fiorio left Alesi without any real reference points. Whereas before he had clearly been the team's number two driver, but with the support of the people who had wanted him in the team, now he was the number two to a Prost who was increasingly nervous, discouraged, and on a collision course with the team, which in fact was to get rid of him one race before the end of the championship. At this point Alesi's role in Ferrari clearly assumed different connotations. From young number two, he became the reference point for the team, which for 1992 flanked him with Ivan Capelli and then from 1993-1995 with Gerhard Berger. Alongside the Austrian driver, who returned to Maranel-

Prost testing in 1991.
The driver and the team were to go separate ways at the end of the season, one race before the end of the championship, amidst blazing controversy

lo where he had worked from 1987 to 1989, Alesi confirmed and maintained his position as a driver who was much-loved, especially by Italian fans. This was despite the fact that Berger was more reliable in technical feedback, testing ability and car development. Although the team officially recognized the role of number one for Berger, Jean continued to love the red cars and drive them sometimes over the limit, often setting extraordinary times to the delight of spectators. His disappointment however grew at the same rate as his stretch without a win, as well as his diminishing chances of taking a world title. When he found out half-way through the 1995 world championship that he was to make way for Schumacher, Alesi had to resign himself to the decision. It was impossible to win with his much-loved Ferrari, especially due to the fact that the team by now believed very little in the French driver. The memory lingers on of five years of high excitement, but also real tension. Five successive seasons with the Prancing Horse: few other drivers had managed to last so long.

MONTEZEMOLO - PART TWO

Luca di Montezemolo came back to Ferrari once again in an official capacity on 20th November 1991. Sixteen years had passed since he had left, since he had relinquished his job of team manager which had culminated with the conquest of the 1975 world title by Niki Lauda.

The Montezemolo years had seen a rebirth of Ferrari. Two seasons, to be exact: 1974, a year when the car had returned to its winning ways, but had mainly been constantly competitive; 1975, a year which will go down in history for a number of different reasons.

It was the year of the 312T, characterized by a revolutionary transversal gearbox, the year of a certain Andreas Nikolaus Lauda, Niki to his friends, who was reared into a great champion by Luca. This success demonstrates how Luca di Montezemolo, at the time a man full of great temperament and capacity to moti-

Luca di Montezemolo shares a joke with Michael Schumacher and Jean Todt. This is the Ferrari of the present, but also of the future

vate all those around him, managed to forge a winning Ferrari, by forgetting all the dark days at Maranello and welding together a strong and unbeatable team of capable men and sheer determination.

These memories probably had a major influence on Fiat's decision to find a successor to President Fusaro. For Luca, the telephone call was an offer which just could not be refused: the invitation to take over the position which once belonged to Enzo Ferrari was mixed with recollections of a time he had always said had been one of the best of his life. Luca di Montezemolo arrived at Maranello and immediately indicated that his plans within Ferrari were on a long-term basis. First he had to resolve the difficult situation linked to the worldwide automobile market: the sale of Ferrari road cars in a period of general economic depression. Once restructuring in this field had got going, the new president could deal with the racing team.

A few weeks into 1992, Luca di Montezemolo decided to intervene. The situation within the team saw all powers concentrated in the hands of Claudio Lombardi, an engineer from Fiat, engine genius and technical brains behind extraordinary rally cars such as the Lancia Delta S4 Group B and the subsequent Delta Group A which won six successive world rally titles. Lombardi had been summoned to Ferrari by Fusaro in May 1991 to fill the power gap left by the traumatic firing of Cesare Fiorio; the very same Fiorio he had replaced at the start of 1989 as head

of Lancia and Alfa Romeo's competition activities, when Fiorio moved to Maranello. Lombardi's management era was a difficult one. Under his leadership, two ex-Ferrari engineers were recalled to Maranello: Harvey Postlethwaite and Claude Migeot. Together the two designed the F1/92, an innovative single-seater which was characterized by a double flat bottom which offered considerable aerodynamic advantage ... in theory at least. In practice, the 1992 Ferrari was never competitive and was overwhelmed not only by Mansell's Williams, but also by the McLaren.

At this point, once he realized the situation was disastrous, Luca di Montezemolo decided to step in with authority. Especially at a planning level. He gradually limited Lombardi to a technical role, and then started up talks with John Barnard.

In the three years since his divorce from Ferrari in autumn 1989, the British designer had not had a happy time: first with Benetton F1, then with the team responsible for the Toyota project run by Tom Walkinshaw, who was at the time not yet involved in Grand Prixs. Barnard had not changed: he still wanted to stay and work in England, so a new "technological centre" was set up for him near Shalford, Surrey, in an area called the "F1 Silicon Valley".

The motivations of the newly-appointed president of the Prancing Horse were clear. Enzo Ferrari had passed away almost four years ago. In this period, the scarlet red cars had occasionally been very competitive, but this was punctuated by confused management and disastrous

internal warfare. Fusaro, Fiorio, Mansell, Prost, Lombardi, Alesi, Capelli .... a lot of projects, planning and ambitions and a lot of disappointments. As the days passed, Luca di Montezemolo began to sit more and more firmly on the throne at Maranello. He began to feel the shadow of the Ferrari legend and he was asked to intervene even more directly and more resolutely within the company. He felt that the team above all needed a real heir to Enzo Ferrari ... and he was the man for the job. And so it was.

Luca di Montezemolo took control of the team's sporting activities. Once John Barnard had been taken on, Montezemolo realized that at Maranello the technical and manpower situation did not hold out great hopes for the future. In 1992 the red cars were struggling and not only were no victories obtained that year, but Ferrari was nowhere near being competitive. The dark days continued in 1993, with Berger and Alesi carrying out endless testing although with disappointing results on the track. Meanwhile however the technical structure of the team was changing. In the engine division, full powers were given to Martinelli, who had come up from within the company. Ferrari also resorted to the experience of the Japanese engineer Goto, formerly with Honda and McLaren. The decision to re-employ Gerhard Berger, who had been with Ferrari from 1987 to 1989 and since then teammate of Senna with McLaren, was also part of this new logic because his experience with the Brazilian and the British team was seen as being of great value.

But the piece which completed the new Ferrari jigsaw was called Jean Todt. The French ex-rally co-driver (he came close to winning the 1981 world title with Guy Fréquelin) was the team manager of the Peugeot team which dominated in rallying, raids and the World Sportscar Championship. Todt came to Maranello on 1st July 1993 and this was the first stone in the construction of the Ferrari of the future.

143

THE LAST ITALIAN

Let's take a step back to 1991: the year of Prost's sensational divorce with Ferrari and the year of the start of an announced new course by Ferrari management at the time closer than it had ever been to Fiat, its men and its methods. Claudio Lombardi was in command of the team when the Prost "time-bomb" stopped ticking. The French champion was in increasing disagreement with the team, with its decisions and its methods. Ferrari came to the Japanese GP, the penultimate round of the championship. The race finished with Prost in difficulty and after the chequered flag he said to a journalist:

"My Ferrari was like a truck to drive". Nothing special: nothing traumatic, at least for a great communicator such as Prost, who had always been able to accompany his driving skills with speaking ability. But this time Prost's declaration left its mark ... and was the straw which broke the camel's back.

It was immediately decided to end his contract: at the final GP of the year in Australia, Prost's Ferrari was given to team tester Gianni Morbidelli. That was a bitter end to a marriage which was born under the best of omens and which was a whisker away from reaching the pinnacle, the world title which had been eluded since Scheckter in 1979 and which Alain had come so close to winning in 1990. The turning-point was much more significant however.

Lombardi's Ferrari was oozing with Fiat influence; the influence which

Prost had wanted at first, then defended and supported (at the time of the Fiorio-Senna negotiations in summer 1990) and finally abandoned after realizing how much the driver and his opinions had become awkward.

The problem was now to find a new Ferrari driver to join the already-confirmed Alesi, who after a difficult 1991 in the political shadow of Alain Prost, now wanted to be the number one driver. The choice of his future team-mate was however pretty limited. The idea of signing Senna, who was not convinced of Ferrari's potential for 1992, was dropped; the possible choices of Mansell and Patrese were considered and rejected, so Lombardi decided to go for Ivan Capelli, for at least two reasons. Firstly, an Italian driver would be positive for the new image of the team, which was capable of standing on its own two feet once again without external intervention. Secondly, Capelli was fast. Memories if the 1990 French GP, won by Prost, the third victory of the season for the Frenchman and the 100th for Ferrari in Formula 1, were still fresh. At Paul Ricard, Prost had a terrific battle with the Leyton House of Ivan Capelli, who was leading for much of the race and was eventually beaten by the Frenchman by nine seconds.

At the end of 1991 the idea of having Capelli in the team seemed an extremely good one. A fast and extremely reliable driver, a good tester, a calm and positive character; in short he had everything required for Ferrari to complete the team along with the fast but unsettled Alesi. It all seemed perfect:

Ferrari couldn't wait to welcome another Italian driver to the team, the first since the split with Alboreto in 1988. What a pity that this idyllic situation was not destined to last very long. Ivan arrived at Maranello and everything seemed marvellous. He tried hard to live up to the sweetness of the Ferrari dream. His statements were full of happiness, gratitude for Ferrari and those who had wanted him in the team, as well as for Alesi, whom he promised he would work well with. But as soon as he tried out the F92A, the famous double flat-bottom Ferrari, the driver's dreams came crashing to the ground.

"The car is fantastic - pouted Alesi to the national and international press - *With this Ferrari, no result will be impossible".* *"The car is undriveable* - responded Capelli - *It's got major problems resulting from design errors".*

The split was immediate. Not only between the two drivers, with Alesi accusing Capelli of a politically negative attitude with the team, but also between Capelli and the team, the large majority of whom preferred to believe in the illusory declarations of Jean and not the criticism of the new driver. The results of the season, when the red cars were sinking into technical and performance trouble despite the numerous modifications made race after race, seem to demonstrate indirectly that Capelli was right. But the split with the team was now irreversible. No-one would admit it, but the causes of the problems of the Ferrari were partly down to Ivan and his scarce com-

petitivity, his lack of desire to risk everything with a car far from perfect, but which was certainly a lot better than the unmitigated engineering disaster the driver described it to be. Not even the views of Niki Lauda, the newly-appointed Ferrari adviser who clearly absolved the drivers of any responsibility for the scarce competitivity of the car, helped to smooth things over. Capelli now had the entire team against him ... or had Alesi against him, which was practically the same thing.

Ivan Capelli's experience at Maranello concluded in the worst possible way - one race before the end of the world championship, exactly the same as what happened to Prost one year before. The man who was "fired" by Ferrari was by now dejected and demotivated. He was not given help by anyone within the team, let alone

by Alesi who did not appreciate the lack of obedience by Capelli, as he should have been "number two" driver and therefore subject to his opinions. Capelli's exit from Ferrari was difficult to digest, and it concluded a totally disappointing season for the Italian; not necessarily from a results point of view, but because a gulf had been created between him and the team and its managers and because he was pushed to one side out of the way.

Capelli found another drive for 1993 with Jordan, who welcomed him with open arms, but who dumped him even more brutally after just one GP for reasons which seriously undermined the professional credibility of the driver.

Ivan Capelli's adventure in Formula 1 terminated here. It was impossible to heal the wounds, especially moral ones, left by his time with Ferrari.

The last Italians at Maranello. Other page, Capelli, Ferrari driver in 1992. Above: Nicola Larini, long-time Ferrari test-driver, who has driven for the team in four Grand Prixs

The cook

A new figure came into being within Ferrari 1979: the team cook. The man given the job was Luigi Montanini, a young 25-year-old who was full of initiative, and wasted as a mechanic. Moreover he had a certain experience in the kitchen, having worked in a famous pastry-shop close to Ferrari headquarters. The idea came from Piero Ferrari; why not organize our own restaurant service instead of continuing to call on the caterers? The choice clearly fell upon Montanini, already nick-named "Pasticcino" (Mr. Pastry).

Ferrari's trackside cook made his debut in Formula 1 in 1979, when the scarlet cars were driven by Jody Scheckter and Gilles Villeneuve. The initial idea was to prepare a few rolls: Montanini soon converted that idea into multi-star cuisine. Since then, Pasticcino has fed a generation of Ferrari drivers, falling back on his experience and imagination to satisfy everyone's tastes.

"I remember one thing above all of Gilles - said Montanini - he liked chocolate. He used to consume vast quantities of chocolate and milk.

But he also liked special dishes such as mushrooms with cream, and generally speaking anything with cream, sauces and butter. Scheckter was the complete opposite. He was obsessed with carrots: he used to eat them in slices or in salads, but often just used to munch them whole, even during technical briefings".

From 1979 to 1993, when he switched to the Benetton team on request from Flavio Briatore, Pasticcino practically "invented" F1 cuisine, and was followed by all the other teams. At his tables have sat drivers of the calibre of Alboreto and Berger, Mansell and Prost ...

"Michele used to eat like all Italians: very little breakfast, light lunch, dinner at the track with plain or tomato-flavoured pasta, a slice of meat. Berger was different: yoghurt for breakfast, a couple of slices of bread with some cheese or butter and jam. At lunch he would often have chicken and rice".

And the menu continued ... with Mansell and Prost.

"Nigel wanted carrots for breakfast: he ate them grated with Parmesan cheese. In the morning, Prost wanted milk and yoghurt with muesli and fruit salad. Both of them, for lunch

and dinner, easily adapted to Italian food: pasta, meat or fresh fish".

Luigi Montanini also has memories of when he used to prepare lunch at the Fiorano track for Enzo Ferrari, who often followed the testing from the track in the early 1980s.

"Ferrari's lunch was light, but complete - he remembered - *Usually I prepared him a risotto with Parmesan cheese, which he liked, then a grilled sirloin seasoned with a good balsamic vinegar and a green salad".*

ALMOST SENNA

The long story of the never-to-be marriage between Ferrari and Senna covered almost the final five years of the life of the Brazilian champion, who died in May 1994. If one considers the respect and admiration expressed by Enzo Ferrari for the great champion and the fact that the story of Ferrari and Senna would almost certainly have continued to the present day, it can safely be said that the rapport between these two cornerstones of the history of motor sport lasted more than a decade.

At the start of the 1990s it was clear that sooner or later Ferrari and Senna were destined to meet. There were many reasons for this, but they all boiled down to one in particular. In a world, sporting or otherwise, in which legends are all too rare, Ferrari had always managed to resist and preserve its aura of being something which went far beyond mere results. When Senna's superiority over all the other drivers became clear half-way through the 1980s, his joining Maranello became one of those social events, like a VIP marriage, which went far beyond love and attraction. It had to take place, for the good of the sport. Moreover in the case of Ayrton and the Prancing Horse, mutual love and attraction were an undeniable value, maybe mitigated by the convenience of the moment, the debatable competitivity of the red cars and the presence of Prost in Ferrari, but in any case undeniable.

We have already spoke of how Fiorio in 1990 had convinced Ayrton to go to Maranello starting from the next season: maybe only after a top-secret test with the scarlet cars organized to convince the driver of the technical validity of the project, as disclo-sed by a number of sources. And maybe - other rumours at the time - after not putting Senna alongside his "enemy" Prost, but at the side of Mansell, leaving Alain free to move at the end of the 1990 championship. The agreement was never concluded, as already mentioned, above all due to the opposition of Prost, who was supported by then-president of Ferrari, Fusaro. When Luca di Montezemolo found himself having to deal with the question of Senna in 1992, his position was perfect: no-one, either in Ferrari or Fiat, could interfere in the plan.

In 1992 the situation within Ferrari was rather serious. From an engineering point of view, the gap with the main competitors (Williams, McLaren and the rapidly-improving Benetton) was plain for all to see. The car was not competitive enough and there was no engineering programme which promised a better short-term future. From a techno-

Ayrton Senna and Ferrari: a long-lasting affair which only the premature death of the driver on 1st May 1994 prevented from turning into a full-scale relationship

logy point of view, Ferrari was undoubtedly way behind the competition, and this became dramatic in the engine field where not even the traditional supremacy of the Prancing Horse could catch Honda and Renault up. Furthermore, Alesi and Capelli were not the right drivers to guarentee that extra advantage that only top drivers can.

This was why the choice of Ayrton Senna was almost a compulsory one. In this area, Ferrari had learnt from recent experience. In 1989-1990 its driver was Nigel Mansell, who had a powerful competitive urge and a capacity to always give 101%, often way over the risk threshold. In 1990-1991 its driver was Alain Prost, who was very skilled in becoming the focal point of the team, creating a perfect car through extraordinary technical finesse. Two top drivers, two aces, two very different human beings. How could the two be united? How could all of this be found in one sin-

THE MAN OF THE FUTURE

gle driver? Obviously the answer was Senna. The Brazilian driver was a combination of Mansell and Prost. Furthermore, he knew how to catalyze the team around himself, how to urge it on, how to talk straight with engineers, gaining their utmost respect. In addition he would have brought with him all the undeniable experience accumulated in the years spent with McLaren and Honda. Finally Senna was not just any champion, he was The Champion. Everyone who loved Ferrari, loved Senna: both inside and outside the team. The team and the driver would in both cases be a perfect match.

The courtship started at once. Niki Lauda, Luca di Montezemolo's special envoy at the circuits, approached the three times world champion and told him basically that Ferrari was waiting for him. Ayrton listened, evaluated the situation, asked for and obtained detailed information. He then replied in a way that could have been a "yes, but not yet". This meant: I would like to come, I will come, but first Ferrari must improve and guarentee, as a minimum condition, a competitive team and car. At that point, it's all up to me. That was summer 1992: the Prancing Horse found itself in a corner and was in desperate need of finding a vastly experienced driver, so it opted for Gerhard Berger. The deal was finalized at the end of August and announced on the eve of the Belgian GP at Spa; with the blessing of Senna, who remained with McLaren, yet did not lose contact with the president of Ferrari.

In fact in September the contacts became even more frequent. Ayrton indicated that he was confident in Ferrari's progress the following year and said he was interested for 1994. Maranello said they were ready for him. The feeling in Ferrari and in the outside world was that the team and the driver were as close as ever to making a deal. The 1993 World Championship got underway. Alain Prost, Senna's sworn "enemy", and his Renault-powered Williams dominated the season. Half-way through the year, the French driver announced that he was leaving Formula 1 at the end of the season. For Ayrton, suffocated by the technical superiority of the Williams which thwarted any possibility of fighting for the championship on level terms, the temptation was irresistible. Frank Williams' swift offer was greeted with an immediate "yes": the perfect technological partnership between the British car and the powerful French Renault engine not only paved the way towards a fourth world title for Senna, equalling Prost, but also

Summer 1995: Jean Alesi learns that from the next season onwards his place in Ferrari will be taken by Michael Schumacher. The German driver came to Maranello after winning two successive F1 titles with Benetton

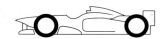

towards a legendary fifth title which only Fangio had ever achieved. Senna's arrival at Ferrari however was only postponed. Commenting on the decision to leave McLaren for Williams, the champion from Sao Paolo did not hesitate to mention that Ferrari would be part of his future plans. Probably it would be the final chapter in a brilliant career which now looked like being unique. It was a real tragedy therefore that fate turned its back on these plans and dreams. On 1st May 1994, the life of Ayrton Senna was cruelly ended at the Imola circuit; without a fourth title, which would almost certainly have been his that year ... and without a fifth title, which maybe he would have won with Ferrari.

Not only Formula 1

Half-way through the Nineties', Ferrari discovered two new categories of motor sport in which it could aim for victory. In 1994, the 333SP made its debut in the North-American IMSA Sportscar Championship, even though it was run by Ferrari clients, not the factory. With the colours of Team Scandia Motorsport, below, the sportscar would dominate the 1995 IMSA season, winning the Drivers' title with Spain's Fermin Velez. Below: heated competition in a Challenge Ferrari race. At first reserved for the 348 and then the 355, the one-make championship has achieved extraordinary success amongst competitors and popularity amongst spectators and races are organized in many countries of the world.

SCHUMACHER

His name is Michael Schumacher. He is young, he has clear ideas and bases his great driving ability on a strong personality which leaves little space for compromise. Ferrari had already been in touch in 1994, the year of his first title with the Ford-powered Benetton, a result which came about after the death of Senna. At this point, defining the German driver as the heir to Ayrton is a logical step. But in a way it is not an exact definition: the motorsport "blood" links between him and the Brazilian champion were already clear when Senna was still alive. Like Ayrton, Schumacher is a naturally fast driver. His performances, often irrespective of the logic imposed by technique and imagination, appear to be so simple, without frills, without the spectacular ability of other drivers. Like Ayrton, Schumacher makes physical training a vital part of his life: when he gets out of the car, at the end of a victorious Grand Prix, he appears to be well-rested, often without a drop of sweat, as if the race had just started. Like Ayrton, Schumacher immediately proved himself to be the focal point of the team. He spends hours and hours in the pits at the end of practice, following the work on his car in neverending dialog with the engineers. He spurs the team on to give its all, motivating it, while not producing any illfeeling, just like Senna. Half-way through 1995, a deal was finally reached for the next two seasons. What Luca di Montezemolo and his entou-

rage - especially team manager Jean Todt - maybe did not expect, was that Schumacher would almost immediately become an object of worship for the Ferrari fans, those hundreds of thousands throughout the world who have a common passion for Ferrari but not necessarily for its drivers.

The miracle came about, almost immediately. Schumacher succeeded in winning with the F310 in Spain, the seventh Grand Prix of the 1996 championship, in a race which was flooded by a downpour. This highlighted the abilities of the driver and levelled the technical performance of the car. Schumacher's incredible performance in the first few laps, when he overtook one car after another and grabbed the lead from a

"rain-master" such as Alesi, was one of those which immediately earn a place in the history of motor racing. The confidence with which he defended his lead in the last few laps despite an engine which was showing worrying signs of not lasting the distance, proved that Schumacher was a great champion. Up there on the Barcelona podium, soaked in rain and champagne, Schumacher earned

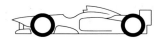

a place in the hall of fame of drivers dear to Ferrari fans. In fact, he had already booked that place months before; right from his first tests with the red cars, right from his first declarations of cautious but firm confidence that the results would come.

Other page: a young Schumacher, together with Mansell and Patrese on his first podium, in the 1992 Mexican GP, where he finished third. Since 1996, Michael has been a Ferrari driver: his team-mate is Eddie Irvine, here with Stirling Moss. Below: the big difference between a Ferrari pit garage in 1924 (Italian GP) and now ... In this page: the world championship aspirations of Schumacher and the Prancing Horse lie with the F310B

Two more wins came in the 1996 World Championship: in Belgium and at Monza. The wins came about due to the misfortunes of others, but in any case they more than lived up to the expectations of the "Ferraristi", and clearly also to the those of the driver, who slowly but surely was being caught up by the legend which was being weaved around him. "Schummy" ended up by being seduced by Ferrari. He finally yielded by accepting a renewal of the contract which would make him a Ferrari driver until the end of 1999, signing one year before the first contract ran out at the end of 1997. As far as Ferrari was concerned, an extension of the contract was the best thing they could have possibly hoped for. There were no doubts about the technical and driving abilities of the German champion; it was the commitment of the man and his involvement in the Ferrari project which had caused a few doubts to be raised. At the end of 1996 Ferrari and Schumacher were forged together. The words of Jean

Alesi a few years before, when the moment for the renewal of his contract came up, spring to mind. At the time Jean was torn between a declaration of love and accusations of scarce technical continuity within the team. *"The truth is - confessed Alesi - that I am in love with Ferrari. I criticize and rebuke Ferrari because they will not guarentee me a contract as number one driver or because they do not pay me as much as I would like. But in reality, when I get into a Ferrari I can feel the weight of motor racing history behind me. I would pay from my own pocket to drive for Ferrari ...".*
For Schumacher, things are different: given the fee guarenteed by his record contract, of this kind declarations would appear to be out of place. But almost certainly, Schumacher himself, when he gets behind the wheel of his single-seater red Ferrari, also feels a discrete and silent presence; the presence of a man, Enzo Ferrari, who almost 100 years ago first came into the world on the outskirts of Modena, with a mission: to create out of nothing the legend that is Ferrari

The future FERRARI

This is the F310B in all its secrets. Right from the first round of the 1997 season, the Ferrari F310B has shown excellent reliability and good performance.
Now it is called upon to open the doors towards a new run of victories.

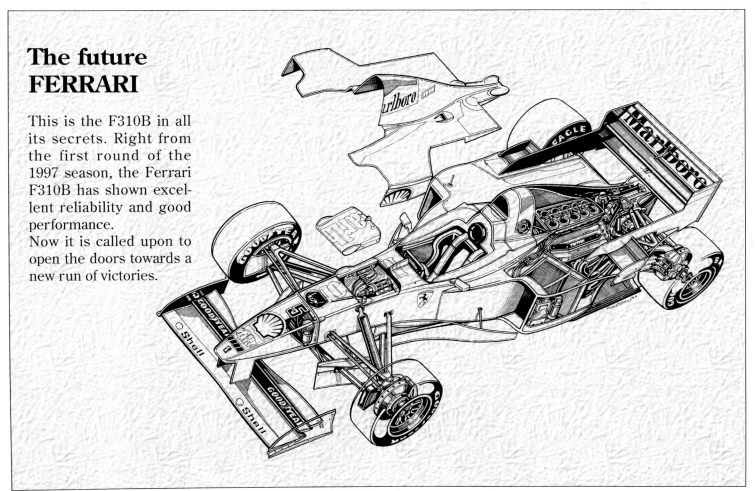

HISTORYCAL DATA

1948

1948: **Modello 125 F1**
Drivers: **Bira - Farina - Sommer**
President: **E. Ferrari**
Technical Director: **G. Colombo**
Sporting Director: **F. Giberti**

Driver	Nat.	GP	Circuit	1°	2°	3°
R. Sommer	FRA	ITA	Del Valentino (Torino)			•

1949

1949: **Modello 125 F1**
Drivers: **Ascari - Villoresi** (Folland - Mays - Richardson - Whitehead)
President: **E. Ferrari**
Technical Director: **G. Colombo**
Sporting Director: **F. Giberti**

Driver	Nat.	GP	Circuit	1°	2°	3°
L. Villoresi	ITA	BEL	Spa		•	
A. Ascari	ITA	BEL	Spa			•
A. Ascari	ITA	SUI	Bremgarten	•		
L. Villoresi	ITA	SUI	Bremgarten		•	
P. Whitehead	GBR	FRA	Reims			•
L. Villoresi	ITA	NED	Zandvoort	•		
A. Ascari	ITA	ITA	Monza	•		
P. Whitehead	GBR	TCH	Brno	•		

1950

1950: **Modelli 125 F1 - 166 F2 - 275 F1 - 375 F1**
Drivers: **Ascari - Serafini - Sommer - Villoresi** (Whitehead)
President: **E. Ferrari**
Technical Director: **G. Colombo - A. Lampredi**
Sporting Director: **F. Giberti**
F1 World Drivers' Champion: **G. Farina** (Ita)

Driver	Nat.	GP	Circuit	1°	2°	3°
A. Ascari	ITA	MON	Montecarlo		•	
P. Whitehead	GBR	FRA	Reims			•
D. Serafini-A. Ascari	ITA	ITA	Monza		•	

1951

1951: **Modello 125 F1 - 212 F1 - 375 F1**
Drivers: **Ascari - Gonzalez - Taruffi - Villoresi** (Fischer - Whitehead)
President: **E. Ferrari**
Technical Director: **A. Lampredi**
Sporting Director: **F. Giberti**
F1 World Drivers' Champion: **J.M. Fangio** (Arg)

Driver	Nat.	GP	Circuit	1°	2°	3°
P. Taruffi	ITA	SUI	Bremgarten		•	
A. Ascari	ITA	BEL	Spa		•	
L. Villoresi	ITA	BEL	Spa			•
A. Ascari-F.	ITA					
Gonzalez	ARG	FRA	Reims		•	
L. Villoresi	ITA	FRA	Reims		•	
F. Gonzalez	ARG	U.K.	Silverstone	•		
L. Villoresi	ITA	U.K.	Silverstone		•	
A. Ascari	ITA	GER	Nürburgring	•		
F. Gonzalez	ARG	GER	Nürburgring		•	
A. Ascari	ITA	ITA	Monza	•		
F. Gonzalez	ARG	ITA	Monza			•
F. Gonzalez	ARG	ESP	Pedralbes		•	

1952

1952: **Modelli 500 F2 - 166 F2**
Drivers: **Ascari - Farina - Taruffi - Villoresi** (Carini - De Tornaco -Fischer - Hirt - Laurent - Rosier - Salvadori - Schoeller - Simon)
President: **E. Ferrari**
Technical Director: **A. Lampredi**
Sporting Director: **N. Ugolini**
F1 World Drivers' Champion: **A. Ascari** (Ita)

Driver	Nat.	GP	Circuit	1°	2°	3°
P. Taruffi	ITA	SUI	Bremgarten	•		
R. Fischer	SUI	SUI	Bremgarten		•	
A. Ascari	ITA	BEL	Spa	•		
G. Farina	ITA	BEL	Spa			•
A. Ascari	ITA	FRA	Rouen	•		
G. Farina	ITA	FRA	Rouen		•	
P. Taruffi	ITA	FRA	Rouen			•
A. Ascari	ITA	U.K.	Silverstone	•		
P. Taruffi	ITA	U.K.	Silverstone		•	
A. Ascari	ITA	GER	Nürburgring	•		
G. Farina	ITA	GER	Nürburgring		•	
R. Fischer	SUI	GER	Nürburgring			•
A. Ascari	ITA	NED	Zandvoort	•		
G. Farina	ITA	NED	Zandvoort		•	
L. Villoresi	ITA	NED	Zandvoort			•
A. Ascari	ITA	ITA	Monza	•		
L. Villoresi	ITA	ITA	Monza			•

1953

1953: **Modelli 550 F2 - 553 F2 - 166 F2**
Drivers: **Ascari - Carini - Farina - Hawthorn - Maglioli - Villoresi** (Adolff - De Terra - Hirt - Rosier -Swaters)
President: **E. Ferrari**
Technical Director: **A. Lampredi**
Sporting Director: **N. Ugolini**
F1 World Drivers' Champion: **A. Ascari** (Ita)

Driver	Nat.	GP	Circuit	1°	2°	3°
A. Ascari	ITA	ARG	Buenos Aires	•		
L. Villoresi	ITA	ARG	Buenos Aires		•	
A. Ascari	ITA	NED	Zandvoort	•		
G. Farina	ITA	NED	Zandvoort		•	
A. Ascari	ITA	BEL	Spa	•		
L. Villoresi	ITA	BEL	Spa		•	
M. Hawthorn	GBR	FRA	Reims	•		
A. Ascari	ITA	U.K.	Silverstone			

Driver	Nat.	GP	Circuit	1°	2°	3°
G. Farina	ITA	U.K.	Silverstone			•
G. Farina	ITA	GER	Nürburgring	•		
M. Hawthorn	GBR	GER	Nürburgring			•
A. Ascari	ITA	SUI	Bremgarten	•		
G. Farina	ITA	SUI	Bremgarten		•	
M. Hawthorn	GBR	SUI	Bremgarten			•
G. Farina	ITA	ITA	Monza		•	
L. Villoresi	ITA	ITA	Monza			•

1954

1954: **Modelli 553 F1 - 625 F1**
Drivers: **Ascari - Farina - Gonzalez - Hawthorn - Maglioli - Manzon - Taruffi - Trintignant** (Parnell - Rosier - Swaters)
President: **E. Ferrari**
Technical Director: **A. Lampredi**
Sporting Director: **N. Ugolini**
F1 World Drivers' Champion: **J.M. Fangio** (Arg)

Driver	Nat.	GP	Circuit	1°	2°	3°
G. Farina	ITA	ARG	Buenos Aires	•		
F. Gonzalez	ARG	ARG	Buenos Aires			•
M. Trintignant	FRA	BEL	Spa		•	
R. Manzon	FRA	FRA	Reims			•
F. Gonzalez	ARG	U.K.	Silverstone	•		
M. Hawthorn	GBR	U.K.	Silverstone		•	
F. Gonzalez-	ARG					
M. Hawthorn	GBR	GER	Nürburgring		•	
M. Trintignant	FRA	GER	Nürburgring			•
F. Gonzalez	ARG	SUI	Bremgarten		•	
M. Hawthorn	GBR	ITA	Monza		•	
F.Gonzalez-	ARG					
U.Maglioli	ITA	ITA	Monza			•
M. Hawthorn	GBR	ESP	Pedralbes	•		

1955

1955: **Modelli 555 F1 - 625 F1**
Drivers: **Castellotti - Farina - Frere - Gonzalez - Hawthorn - Maglioli - Schell - Taruffi - Trintignant** (Claes)
President: **E. Ferrari**
Technical Director: **A. Lampredi**
Sporting Director: **N. Ugolini**
F1 World Drivers' Champion: **J.M. Fangio** (Arg)

Driver	Nat.	GP	Circuit	1°	2°	3°
Gonzalez-Farina-	ARG/ITA					
Trintignant	FRA	ARG	Buenos Aires		•	
Farina-Maglioli	ITA/ITA					
Trintignant	FRA	ARG	Buenos Aires			•
M. Trintignant	FRA	MON	Montecarlo	•		
G. Farina	ITA	BEL	Spa			•
E. Castellotti	ITA	ITA	Monza			•

1956

1956: **Modello D50**
Drivers: **Castellotti - Collins - De Portago - Fangio - Frere - Gendebien - Musso - Pilette**
President: **E. Ferrari**
Technical Director: **A. Fraschetti**
Sporting Director: **E. Sculati**
F1 World Drivers' Champion: **J.M. Fangio** (Arg)

Driver	Nat.	GP	Circuit	1°	2°	3°
L. Musso-	ITA					
J.M. Fangio	ARG	ARG	Buenos Aires	•		
P. Collins-	GBR					
J.M. Fangio	ARG	MON	Montecarlo		•	
P. Collins	GBR	BEL	Spa	•		
P. Frere	BEL	BEL	Spa		•	
P. Collins	GBR	FRA	Reims	•		
E. Castellotti	ITA	FRA	Reims		•	
J.M. Fangio	ARG	U.K.	Silverstone	•		
A.De Portago-	SPA					
P.Collins	GBR	U.K.	Silversone		•	
J.M. Fangio	ARG	GER	Nürburgring	•		
P.Collins-	GBR					
J.M.Fangio	ARG	ITA	Monza		•	

1957

1957: **Modelli D50 - 801 F1**
Drivers: **Castellotti - Collins - De Portago - Hawthorn - Musso - Perdisa - Trintignant - Von Trips**
President: **E. Ferrari**
Technical Director: **A. Fraschetti**
Sporting Director: **O. Tavoni**
F1 World Drivers' Champion: **J.M. Fangio** (Arg)

Driver	Nat.	GP	Circuit	1°	2°	3°
L. Musso	ITA	FRA	Rouen		•	
P. Collins	GBR	FRA	Rouen			•
L. Musso	ITA	U.K.	Aintree		•	
M. Hawthorn	GBR	U.K.	Aintree			•
M. Hawthorn	GBR	GER	Nürburgring		•	
P. Collins	GBR	GER	Nürburgring			•
W. Von Trips	GER	ITA	Monza			•

1958

1958: **Modello 246 F1**
Drivers: **Collins - Gendebien - Hawthorn - P. Hill - Musso - Von Trips**
President: **E. Ferrari**
Technical Director: **C. Chiti**
Sporting Director: **O. Tavoni**
F1 World Drivers' Champion: **M. Hawthorn** (GBR)
F1 Manufacturers' Cup: **Vanwall**

Driver	Nat.	GP	Circuit	1°	2°	3°
L. Musso	ITA	ARG	Buenos Aires		•	
M. Hawthorn	GBR	ARG	Buenos Aires			•
L. Musso	ITA	MON	Montecarlo		•	
P. Collins	GBR	MON	Montecarlo			•
M. Hawthorn	GBR	BEL	Spa		•	
M. Hawthorn	GBR	FRA	Reims	•		
W. Von Trips	GER	FRA	Reims			•
P. Collins	GBR	U.K.	Silverstone	•		
M. Hawthorn	GBR	U.K.	Silverstone		•	
M. Hawthorn	GBR	POR	Oporto		•	
M. Hawthorn	GBR	ITA	Monza		•	
P. Hill	USA	ITA	Monza			•
M. Hawthorn	GBR	MAR	Casablanca		•	
P. Hill	USA	MAR	Casablanca			•

1959

1959: **Modello 256 F1**
Drivers: **Allison - Behra - Brooks - Gendebien - Gurney - P. Hill - Von Trips**
President: **E. Ferrari**
Technical Director: **C. Chiti**
Sporting Director: **O. Tavoni**
F1 World Drivers' Champion: **J. Brabham** (AUS)
F1 Manufacturers' Cup: **Cooper**

Driver	Nat.	GP	Circuit	1°	2°	3°
T. Brooks	GBR	MON	Montecarlo		•	
T. Brooks	GBR	FRA	Reims	•		
P. Hill	USA	FRA	Reims		•	
T. Brooks	GBR	GER	Avus	•		
D. Gurney	USA	GER	Avus		•	
P. Hill	USA	GER	Avus			•
D. Gurney	USA	POR	Monsanto			•
P. Hill	USA	ITA	Monza		•	
T. Brooks	GBR	USA	Sebring			•

1960

1960: **Modelli 256 F1 - 256 P F1**
Drivers: **Allison - Ginther - Gonzalez - P. Hill - Mairesse - Von Trips**
President: **E. Ferrari**
Technical Director: **C. Chiti**
Sporting Director: **O. Tavoni**
F1 World Drivers' Champion: **J. Brabham** (AUS)
F1 Manufacturers' Cup: **Cooper**

Driver	Nat.	GP	Circuit	1°	2°	3°
C. Allison	GBR	ARG	Buenos Aires		•	
P. Hill	USA	MON	Montecarlo			•
P. Hill	USA	ITA	Monza	•		
R. Ginther	USA	ITA	Monza		•	
W. Mairesse	BEL	ITA	Monza			•

1961

1961: **Modello 156 F1**
Drivers: **Baghetti - Gendebien - Ginther - P. Hill - Mairesse - R. Rodriguez - Von Trips**
President: **E. Ferrari**
Technical Director: **C. Chiti**
Sporting Director: **O. Tavoni**
F1 World Drivers' Champion: **P. Hill** (USA)
F1 manufacturers' Cup: **Ferrari**

Driver	Nat.	GP	Circuit	1°	2°	3°
R. Ginther	USA	MON	Montecarlo		•	
P. Hill	USA	MON	Montecarlo			•
W. Von Trips	GER	NED	Zandvoort	•		
P. Hill	USA	NED	Zandvoort		•	
P. Hill	USA	BEL	Spa	•		
W. Von Trips	GER	BEL	Spa		•	
R. Ginther	USA	BEL	Spa			•
G. Baghetti	ITA	FRA	Reims	•		
W. Von Trips	GER	U.K.	Aintree	•		
P. Hill	USA	U.K.	Aintree		•	
R. Ginther	USA	U.K.	Aintree			•
W. Von Trips	GER	GER	Nürburgring		•	
P. Hill	USA	GER	Nürburgring		•	
P. Hill	USA	ITA	Monza	•		

1962

1962: **Modello 156 F1**
Drivers: **Baghetti - Bandini - P. Hill - Mairesse - R. Rodriguez**
President: **E. Ferrari**
Technical Director: **M. Forghieri**
Sporting Director: **E. Dragoni**
F1 World Drivers' Champion: **G. Hill** (GBR)
F1 Manufacturers' Cup: **BRM**

Driver	Nat.	GP	Circuit	1°	2°	3°
P. Hill	USA	NED	Zandvoort			•
P. Hill	USA	MON	Montecarlo		•	
L. Bandini	ITA	MON	Montecarlo			•
P. Hill	USA	BEL	Spa			•

1963

1963: **Modello 156 F1-63**
Drivers: **Bandini - Mairesse - Scarfiotti - Surtees**
President: **E. Ferrari**
Technical Director: **M. Forghieri**
Sporting Director: **E. Dragoni**
F1 World Drivers' Champion: **J. Clark** (GBR)
F1 Manufacturers' Cup: **Lotus**

Driver	Nat.	GP	Circuit	1°	2°	3°
J. Surtees	GBR	NED	Zandvoort			•
J. Surtees	GBR	U.K.	Silverstone		•	
J. Surtees	GBR	GER	Nürburgring	•		

1964

1964: **Modelli 156 F1-63 - 158 F1 - 512 F1**
Drivers: **Bandini - P. Rodriguez - Scarfiotti - Surtees**
President: **E. Ferrari**
Technical Director: **M. Forghieri**
Sporting Director: **E. Dragoni**
F1 World Drivers' Champion: **J. Surtees** (GBR)
F1 Manufacturers' Cup: **Ferrari**

Driver	Nat.	GP	Circuit	1°	2°	3°
J. Surtees	GBR	NED	Zandvoort		•	
J. Surtees	GBR	U.K.	Brands Hatch			•
J. Surtees	GBR	GER	Nürburgring	•		
L. Bandini	ITA	GER	Nürburgring			•
L. Bandini	ITA	AUT	Zeltweg	•		
J. Surtees	GBR	ITA	Monza	•		
L. Bandini	ITA	ITA	Monza			•
J. Surtees	GBR	USA	Watking Glen		•	
J. Surtees	GBR	MEX	C. del Messico		•	
L. Bandini	ITA	MEX	C. del Messico			•

1965

1965: Modelli 158 F1 - 512 F1
Drivers: **Bandini - Bondurant - P. Rodriguez - Scarfiotti - Surtees - Vaccarella**
President: **E. Ferrari**
Technical Director: **M. Forghieri**
Sporting Director: **E. Dragoni**
F1 World Drivers' Champion: **J. Clark** (GBR)
F1 Manufacturers' Cup: **Lotus**

Driver	Nat.	GP	Circuit	1°	2°	3°
J. Surtees	GBR	SAF	East London	•		
L. Bandini	ITA	MON	Montecarlo	•		
J. Surtees	GBR	FRA	Clermont			•
J. Surtees	GBR	U.K.	Silverstone			•

1966

1966: Modelli 246 F1-66 - 312 F1-66
Drivers: **Bandini - Parkes - Scarfiotti - Surtees**
President: **E. Ferrari**
Technical Director: **M. Forghieri**
Sporting Director: **E. Dragoni**
F1 World Drivers' Champion: **J. Brabham** (AUS)
F1 Manufacturers' Cup: **Brabham**

Driver	Nat.	GP	Circuit	1°	2°	3°
L. Bandini	ITA	MON	Montecarlo		•	
J. Surtees	GBR	BEL	Spa	•		
L. Bandini	ITA	BEL	Spa			•
M. Parkes	GBR	FRA	Reims		•	
L. Scarfiotti	ITA	ITA	Monza	•		
M. Parkes	GBR	ITA	Monza		•	

1967

1967: Modello 312 F1-67
Drivers: **Amon - Bandini - Parkes - Scarfiotti**
President: **E. Ferrari**
Technical Director: **M. Forghieri**
Sporting Director: **F. Lini**
F1 World Drivers' Champion: **D. Hulme** (NZL)
F1 Manufacturers' Cup: **Brabham**

Driver	Nat.	GP	Circuit	1°	2°	3°
C. Amon	NZL	MON	Montecarlo			•
C. Amon	NZL	BEL	Spa			•
C. Amon	NZL	U.K.	Silverstone			•
C. Amon	NZL	GER	Nürburgring			•

1968

1968: Modello 312 F1-68
Drivers: **Amon - Bell - De Adamich - Ickx**
President: **E. Ferrari**
Technical Director: **M. Forghieri**
Sporting Director: **F. Gozzi**

F1 World Drivers' Champion: **G. Hill** (GBR)
F1 Manufacturers' Cup: **Lotus**

Driver	Nat.	GP	Circuit	1°	2°	3°
J. Ickx	BEL	BEL	Spa			•
J. Ickx	BEL	FRA	Rouen	•		
C. Amon	NZL	U.K.	Brands Hiatch		•	
J. Ickx	BEL	U.K.	Brands Hiatch			•
J. Ickx	BEL	ITA	Monza			•

1969

1969: Modello 312 F1-69
Drivers: **Amon - P. Rodriguez**
President: **E. Ferrari**
Technical Director: **M. Forghieri**
Sporting Director: **F. Gozzi**
F1 World Drivers' Champion: **J. Stewart** (GBR)
F1 Manufacturers' Cup: **Matra**

Driver	Nat.	GP	Circuit	1°	2°	3°
C. Amon	NZL	NED	Zandvoort			•

1970

1970: Modello 312 B
Drivers: **Giunti - Ickx - Regazzoni**
President: **E. Ferrari**
Technical Director: **M. Forghieri**
Sporting Director: **F. Gozzi**
F1 World Drivers' Champion: **J. Rindt** (AUT)
F1 Manufacturers' Cup: **Lotus**

Driver	Nat.	GP	Circuit	1°	2°	3°
J. Ickx	BEL	NED	Zandvoort			•
J. Ickx	BEL	GER	Hockenheim		•	
J. Ickx	BEL	AUT	Osterreichring	•		
C. Regazzoni	SUI	AUT	Osterreichring		•	
C. Regazzoni	SUI	ITA	Monza	•		
J. Ickx	BEL	CAN	St. Jovite	•		
C. Regazzoni	SUI	CAN	St. Jovite		•	
J. Ickx	BEL	MEX	C. del Messico	•		
C. Regazzoni	SUI	MEX	C. del Messico		•	

1971

1971: Modelli 312 B - 312 B2
Drivers: **Andretti - Ickx - Regazzoni**
President: **E. Ferrari**
Technical Director: **M. Forghieri - A. Colombo**
Sporting Director: **P. Schetty**
F1 World Drivers' Champion: **J. Stewart** (GBR)
F1 Manufacturers' Cup: **Tyrrell**

Driver	Nat.	GP	Circuit	1°	2°	3°
M. Andretti	USA	SAF	Kyalami	•		
C. Regazzoni	SUI	SAF	Kyalami			•
J. Ickx	BEL	ESP	Montjuich Park		•	
J. Ickx	BEL	MON	Montecarlo			•
J. Ickx	BEL	NED	Zandvoort	•		
C. Regazzoni	SUI	NED	Zandvoort			•
C. Regazzoni	SUI	GER	Nürburgring			•

155

HISTORYCAL DATA

1972

1972: **Modello 312 B2**
Drivers: **Andretti - Galli - Ickx - Merzario - Regazzoni**
President: **E. Ferrari**
Technical Director: **A. Colombo**
Sporting Director: **P. Schetty**
F1 World Drivers' Champion: **E. Fittipaldi** (BRA)
F1 Manufacturers' Cup: **Lotus**

Driver	Nat.	GP	Circuit	1°	2°	3°
J. Ickx	BEL	ARG	Buenos Aires			•
J. Ickx	BEL	ESP	Jarama		•	
C. Regazzoni	SUI	ESP	Jarama		•	
J. Ickx	BEL	MON	Montecarlo		•	
J. Ickx	BEL	GER	Nürburgring	•		
C. Regazzoni	SUI	GER	Nürburgring		•	

1973

1973: **Modelli 312 B2 - 312 B2-73**
Drivers: **Ickx - Merzario**
President: **E. Ferrari**
Technical Director: **A. Colombo - M. Forghieri**
Sporting Director: **G. Rosani - L. di Montezemolo**
F1 World Drivers' Champion: **J. Stewart** (GBR)
F1 Manufacturers' Cup: **Lotus**

1974

1974: **Modello 312 B3-74**
Drivers: **Lauda - Regazzoni**
President: **E. Ferrari**
Technical Director: **M. Forghieri**
Sporting Director: **L. di Montezemolo**
F1 World Drivers' Champion: **E. Fittipaldi** (BRA)
F1 Manufacturers' Cup: **McLaren**

Driver	Nat.	GP	Circuit	1°	2°	3°
N. Lauda	AUT	ARG	Buenos Aires	•		
C. Regazzoni	SUI	ARG	Buenos Aires			•
C. Regazzoni	SUI	BRA	Interlagos			•
N. Lauda	AUT	ESP	Jarama		•	
C. Regazzoni	SUI	ESP	Jarama			•
N. Lauda	AUT	BEL	Spa - Francorchamps		•	
N. Lauda	AUT	NED	Zandvoort		•	
C. Regazzoni	SUI	NED	Zandvoort		•	
N. Lauda	AUT	FRA	Digione		•	
C. Regazzoni	SUI	FRA	Digione			•
C. Regazzoni	SUI	GER	Nürburgring	•		
C. Regazzoni	SUI	CAN	Mosport			•

1975

1975: **Modelli 312 B3-74 - 312 T**
Drivers: **Lauda - Regazzoni**
President: **E. Ferrari**
Technical Director: **M. Forghieri**
Sporting Director: **L. di Montezemolo**
F1 World Drivers' Champion: **N. Lauda** (AUT)
F1 Manufacturers' Cup: **Ferrari**

Driver	Nat.	GP	Circuit	1°	2°	3°
N. Lauda	AUT	MON	Montecarlo	•		
N. Lauda	AUT	BEL	Zolder	•		
N. Lauda	AUT	SWE	Anderstorp	•		
C. Regazzoni	SUI	SWE	Anderstorp			•
N. Lauda	AUT	NED	Zandvoort		•	
C. Regazzoni	SUI	NED	Zandvoort			•
N. Lauda	AUT	FRA	Paul Ricard	•		
N. Lauda	AUT	GER	Nürburgring			•
C. Regazzoni	SUI	ITA	Monza	•		
N. Lauda	AUT	ITA	Monza			•
N. Lauda	AUT	USA	Watkins Glen	•		

1976

1976: **Modelli 312 T - 312 T2**
Drivers: **Lauda - Regazzoni - Reutemann**
President: **E. Ferrari**
Technical Director: **M. Forghieri**
Sporting Director: **D. Audetto**
F1 World Drivers' Champion: **J. Hunt** (GBR)
F1 Manufacturers' Cup: **Ferrari**

Driver	Nat.	GP	Circuit	1°	2°	3°
N. Lauda	AUT	BRA	Interlagos	•		
N. Lauda	AUT	SAF	Kyalami	•		
C. Regazzoni	SUI	USA West	Long Beach	•		
N. Lauda	AUT	USA West	Long Beach		•	
N. Lauda	AUT	ESP	Jarama		•	
N. Lauda	AUT	BEL	Zolder	•		
C. Regazzoni	SUI	BEL	Zolder			•
N. Lauda	AUT	MON	Montecarlo	•		
N. Lauda	AUT	SWE	Anderstorp			•
N. Lauda	AUT	U.K.	Brands Hatch	•		
C. Regazzoni	SUI	NED	Zandvoort		•	
C. Regazzoni	SUI	ITA	Monza		•	
N. Lauda	AUT	USA	Watkins Glen			•

1977

1977: **Modello 312 T2**
Drivers: **Lauda - Reutemann - Villeneuve**
President: **E. Ferrari**
Technical Director: **M. Forghieri**
Sporting Director: **R. Nosetto**
F1 World Drivers' Champion: **N. Lauda** (AUT)
F1 Manufacturers' Cup: **Ferrari**

Driver	Nat.	GP	Circuit	1°	2°	3°
C. Reutemann	ARG	ARG	Buenos Aires			•
G. Reutemann	ARG	BRA	Interlagos	•		
N. Lauda	AUT	BRA	Interlagos			•
N. Lauda	AUT	SAF	Kyalami	•		
N. Lauda	AUT	USA West	Long Beach		•	
C. Reutemann	ARG	ESP	Jarama			•
N. Lauda	AUT	MON	Montecarlo		•	
C. Reutemann	ARG	MON	Montecarlo			•
N. Lauda	AUT	BEL	Zolder		•	
C. Reutemann	ARG	SWE	Anderstorp			•
N. Lauda	AUT	U.K.	Silverstone		•	
N. Lauda	AUT	GER	Hockenheim	•		

Driver	Nat.	GP	Circuit	1°	2°	3°
N. Lauda	AUT	AUT	Osterreichring		•	
N. Lauda	AUT	NED	Zandvoort	•		
N. Lauda	AUT	ITA	Monza		•	
C. Reutemann	ARG	JPN	Fuji		•	

1978

1978: Modelli 312 T2 - 312 T3
Drivers: **Reutemann - Villeneuve**
President: **E. Ferrari**
Technical Director: **M. Forghieri**
Sporting Director: **M. Piccinini**
F1 World Drivers' Champion: **M. Andretti** (USA)
F1 Manufacturers' Cup: **Lotus**

Driver	Nat.	GP	Circuit	1°	2°	3°
C. Reutemann	ARG	BRA	Rio	•		
C. Reutemann	ARG	USA West	Long Beach	•		
C. Reutemann	ARG	BEL	Zolder			•
C. Reutemann	ARG	U.K.	Brands Hatch	•		
G. Villeneuve	CAN	AUT	Osterreichring			•
C. Reutemann	ARG	ITA	Monza			•
C. Reutemann	ARG	USA	Watkins Glen	•		
G. Villeneuve	CAN	CAN	Montreal	•		
C. Reutemann	ARG	CAN	Montreal			•

1979

1979: Modelli 312 T3 - 312 T4
Drivers: **Scheckter - Villeneuve**
President: **E. Ferrari**
Technical Director: **M. Forghieri**
Sporting Director: **M. Piccinini**
F1 World Drivers' Champion: **J. Scheckter** (SA)
F1 Manufacturers' Cup: **Ferrari**

Driver	Nat.	GP	Circuit	1°	2°	3°
G. Villeneuve	CAN	SAF	Kyalami	•		
J. Scheckter	SA	SAF	Kyalami		•	
G. Villeneuve	CAN	USA West	Long Beach	•		
J. Scheckter	SA	USA West	Long Beach		•	
J. Scheckter	SA	BEL	Zolder	•		
J. Scheckter	SA	MON	Montecarlo	•		
G. Villeneuve	CAN	FRA	Digione		•	
G. Villeneuve	CAN	AUT	Osterreichring		•	
J. Schectker	SA	NED	Zandvoort		•	
J. Scheckter	SA	ITA	Monza	•		
G. Villeneuve	CAN	ITA	Monza		•	
G. Villeneuve	CAN	CAN	Montreal		•	
G. Villeneuve	CAN	USA	Watkins Glen	•		

1980

1980: Modello 312 T5
Drivers: **Scheckter - Villeneuve**
President: **E. Ferrari**
Technical Director: **M. Forghieri**
Sporting Director: **M. Piccinini**
F1 World Drivers' Champion: **A. Jones** (AUS)
F1 Manufacturers' Cup: **Williams**

1981

1981: Modello 126 CK
Drivers: **Pironi - Villeneuve**
President: **E. Ferrari**
Technical Director: **M. Forghieri**
Sporting Director: **M. Piccinini**
F1 World Drivers' Champion: **N. Piquet** (BRA)
F1 Manufacturers' Cup: **Williams**

Driver	Nat.	GP	Circuit	1°	2°	3°
G. Villeneuve	CAN	MON	Montecarlo	•		
G. Villeneuve	CAN	ESP	Jarama	•		
G. Villeneuve	CAN	CAN	Montreal			•

1982

1982: Modello 126 C2
Drivers: **Andretti - Pironi - Tambay - Villeneuve**
President: **E. Ferrari**
Technical Director: **M. Forghieri**
Sporting Director: **M. Piccinini**
F1 World Drivers' Champion: **K. Rosberg** (FIN)
F1 World Manufacturers' Champion: **Ferrari**

Driver	Nat.	GP	Circuit	1°	2°	3°
D. Pironi	FRA	SMR	Imola	•		
G. Villeneuve	CAN	SMR	Imola		•	
D. Pironi	FRA	MON	Montecarlo		•	
D. Pironi	FRA	USA East	Detroit			•
D. Pironi	FRA	NED	Zandvoort	•		
D. Pironi	FRA	U.K.	Brands Hatch		•	
P. Tambay	FRA	U.K.	Brands Hatch			•
D. Pironi	FRA	FRA	Paul Richard			•
P. Tambay	FRA	GER	Hockenheim	•		
P. Tambay	FRA	ITA	Monza		•	
M. Andretti	USA	ITA	Monza			•
P. Tambay	FRA	USA	Las Vegas		•	

1983

1983: Modelli 126 C2 - 126 C3
Drivers: **Arnoux - Tambay**
President: **E. Ferrari**
Technical Director: **M. Forghieri**
Sporting Director: **M. Piccinini**
F1 World Drivers' Champion: **N. Piquet** (BRA)
F1 World Manufacturers' Champion: **Ferrari**

Driver	Nat.	GP	Circuit	1°	2°	3°
R. Arnoux	FRA	USA	Long Beach			•
P. Tambay	FRA	SMR	Imola	•		
R. Arnoux	FRA	SMR	Imola			•
P. Tambay	FRA	BEL	Spa		•	
R. Arnoux	FRA	CAN	Montreal	•		
P. Tambay	FRA	CAN	Montreal		•	
P. Tambay	FRA	U.K.	Silverstone			•
R. Arnoux	FRA	GER	Hockenheim	•		
R. Arnoux	FRA	AUT	Osterreichring	•		
R. Arnoux	FRA	NED	Zandvoort	•		
P. Tambay	FRA	NED	Zandvoort		•	
R. Arnoux	FRA	ITA	Monza	•		

1984

1984: Modello 126 C4
Drivers: **Alboreto - Arnoux**
President: **E. Ferrari**
Technical Director: **M. Forghieri - H. Postlethwaite**
Sporting Director: **M. Piccinini**
F1 World Drivers' Champion: **N. Lauda** (AUT)
F1 World Manufacturers' Champion: **McLaren**

Driver	Nat.	GP	Circuit	1°	2°	3°
M. Alboreto	ITA	BEL	Zolder	•		
R. Arnoux	FRA	BEL	Zolder			•
R. Arnoux	FRA	SMR	Imola		•	
R. Arnoux	FRA	USA	Dallas		•	
M. ALboreto	ITA	AUT	Osterreichring			•
M. Alboreto	ITA	ITA	Monza		•	
M. Alboreto	ITA	Europe	Nürburgring		•	

1985

1985: Modello 156-85
Drivers: **Alboreto - Arnoux - Johansson**
President: **E. Ferrari**
Technical Director: **H. Postlethwaite**
Sporting Director: **M. Piccinini**
F1 World Drivers' Champion: **A. Prost** (FRA)
F1 World Manufacturers' Champion: **McLaren**

Driver	Nat.	GP	Circuit	1°	2°	3°
M. Alboreto	ITA	BRA	Rio		•	
M. Alboreto	ITA	POR	Estoril		•	
M. Alboreto	ITA	MON	Montecarlo		•	
M. Alboreto	ITA	CAN	Montreal	•		
S. Johansson	SWE	CAN	Montreal		•	
S. Johansson	SWE	USA	Detroit		•	
M. Alboreto	ITA	USA	Detroit			•
M. Alboreto	ITA	U.K.	Silverstone		•	
M. Alboreto	ITA	GER	Nürburgring	•		
M. Alboreto	ITA	AUT	Osterreichring			•

1986

1986: Modello F1-86
Drivers: **Alboreto - Johansson**
President: **E. Ferrari**
Technical Director: **H. Postlethwaite**
Sporting Director: **M. Piccinini**
F1 World Drivers' Champion: **A. Prost** (FRA)
F1 World Manufacturers' Champion: **Williams**

Driver	Nat.	GP	Circuit	1°	2°	3°
S. Johansson	SWE	BEL	Spa			•
M. Alboreto	ITA	AUT	Osterreichring		•	
S. Johansson	SWE	AUT	Osterreichring			•
S. Johansson	SWE	ITA	Monza			•
S. Johansson	SWE	AUS	Adelaide			•

1987

1987: Modello F1-87   Drivers: **Alboreto - Berger**
President: **E. Ferrari**
Technical Director: **J. Barnard**
Sporting Director: **M. Piccinini**
F1 World Drivers' Champion: **N. Piquet** (BRA)
F1 World Manufacturers' Champion: **Williams**

Driver	Nat.	GP	Circuit	1°	2°	3°
M. Alboreto	ITA	SMR	Imola			•
M. Alboreto	ITA	MON	Montecarlo			•
G. Berger	AUT	POR	Estoril		•	
G. Berger	AUT	JPN	Suzuka	•		
G. Berger	AUT	AUS	Adelaide	•		
M. Alboreto	ITA	AUS	Adelaide		•	

1988

1988: Modello F1-87/88C   Drivers: **Alboreto - Berger**
President: **E. Ferrari**
Technical Director: **H. Postlethwaite - J. Barnard**
Sporting Director: **M. Piccinini**
F1 World Drivers' Champion: **A. Senna** (BRA)
F1 World Manufacturers' Champion: **McLaren**

Driver	Nat.	GP	Circuit	1°	2°	3°
G. Berger	AUT	BRA	Rio		•	
M. Alboreto	ITA	MON	Montecarlo		•	
G. Berger	AUT	MON	Montecarlo			•
G. Berger	AUT	MEX	C. del Messico			•
M. Alboreto	ITA	FRA	Paul Ricard			•
G. Berger	AUT	GER	Hockenheim			•
G. Berger	AUT	ITA	Monza		•	
M. Alboreto	ITA	ITA	Monza			•

1989

1989: Modello F1-89   Driver: **Berger - Mansell**
President: **P. Fusaro**
Technical Director: **J. Barnard**
Sporting Director: **C. Fiorio**
F1 World Drivers' Champion: **A. Prost** (FRA)
F1 World Manufacturers' Champion: **McLaren**

Driver	Nat.	GP	Circuit	1°	2°	3°
N. Mansell	GBR	BRA	Rio	•		
N. Mansell	GBR	FRA	Paul Ricard		•	
N. Mansell	GBR	U.K.	Silverstone		•	
N. Mansell	GBR	GER	Hockenheim			•
N. Mansell	GBR	HUN	Hungaroring	•		
N. Mansell	GBR	BEL	Spa			•
G. Berger	AUT	ITA	Monza		•	
G. Berger	AUT	POR	Estoril		•	
G. Berger	AUT	ESP	Jèrez			•

1990

1990: Modello F1-90
Drivers: **Mansell - Prost**
President: **P. Fusaro**

Driver	Nat.	GP	Circuit	1°	2°	3°
A. Prost	FRA	BRA	Interlagos	•		
N. Mansell	GBR	CAN	Montreal			•
A. Prost	FRA	MEX	Città Messico	•		
N. Mansell	GBR	MEX	Città Messico		•	
A. Prost	FRA	FRA	Paul Ricard	•		
A. Prost	FRA	U.K.	Silverstone	•		
A. Prost	FRA	BEL	Spa		•	
A. Prost	FRA	ITA	Monza		•	
N. Mansell	GBR	POR	Estoril	•		
A. Prost	FRA	POR	Estoril			•
A. Prost	FRA	ESP	Jèrez	•		
N. Mansell	GBR	ESP	Jèrez		•	
N. Mansell	GBR	AUT	Adelaide		•	
A. Prost	FRA	AUS	Adelaide			•

Team Manager: **C. Fiorio**
F1 World Drivers' Champion: **A. Senna** (BRA)
F1 World Manufacturers' Champion: **McLaren**

1991

1991: **Modello F1-91**
Drivers: **Alesi - Morbidelli - Prost**
President: **P. Fusaro - L. di Montezemolo**
Team Manager: **C. Fiorio - C. Lombardi**
F1 World Drivers' Champion: **A. Senna** (BRA)
F1 World Manufacturers' Champion: **McLaren**

Driver	Nat.	GP	Circuit	1°	2°	3°
A. Prost	FRA	USA	Phoenix		•	
J. Alesi	FRA	MON	Montecarlo			•
A. Prost	FRA	FRA	Magny Cours		•	
A. Prost	FRA	U.K.	Silverstone			•
J. Alesi	FRA	GER	Hockenheim			•
A. Prost	FRA	ITA	Monza			•
J. Alesi	FRA	POR	Estoril			•
A. Prost	FRA	ESP	Barcellona		•	

1992

1992: **Modello F92 A**
Drivers: **Alesi - Capelli - Larini**
President: **L. di Montezemolo**
Team Manager: **C. Lombardi**
F1 World Drivers' Champion: **N. Mansell** (GBR)
F1 World Manufacturers' Champion: **Williams**

Driver	Nat.	GP	Circuit	1°	2°	3°
J. Alesi	FRA	ESP	Barcellona			•
J. Alesi	FRA	CAN	Montreal			•

1993

1993: **Modello F93 A**
Driver: **Alesi - Berger**
President: **L. di Montezemolo**
Team Manager: **H. Postlethwaite - J. Todt**
F1 World Drivers' Champion: **A. Prost** (FRA)
F1 World Manufacturers' Champion: **Williams**

Driver	Nat.	GP	Circuit	1°	2°	3°
J. Alesi	FRA	MON	Montecarlo			•

1994

1994: **Modello 412 T1**
Drivers: **Alesi - Berger - Larini**
President: **L. di Montezemolo**
Team Manager: **J. Todt**
F1 World Drivers' Champion: **M. Schumacher** (GER)
F1 World Manufacturers' Champion: **Williams**

Driver	Nat.	GP	Circuit	1°	2°	3°
J. Alesi	FRA	BRA	Interlagos			•
G. Berger	AUT	Pacific	Aida		•	
N. Larini	ITA	SMR	Imola		•	
G. Berger	AUT	MON	Montecarlo			•
J. Alesi	FRA	CAN	Villeneuve			•
G. Berger	AUT	FRA	Magny-Cours			•
J. Alesi	FRA	U.K.	Silverstone			•
G. Berger	AUT	GER	Hockenheim	•		
G. Berger	AUT	ITA	Monza		•	
J. Alesi	FRA	JPN	Suzuka			•
G. Berger	AUT	AUS	Adelaide		•	

1995

1995: **Modello 412 T2**
Drivers: **Alesi - Berger**
President: **L. di Montezemolo**
Team Manager: **J. Todt**
F1 World Drivers' Champion: **M. Schumacher** (GER)
F1 World Manufacturers' Champion: **Benetton**

Driver	Nat.	GP	Circuit	1°	2°	3°
G. Berger	AUT	BRA	Interlagos		•	
J. Alesi	FRA	BRA	Interlagos			•
J. Alesi	FRA	ARG	O. F.Galvez		•	
J. Alesi	FRA	SMR	Imola			•
G. Berger	AUT	SMR	Imola			•
G. Berger	AUT	ESP	Catalunya			•
G. Berger	AUT	MON	Montecarlo			•
J. Alesi	FRA	CAN	G. Villeneuve	•		
J. Alesi	FRA	U.K.	Silverstone		•	
G. Berger	AUT	GER	Hockenheim			•
G. Berger	AUT	HUN	Hungaroring			•
J. Alesi	FRA	Europe	Nürburgring		•	

1996

1996: **Modello F310**
Drivers: **Irvine - Schumacher**
President: **L. di Montezemolo**
Team Manager: **J. Todt**
F1 World Drivers' Champion: **D. Hill** (GBR)
F1 World Manufacturers' Champion: **Williams**

Driver	Nat.	GP	Circuit	1°	2°	3°
E. Irvine	IRL	AUS	Melbourne			•
M. Schumacher	GER	BRA	José C. Pace			•
M. Schumacher	GER	Europe	Nürburgring		•	
M. Schumacher	GER	SMR	E. e D. Ferrari		•	
M. Schumacher	GER	ESP	Catalunya	•		
M. Schumacher	GER	BEL	Spa	•		
M. Schumacher	GER	ITA	Monza	•		
M. Schumacher	GER	POR	Estoril			•
M. Schumacher	GER	JPN	Suzuka		•	

I was asked to write a few words about Enzo Ferrari, but I've got to admit it wasn't an easy job. Having shared moments of great joy as well as moments of deep dejection with such a legendary figure, I had to watch out and not let my emotional envolvement make me say banal or obvious things, and I especially didn't want to go overboard. What I also felt was important was not to repeat what so many others have already said about him. In brief, therefore, I can say, first of all, that having had the privilege of collaborating with Enzo Ferrari is something that I'm indeed very proud of.

Furthermore, during the five years I was at Maranello, there was never a day that went by that I wasn't able to see for myself what an uncomplicated man he was, in contrast to what many have said about him. What seemed to be an enigmatic behavior on his part was actually a pose and not the way he really was, because he fully realized that the secret to his success lay in the fact that others considered him to be unapproachable, and he stuck to this principle through thick and thin.

He also had a rare gift when it came to overcoming problems. His interior force and composure, even when things got rough, was an example and inspiration for all of his collaborators.

Racing was his life, his sustenance, the air he breathed. Building and selling prestigious automobiles was only an expedient for obtaining his principle objective: to race, win and continue reaping greater glory.

Although becoming a legend was never Enzo Ferrari's real intention, it was inevitable.

Michele Alboreto